0500000454426 3

D0461815

JUL 13 2010

MOVING PICTURES

ISBN 978-1-60309-049-0
1. Graphic Novels
2. Historical Fiction

Edited by Chris Staros. Published by Top Shelf Productions, PO Box 1282, Marietta GA 30061-1282,
USA. Publishers: Brett Warnock and Chris Staros. Top Shelf Productions® and the Top Shelf logo are
registered trademarks of Top Shelf Productions, Inc.

Visit our online catalog at www.topshelfcomix.com.

First printing, April 2010. Printed in China

10 9 8 7 6 5 4 3 2 1

GRAPHIC NOVEL F Imm

MOVING PICTURES

Kathryn & Stuart Immonen

Top Shelf Productions
Atlanta / Portland

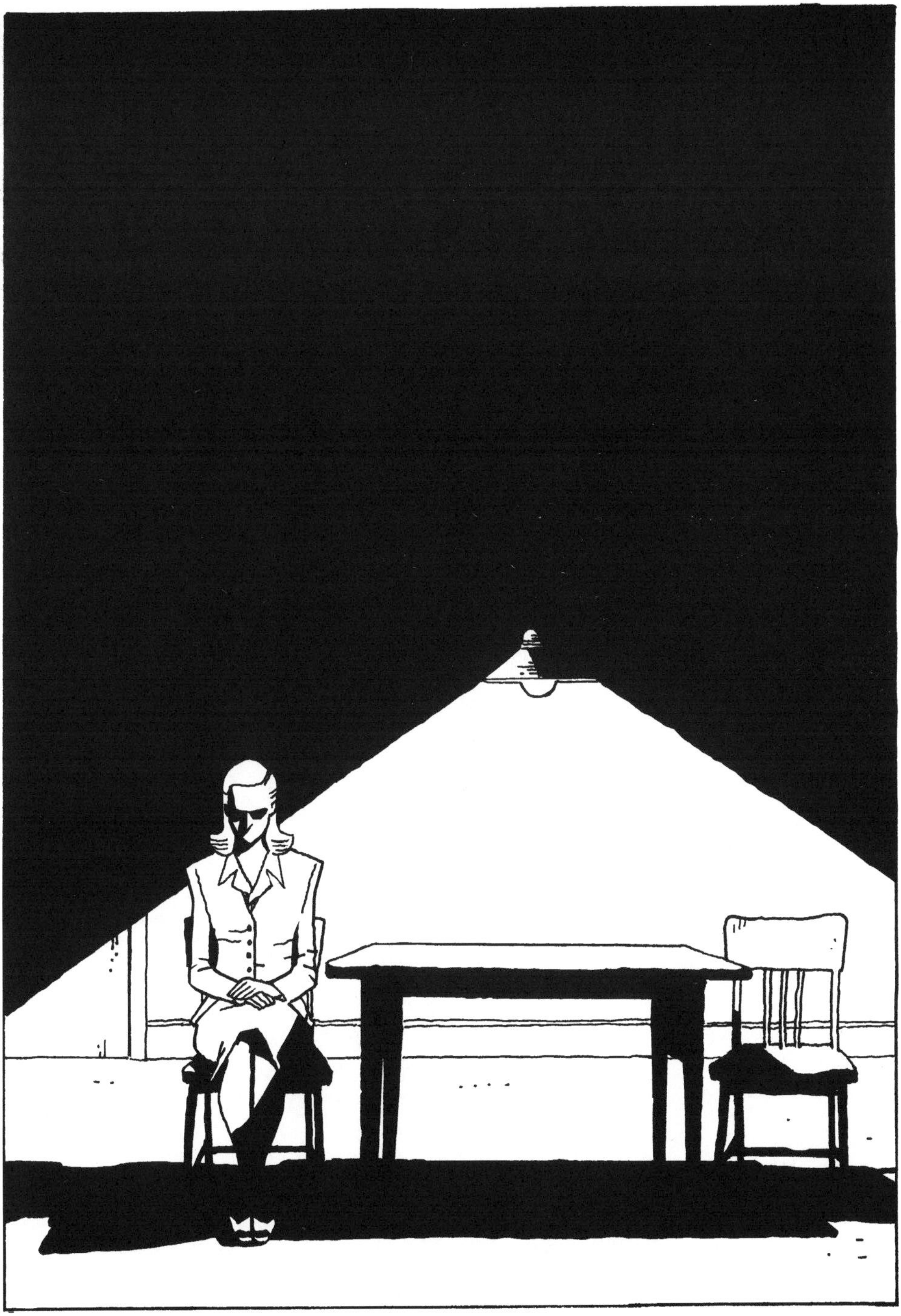

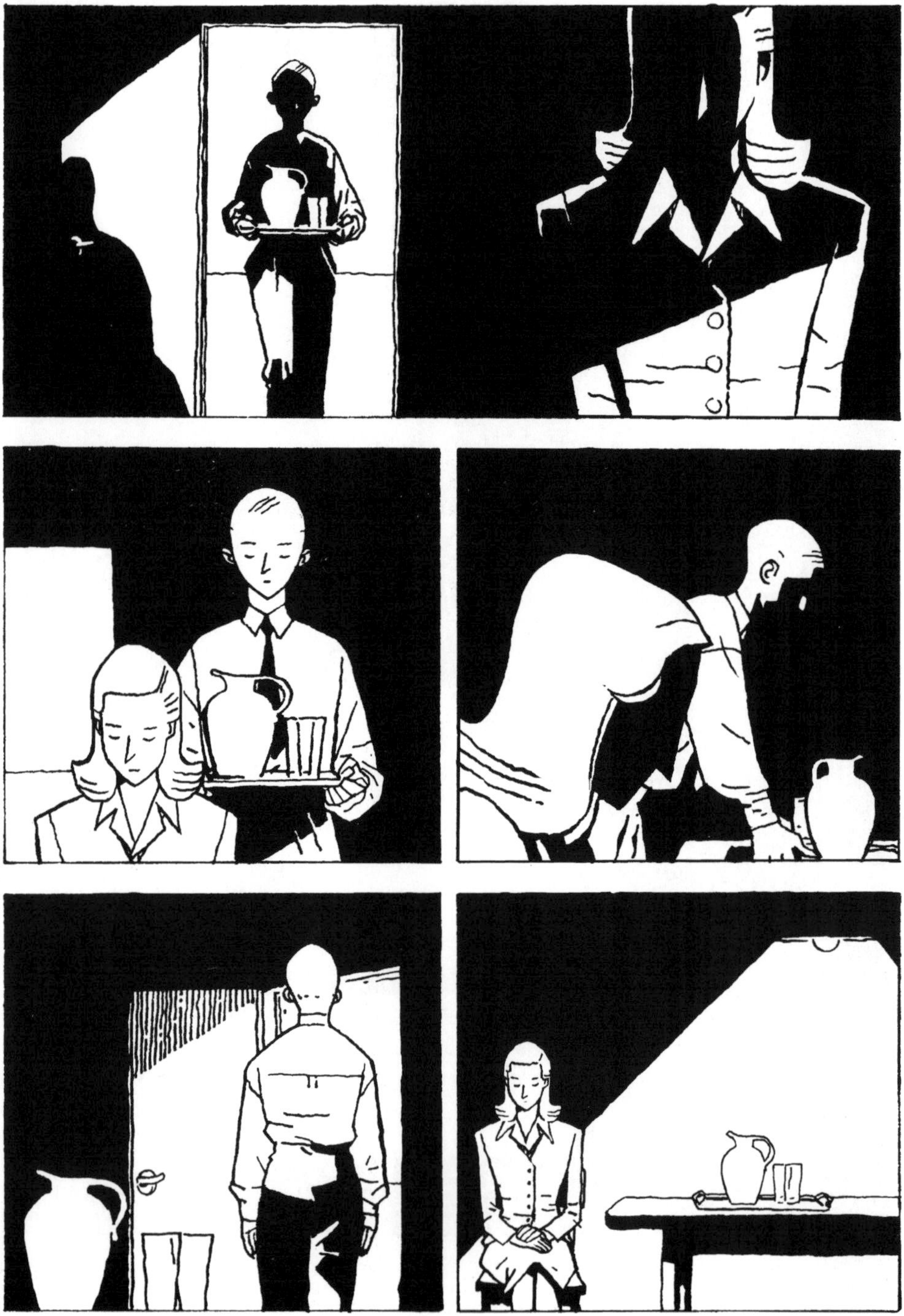

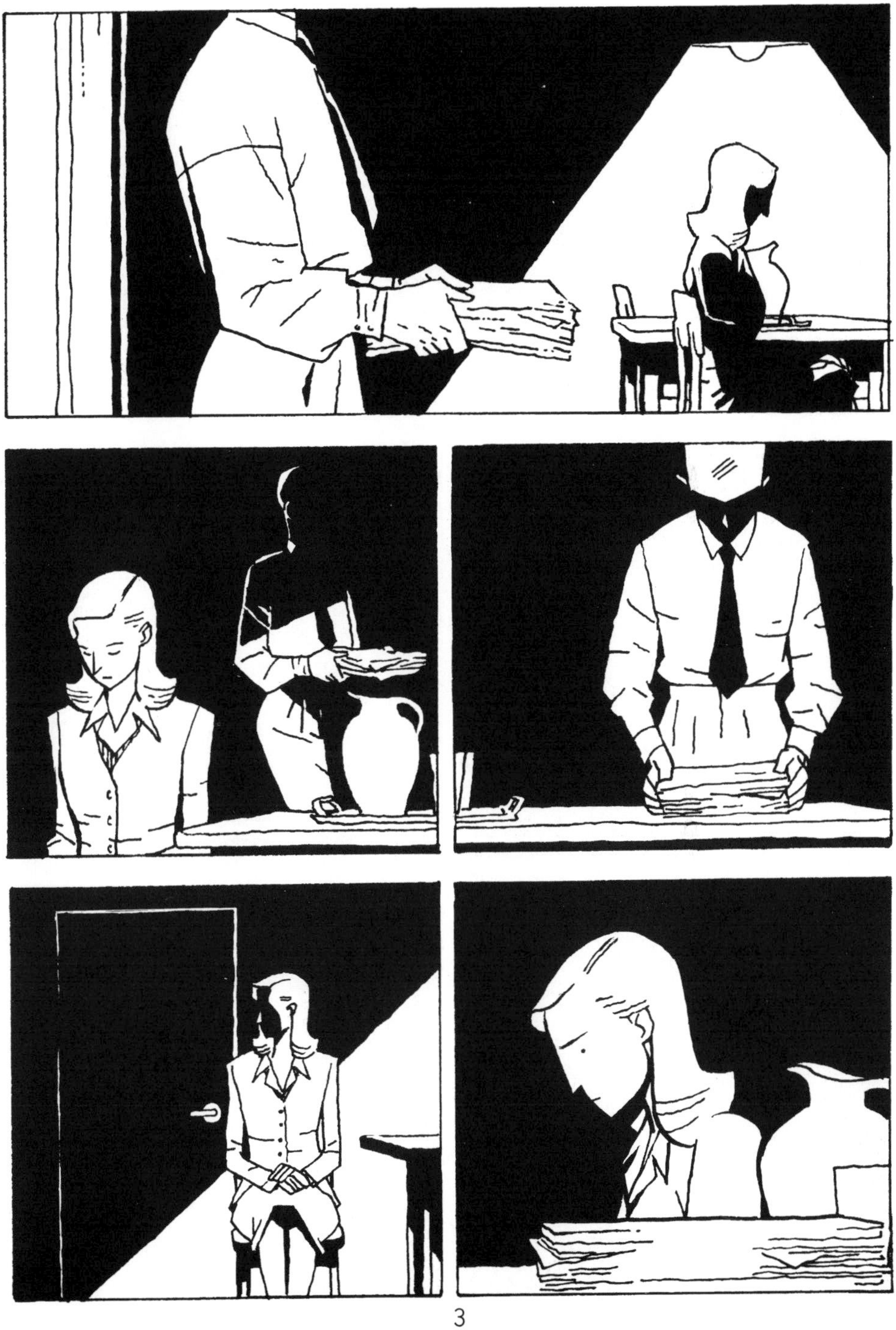

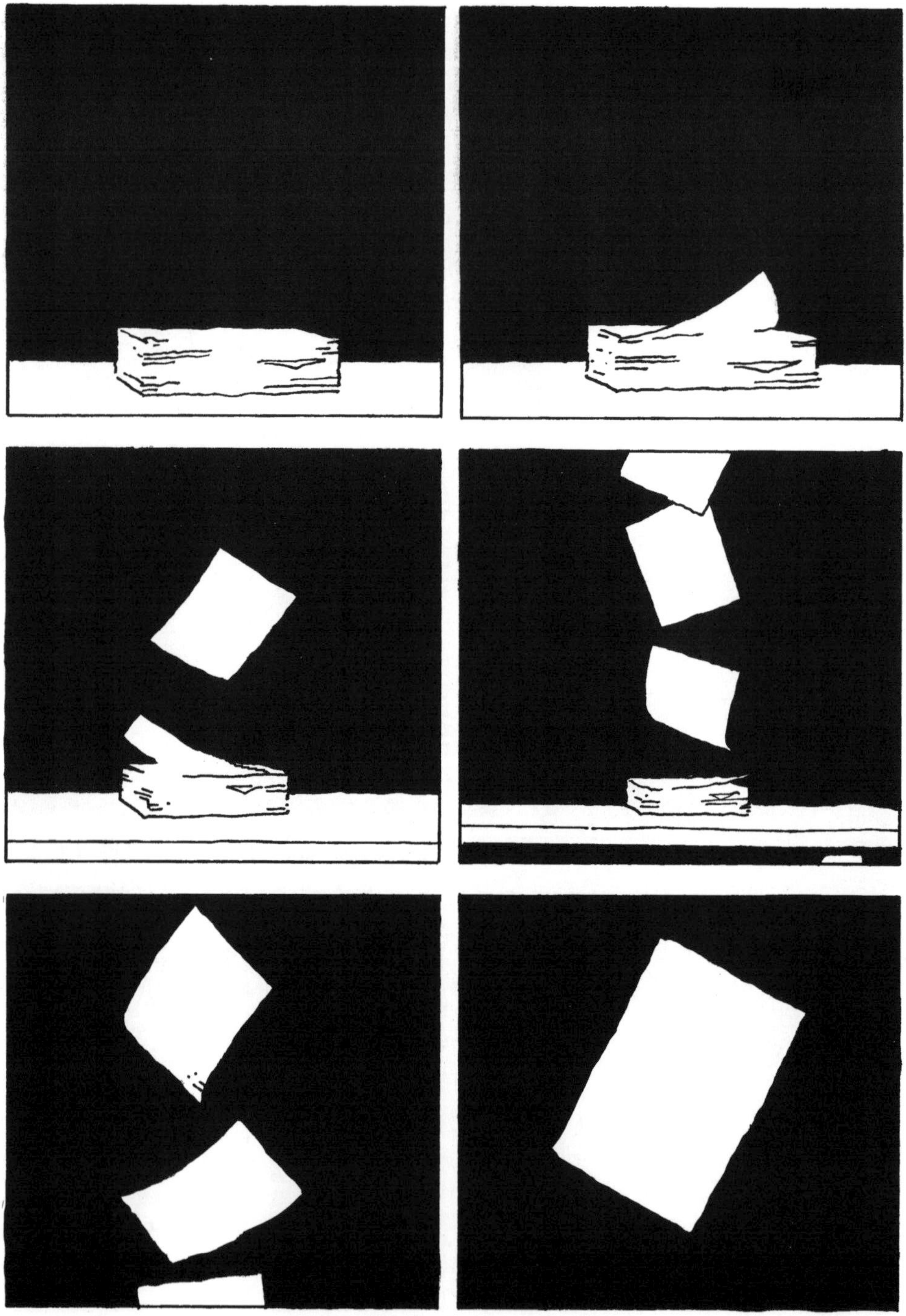

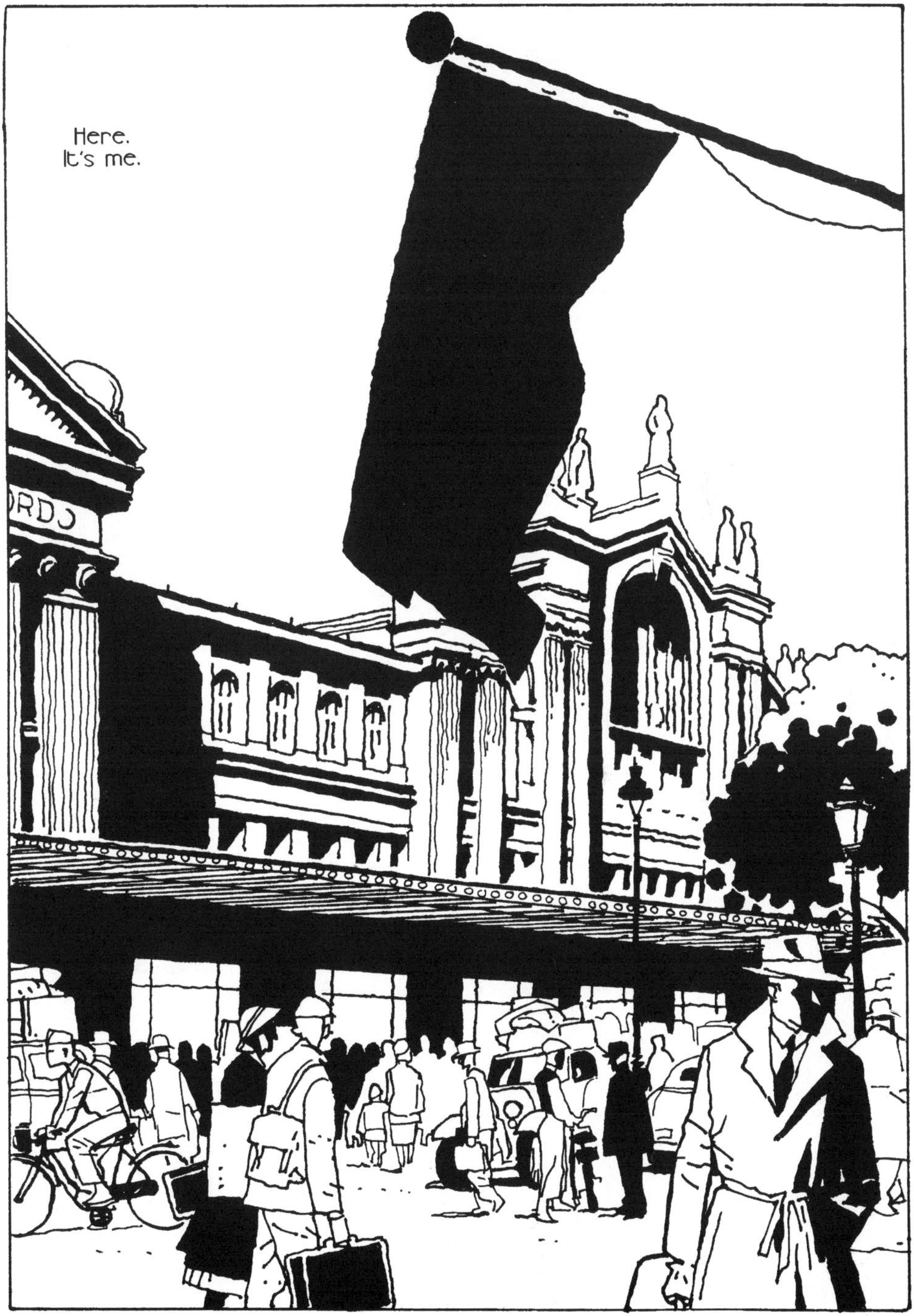
Here.
It's me.
ORDJ

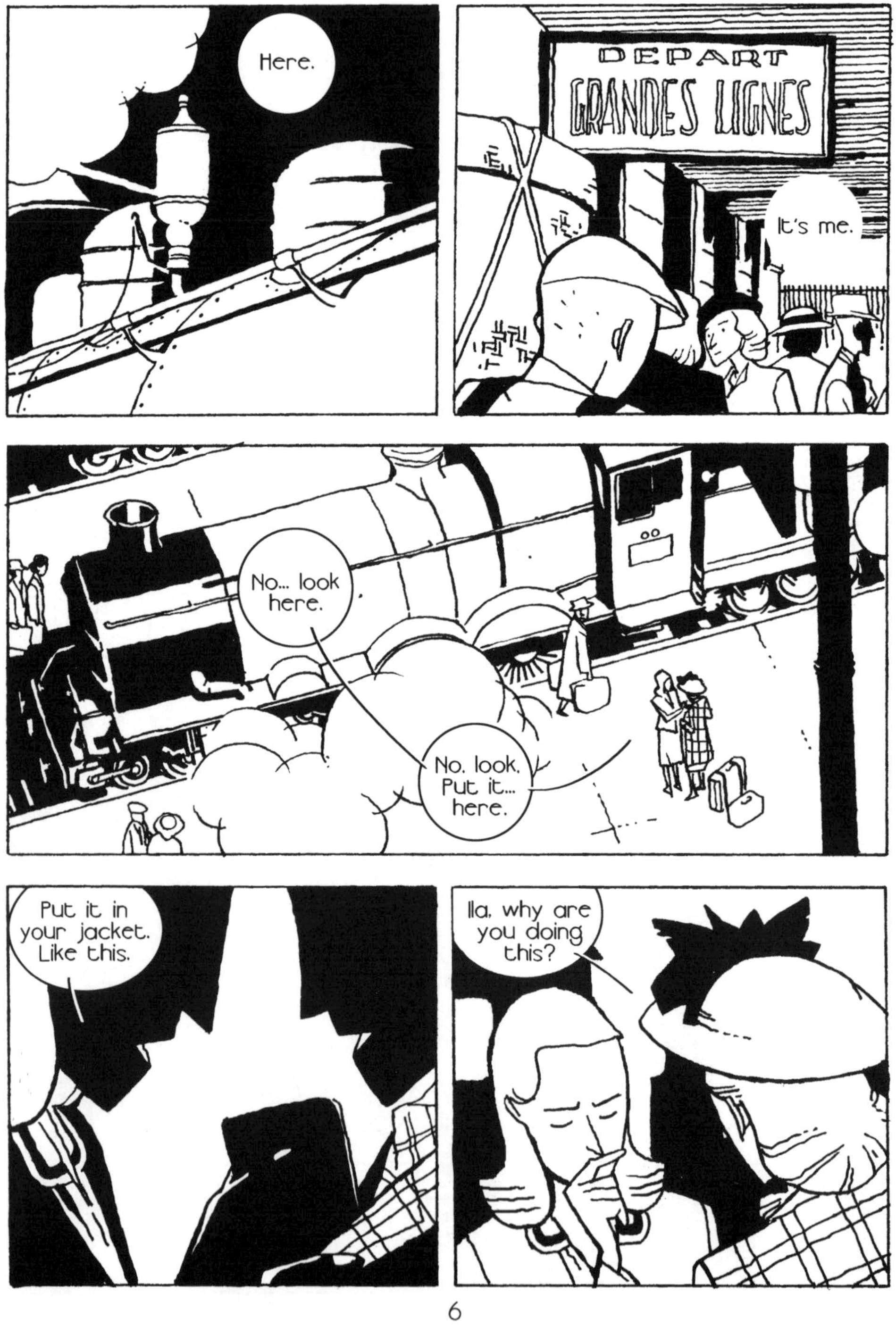
Here.
DEPART
GRANDES LIGNES
It's me.
No... look here.
No. look. Put it... here.
Put it in your jacket. Like this.
Ila, why are you doing this?

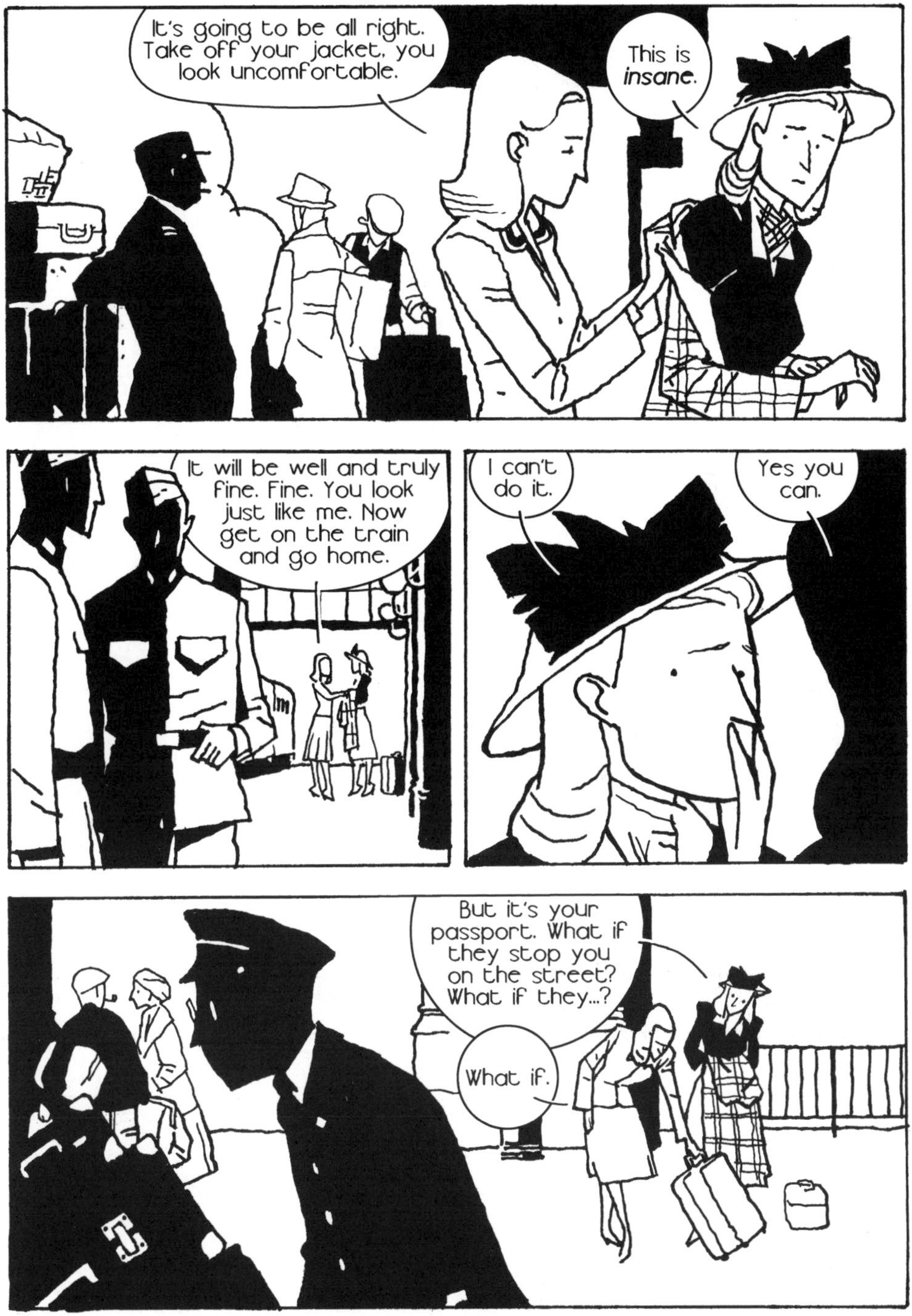
It's going to be all right. Take off your jacket, you look uncomfortable.
This is *insane*.
It will be well and truly fine. Fine. You look just like me. Now get on the train and go home.
I can't do it.
Yes you can.
But it's your passport. What if they stop you on the street? What if they...?
What if.

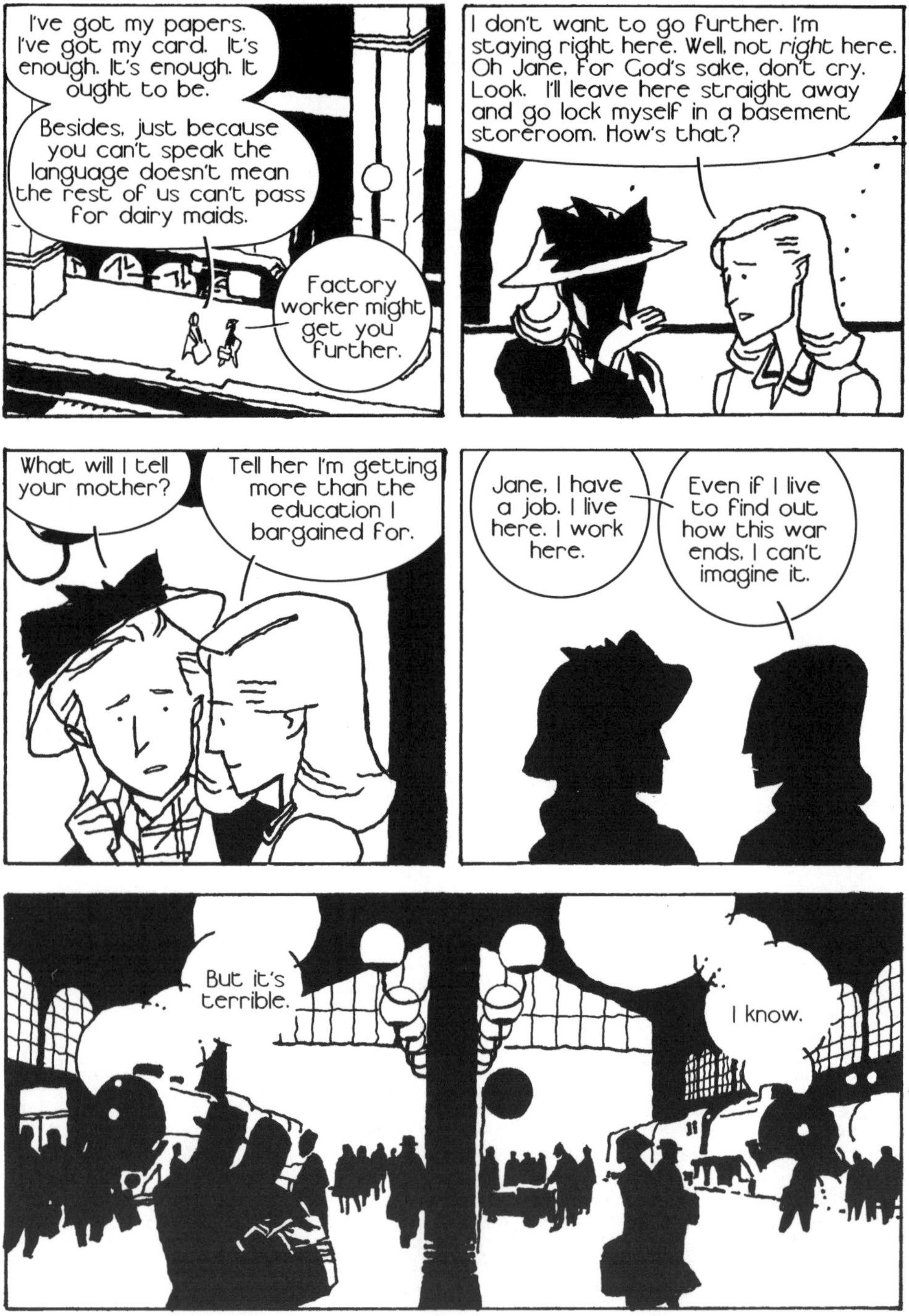
I've got my papers. I've got my card. It's enough. It's enough. It ought to be.
Besides, just because you can't speak the language doesn't mean the rest of us can't pass for dairy maids.
Factory worker might get you further.
I don't want to go further. I'm staying right here. Well, not *right* here. Oh Jane, for God's sake, don't cry. Look. I'll leave here straight away and go lock myself in a basement storeroom. How's that?
What will I tell your mother?
Tell her I'm getting more than the education I bargained for.
Jane, I have a job. I live here. I work here.
Even if I live to find out how this war ends, I can't imagine it.
But it's terrible.
I know.

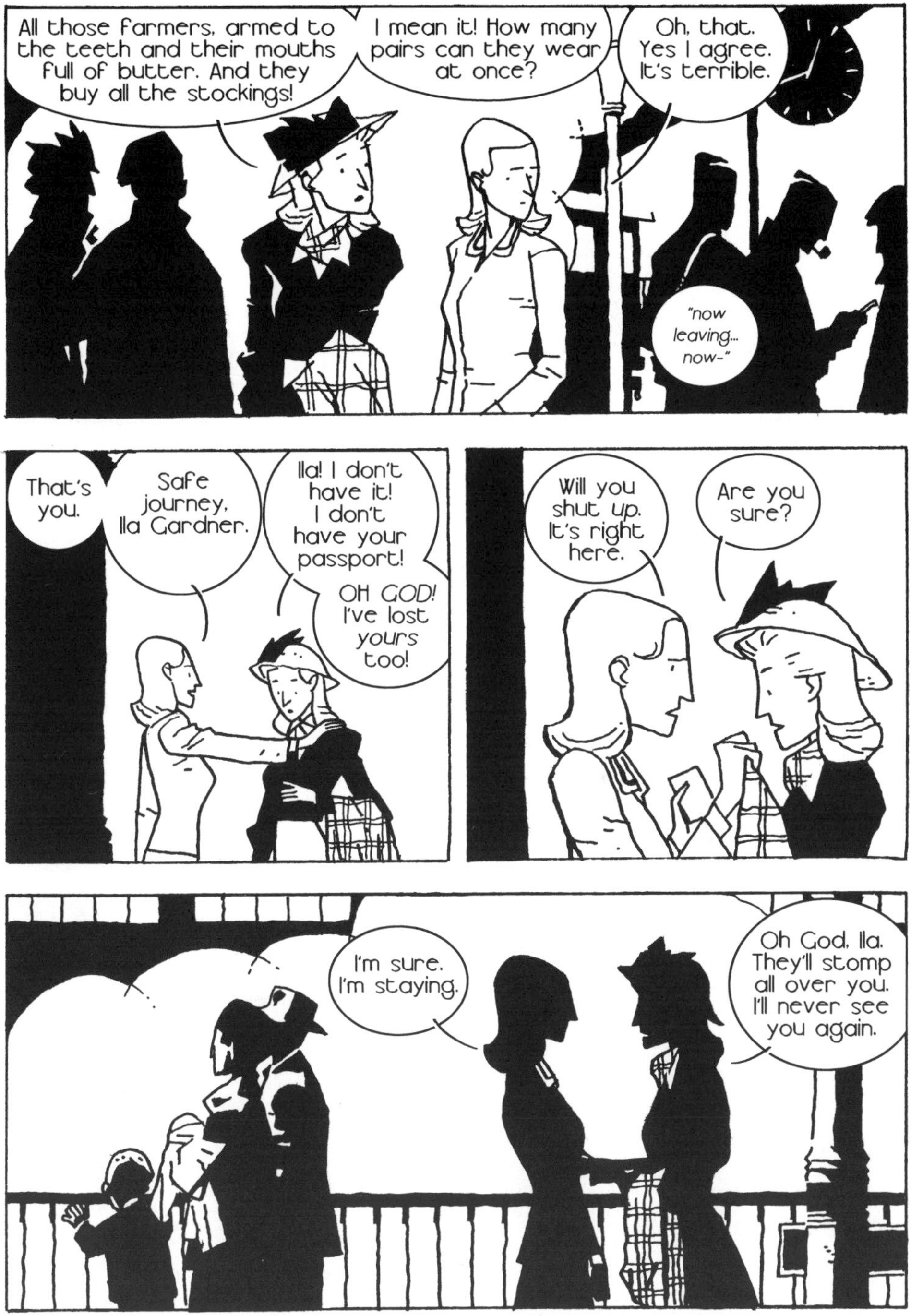
All those farmers, armed to the teeth and their mouths full of butter. And they buy all the stockings!
I mean it! How many pairs can they wear at once?
Oh, that. Yes I agree. It's terrible.
"now leaving... now-"
That's you.
Safe journey, Ila Gardner.
Ila! I don't have it! I don't have your passport!
OH *GOD*! I've lost *yours* too!
Will you shut *up*. It's right here.
Are you sure?
I'm sure. I'm staying.
Oh God, Ila. They'll stomp all over you. I'll never see you again.

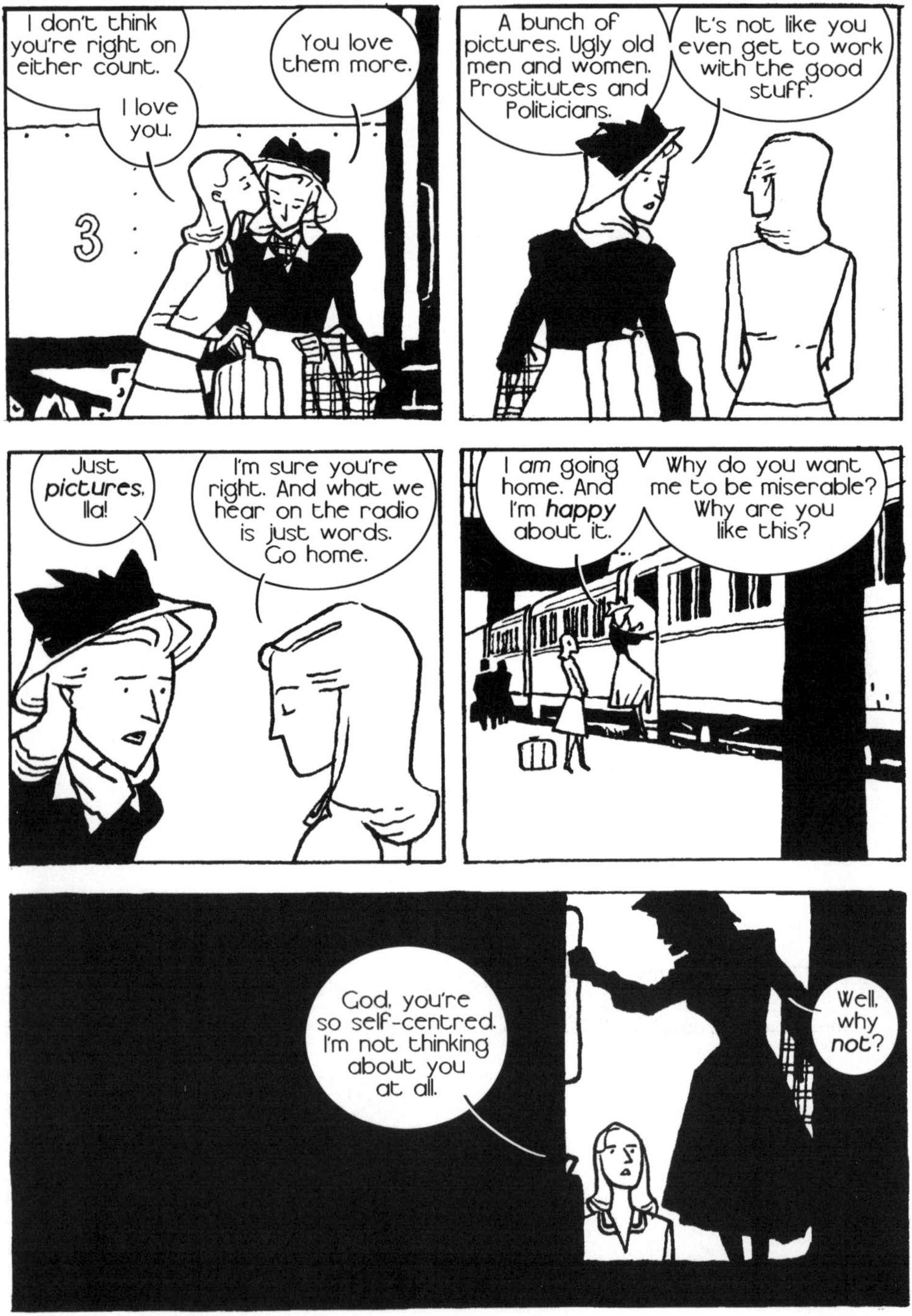
I don't think you're right on either count.
I love you.
You love them more.
A bunch of pictures. Ugly old men and women. Prostitutes and Politicians.
It's not like you even get to work with the good stuff.
3
Just *pictures*, Ila!
I'm sure you're right. And what we hear on the radio is just words. Go home.
I *am* going home. And I'm *happy* about it.
Why do you want me to be miserable? Why are you like this?
God, you're so self-centred. I'm not thinking about you at all.
Well, why *not*?

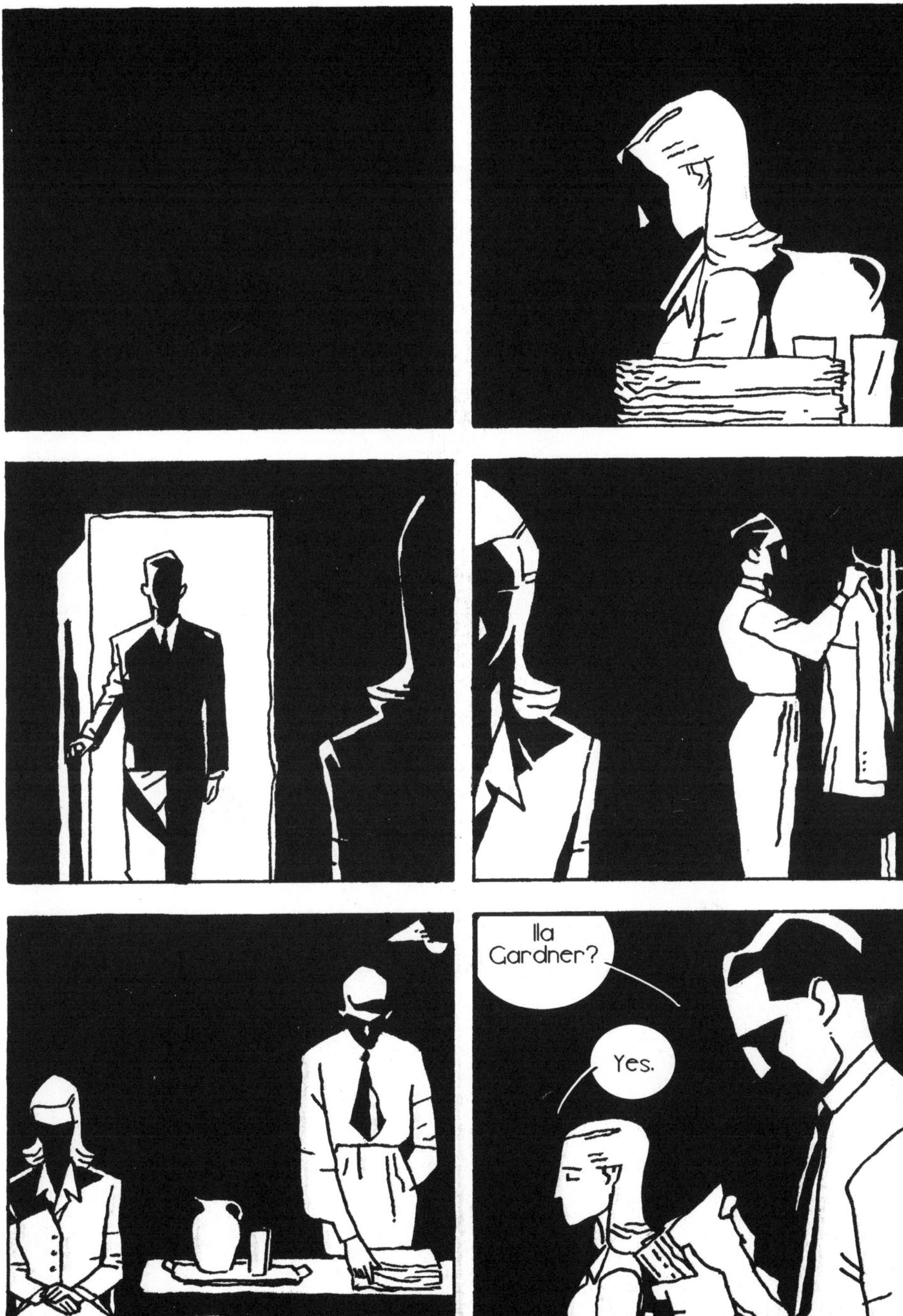

Ila Gardner?
Yes.

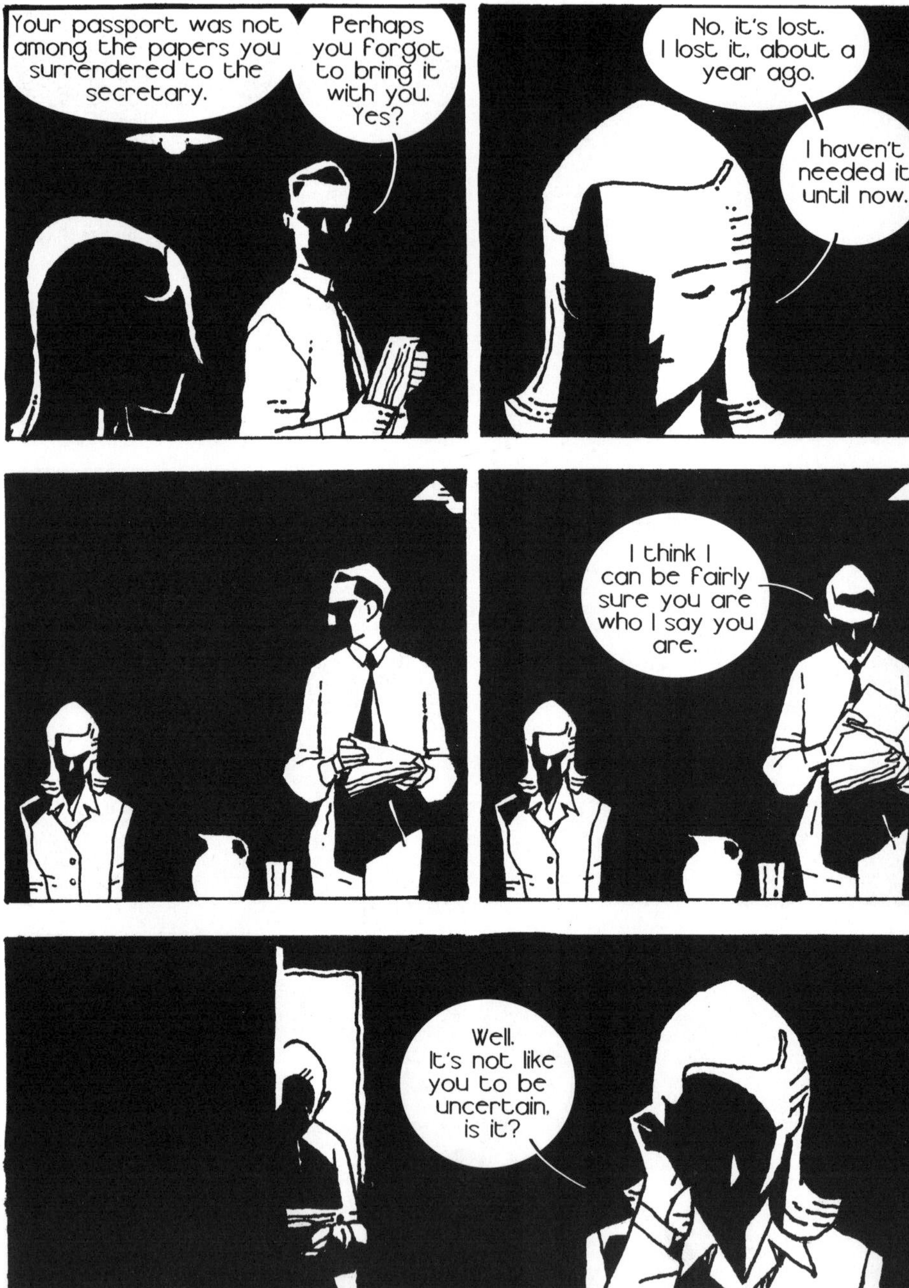
Your passport was not among the papers you surrendered to the secretary.
Perhaps you forgot to bring it with you. Yes?
No, it's lost. I lost it, about a year ago.
I haven't needed it until now.
I think I can be fairly sure you are who I say you are.
Well. It's not like you to be uncertain, is it?

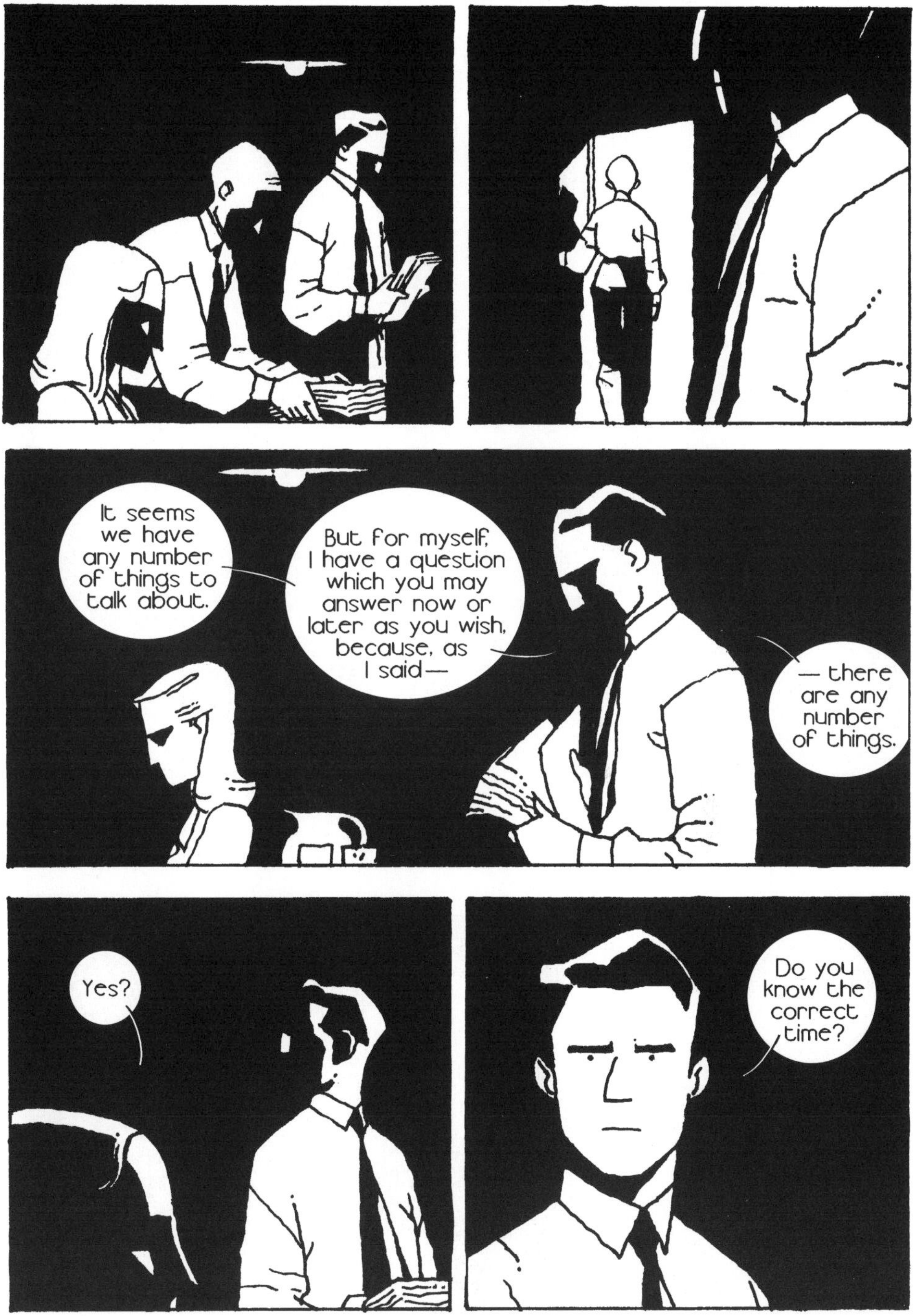
It seems we have any number of things to talk about.
But for myself, I have a question which you may answer now or later as you wish, because, as I said—
— there are any number of things.
Yes?
Do you know the correct time?

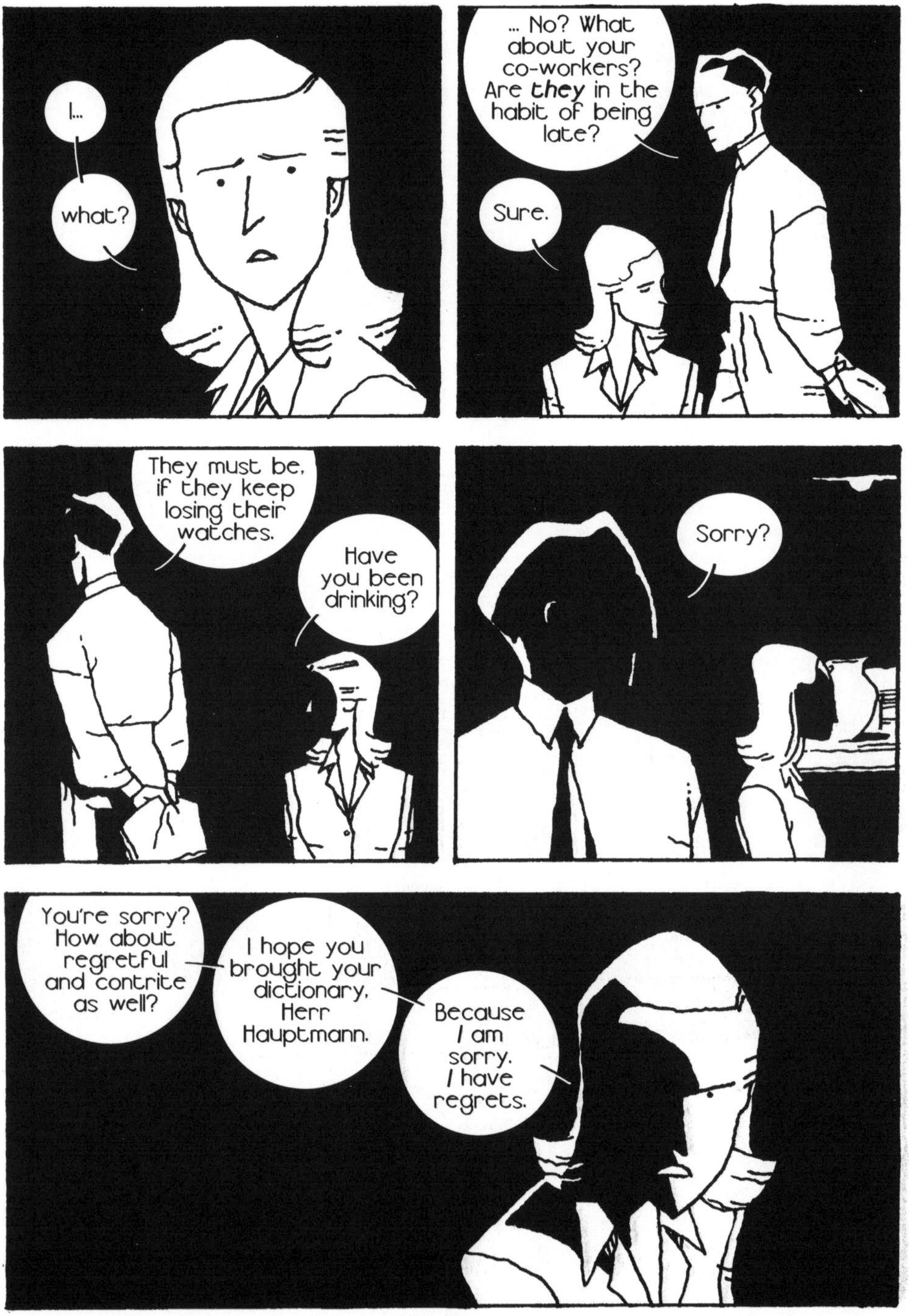
I...
what?
... No? What about your co-workers? Are *they* in the habit of being late?
Sure.
They must be, if they keep losing their watches.
Have you been drinking?
Sorry?
You're sorry? How about regretful and contrite as well?
I hope you brought your dictionary, Herr Hauptmann.
Because *I* am sorry. I have regrets.

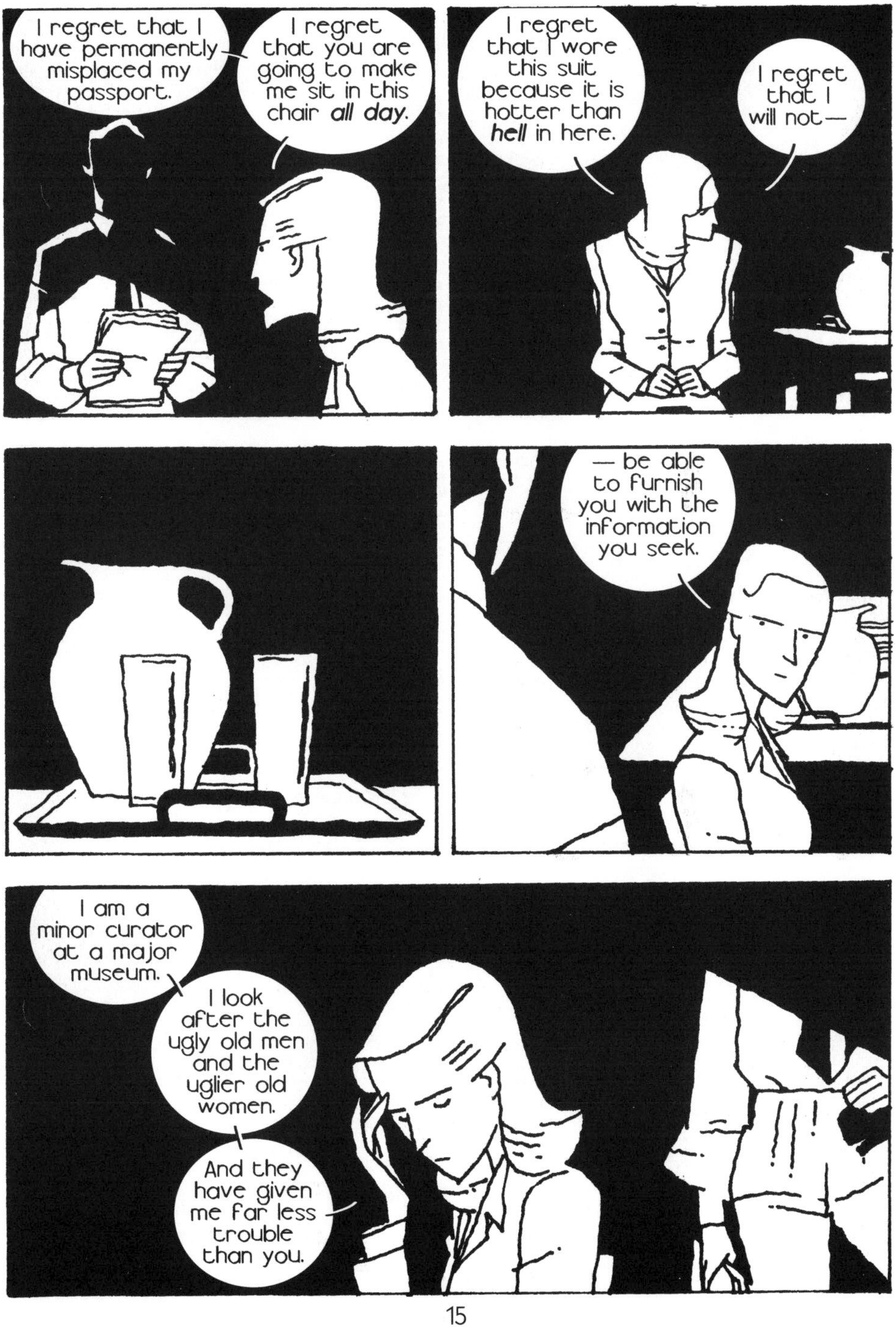
I regret that I have permanently misplaced my passport.
I regret that you are going to make me sit in this chair *all day*.
I regret that I wore this suit because it is hotter than *hell* in here.
I regret that I will not—
— be able to furnish you with the information you seek.
I am a minor curator at a major museum.
I look after the ugly old men and the uglier old women.
And they have given me far less trouble than you.

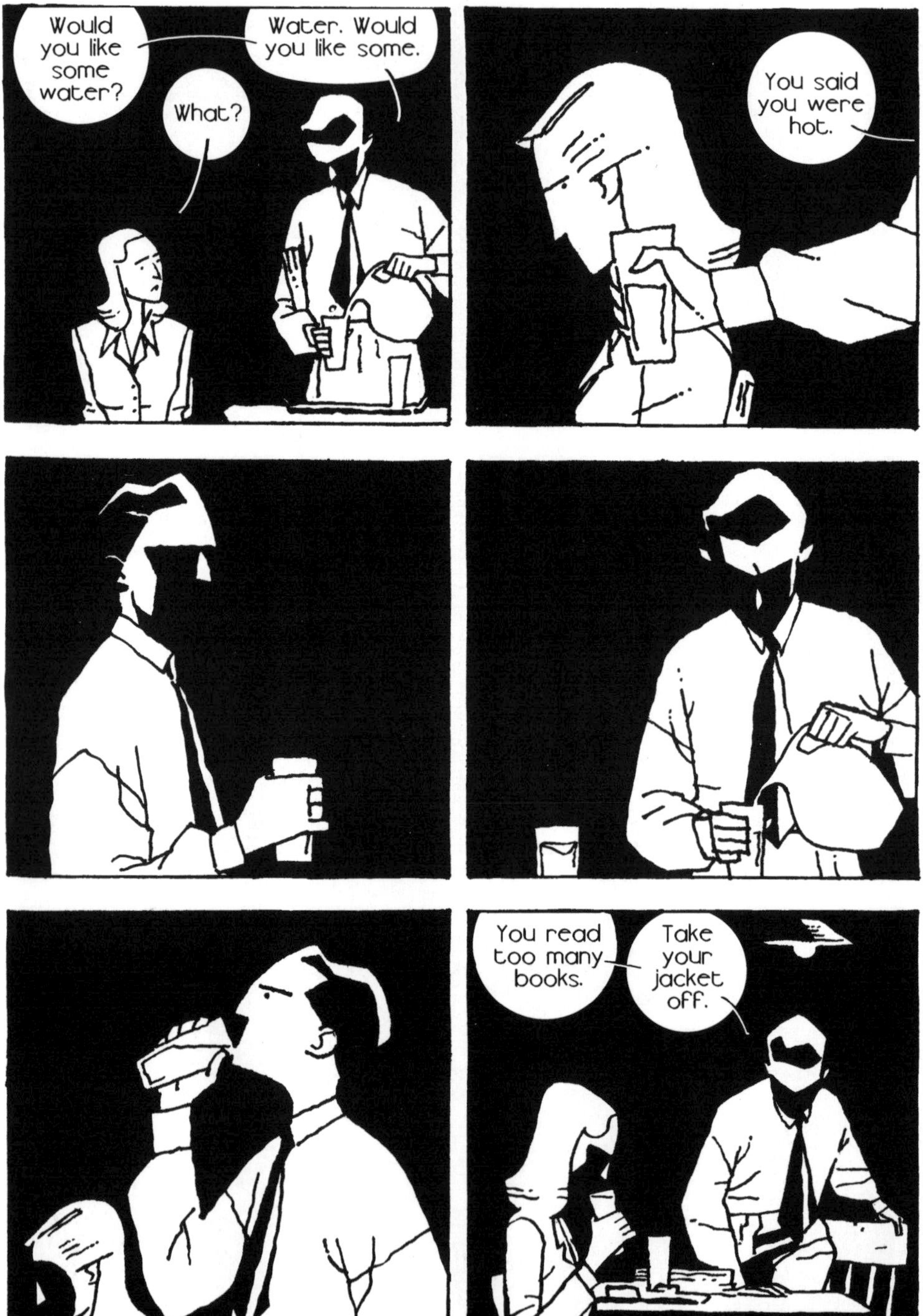
Would you like some water?
What?
Water. Would you like some.
You said you were hot.
You read too many books.
Take your jacket off.

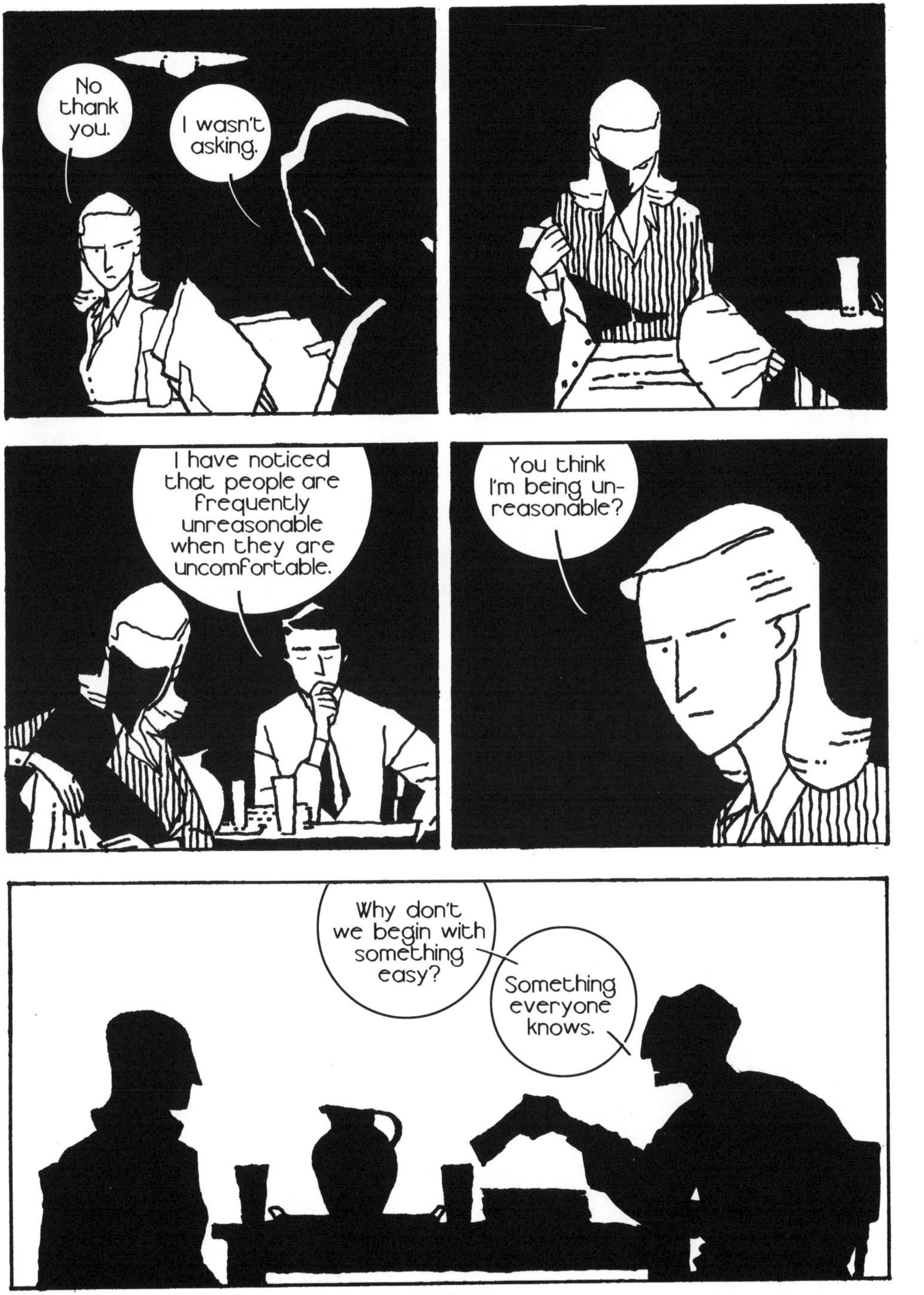
No thank you.
I wasn't asking.
I have noticed that people are frequently unreasonable when they are uncomfortable.
You think I'm being unreasonable?
Why don't we begin with something easy?
Something everyone knows.

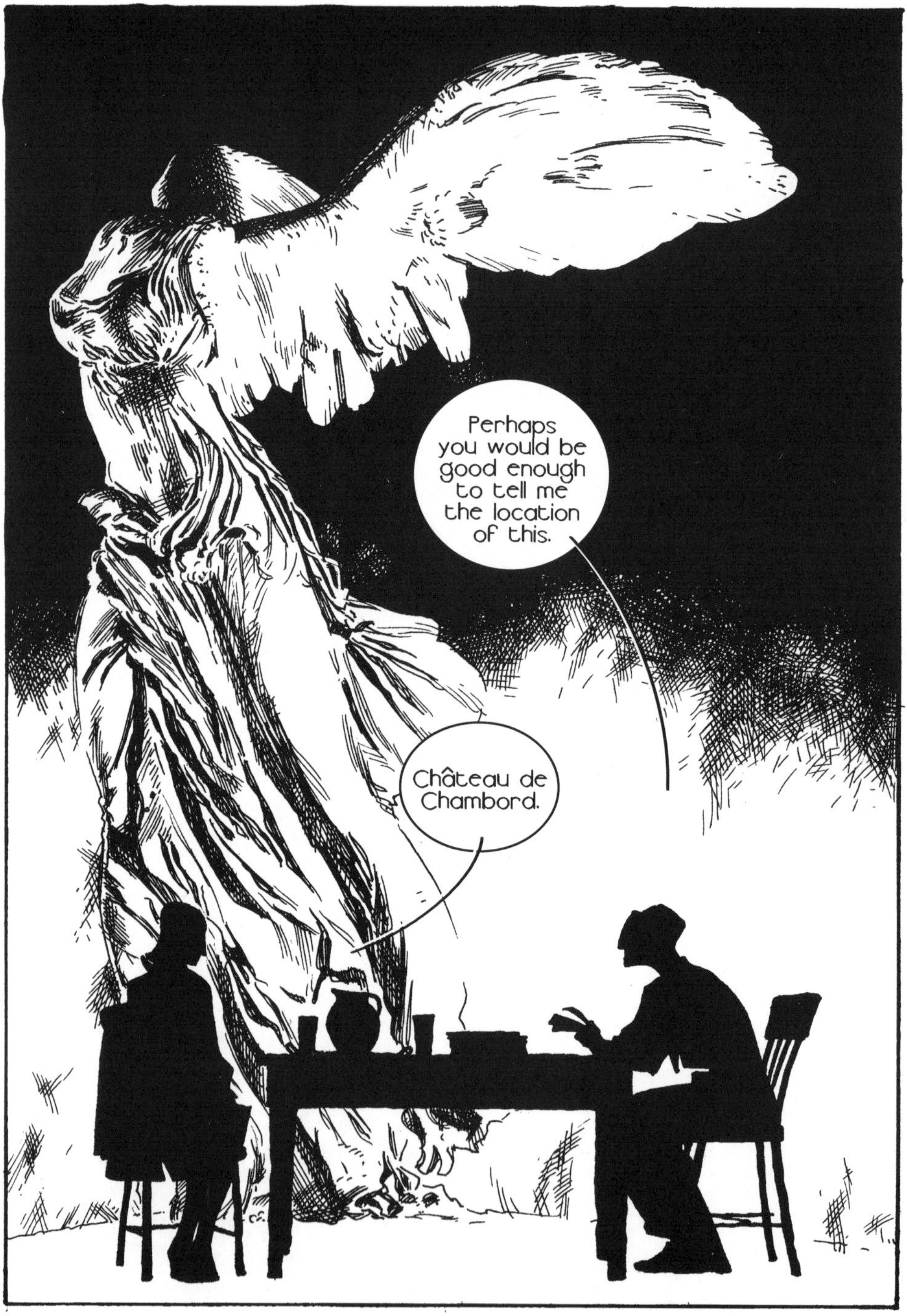
Perhaps you would be good enough to tell me the location of this.
Château de Chambord.

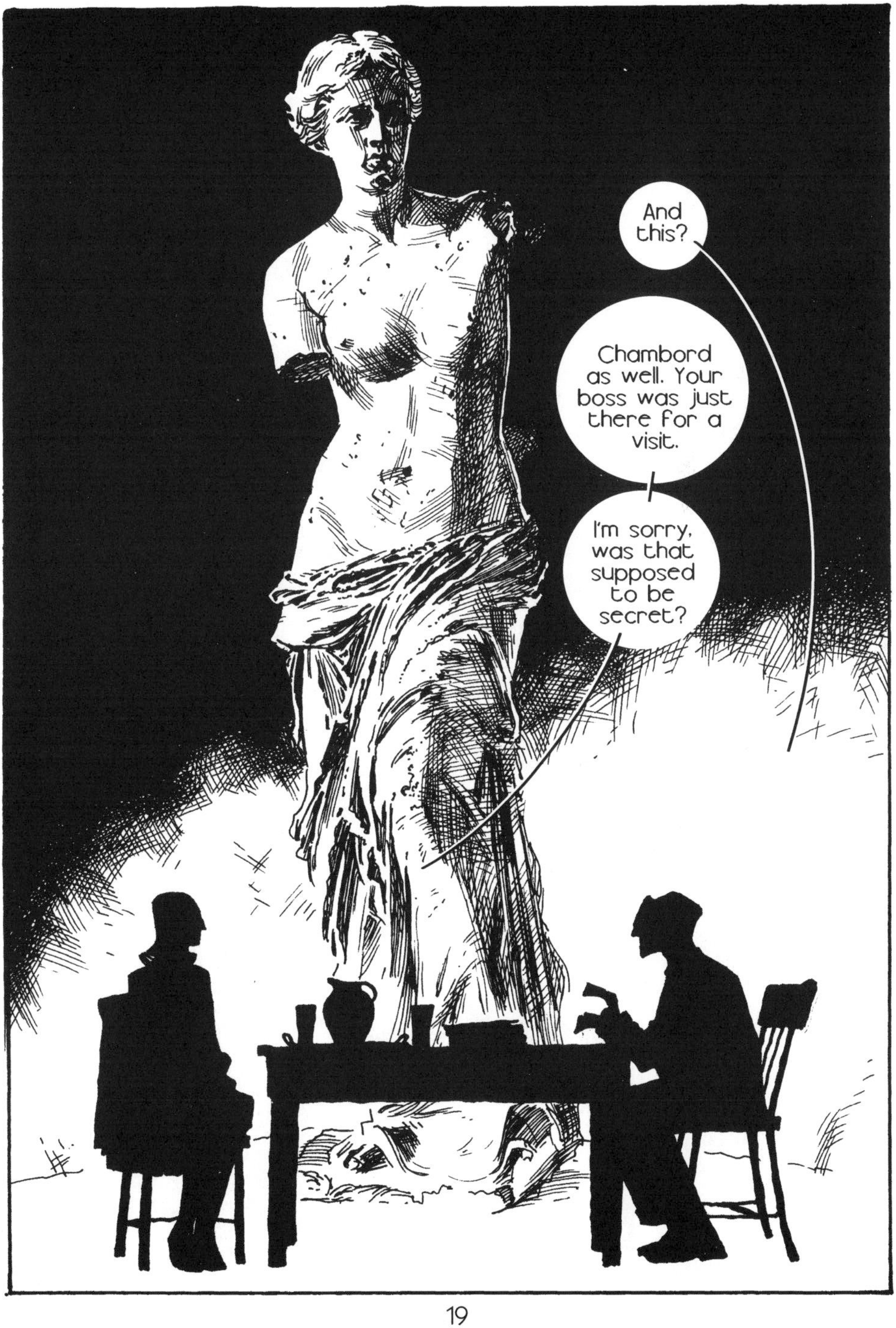
And this?
Chambord as well. Your boss was just there for a visit.
I'm sorry, was that supposed to be secret?

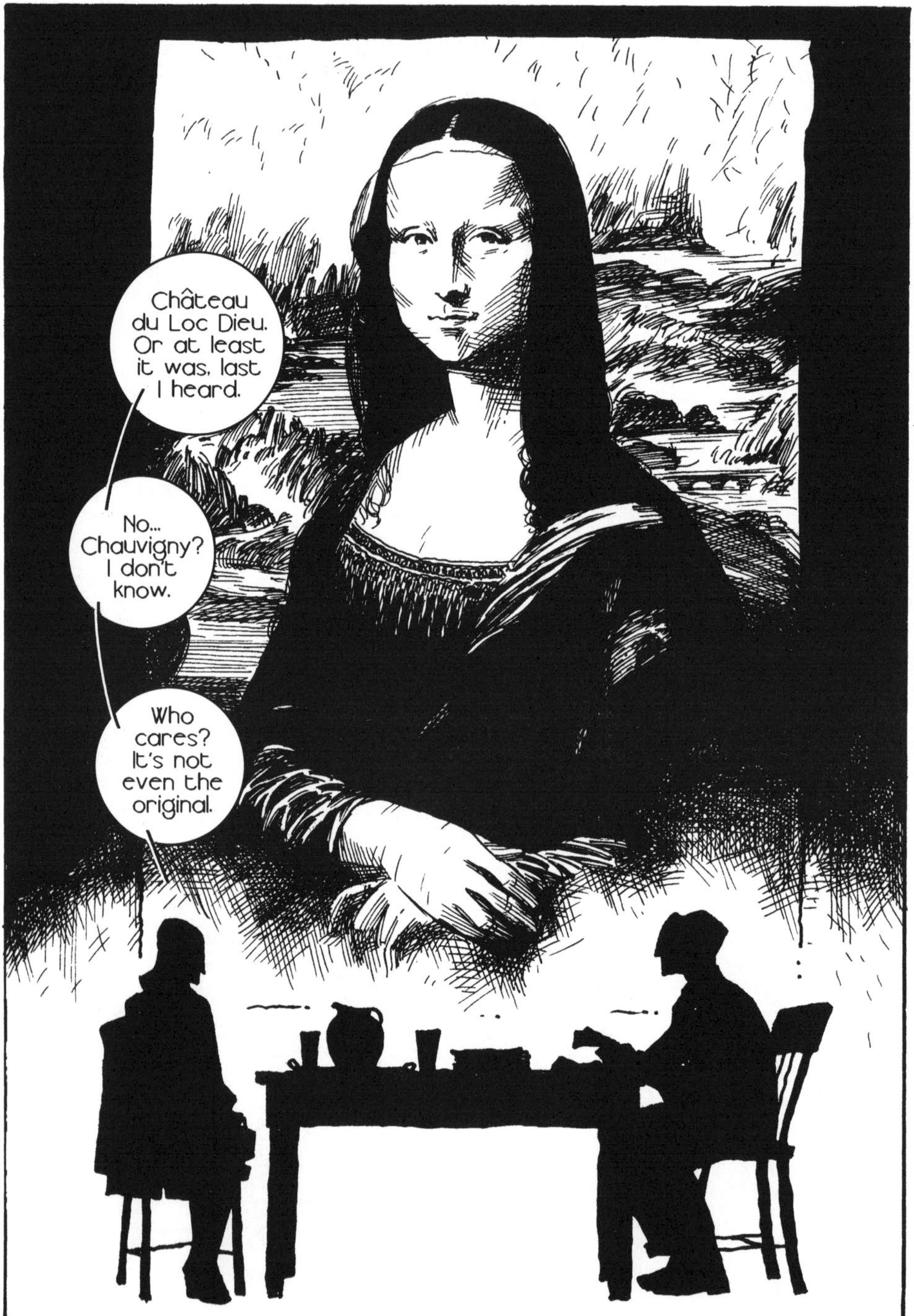
Château du Loc Dieu. Or at least it was, last I heard.
No... Chauvigny? I don't know.
Who cares? It's not even the original.

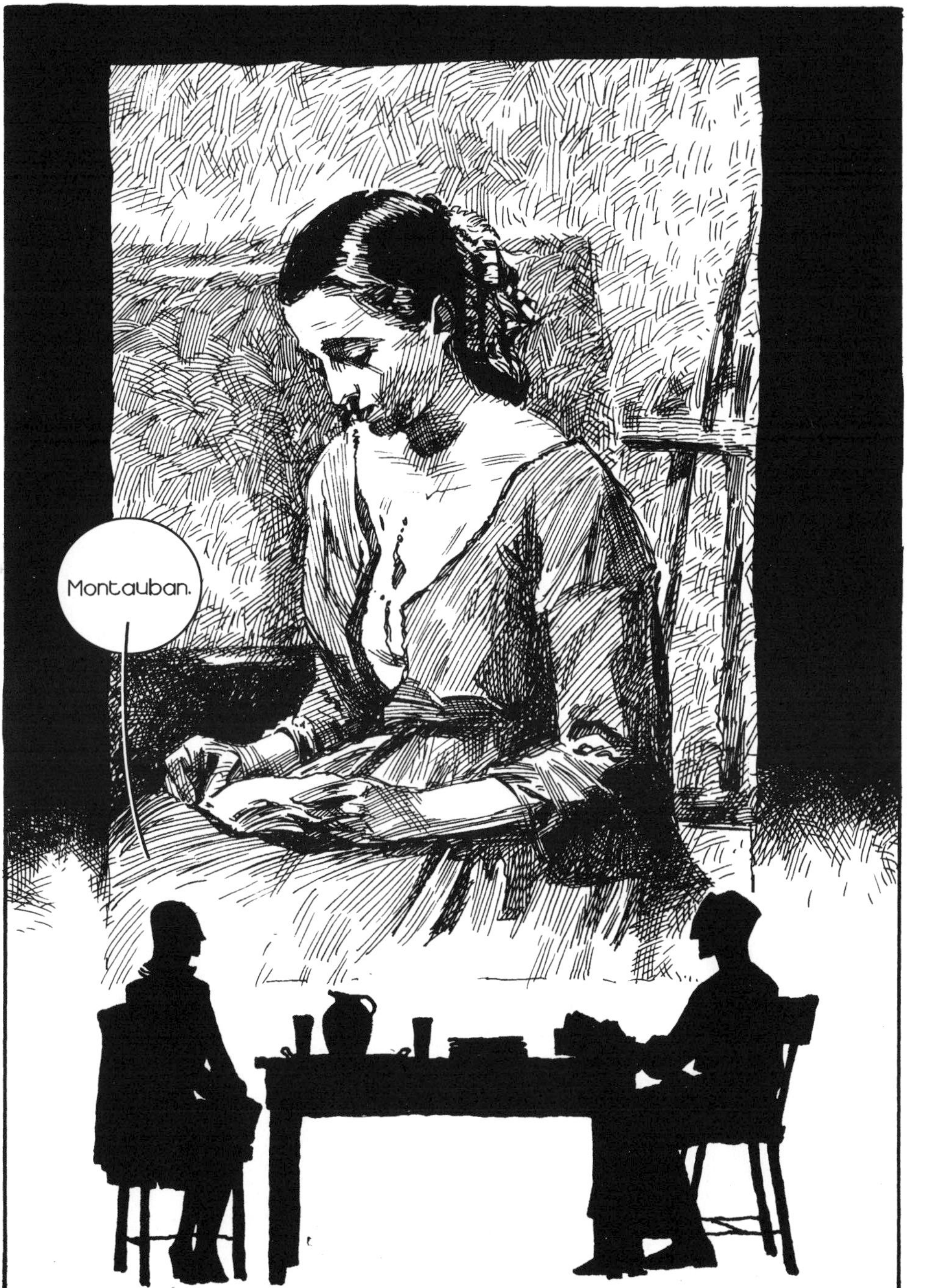
Montauban.

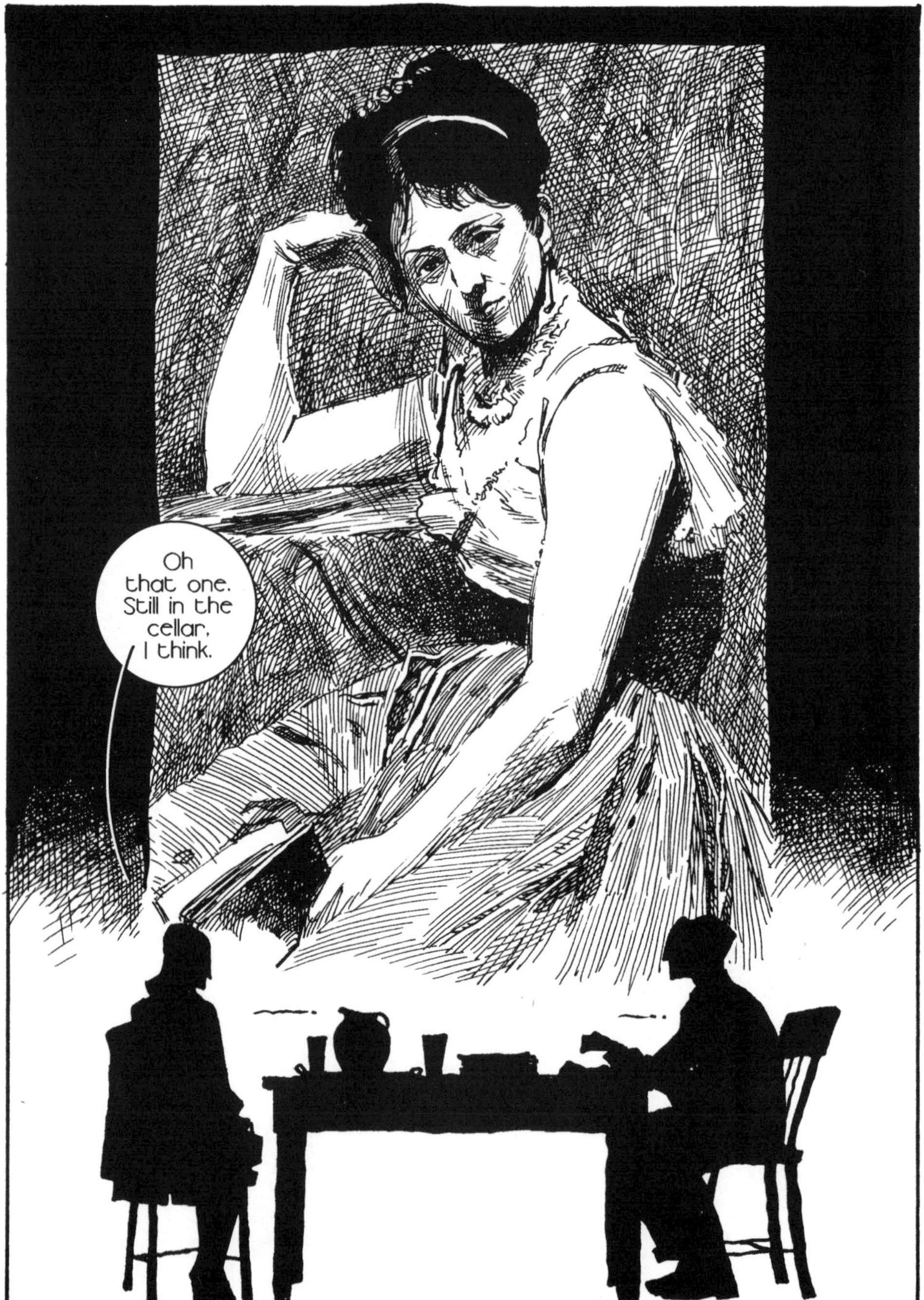
Oh that one. Still in the cellar, I think.

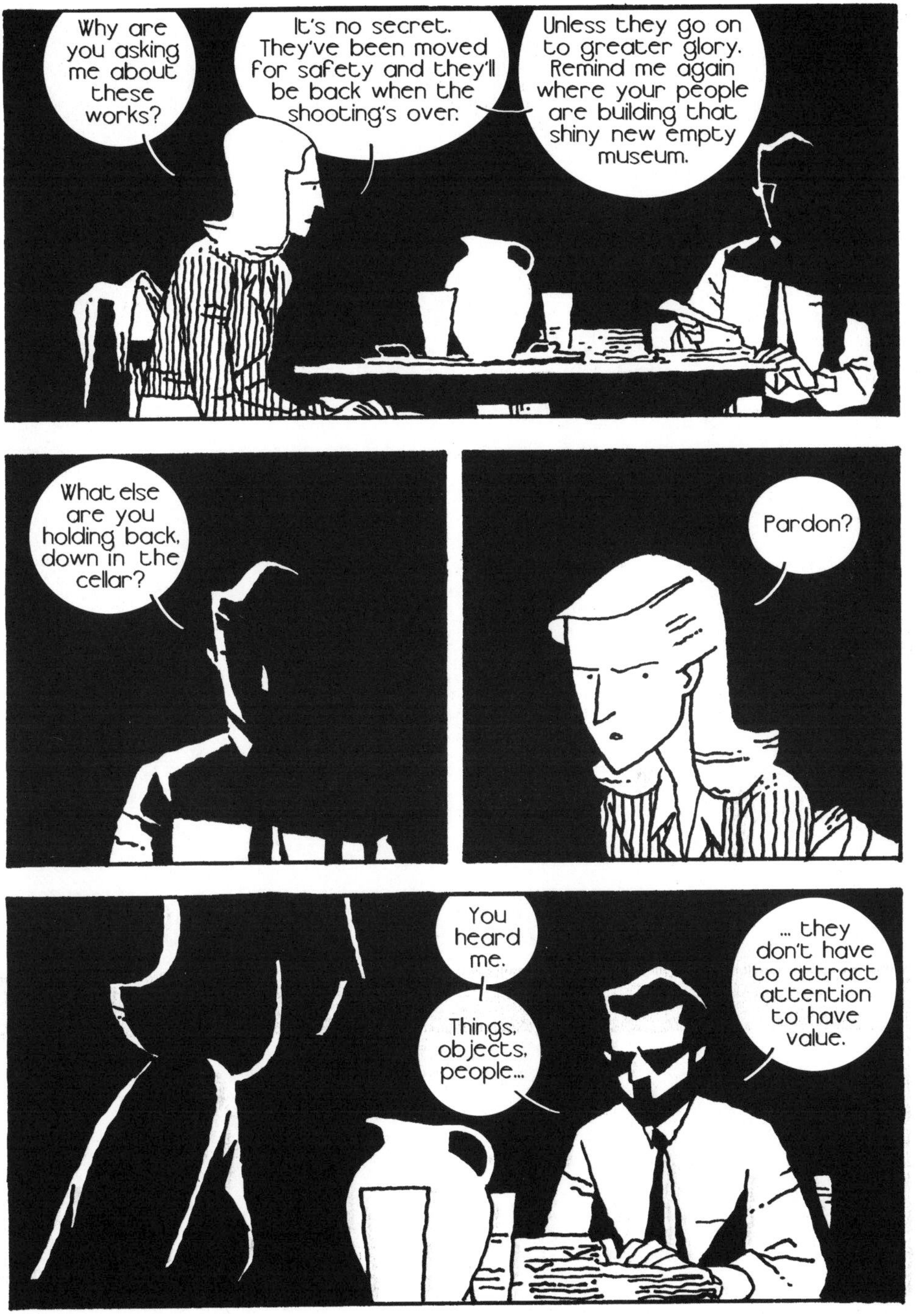
Why are you asking me about these works?
It's no secret. They've been moved for safety and they'll be back when the shooting's over.
Unless they go on to greater glory. Remind me again where your people are building that shiny new empty museum.
What else are you holding back, down in the cellar?
Pardon?
You heard me.
Things, objects, people...
... they don't have to attract attention to have value.

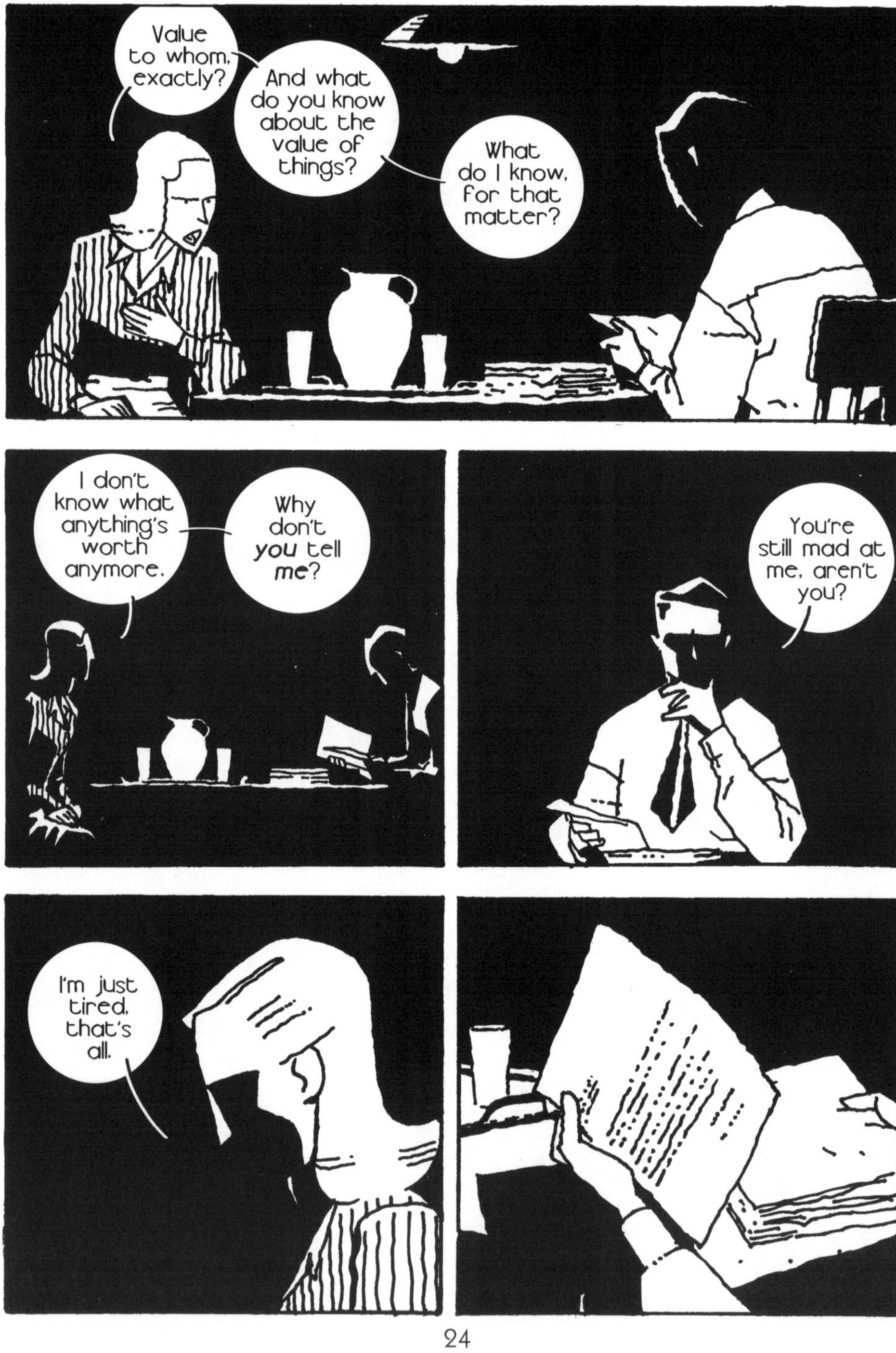
Value to whom, exactly?
And what do you know about the value of things?
What do I know, for that matter?
I don't know what anything's worth anymore.
Why don't *you* tell *me*?
You're still mad at me, aren't you?
I'm just tired, that's all.

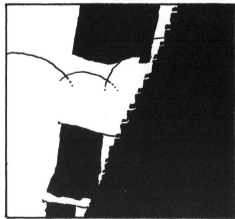

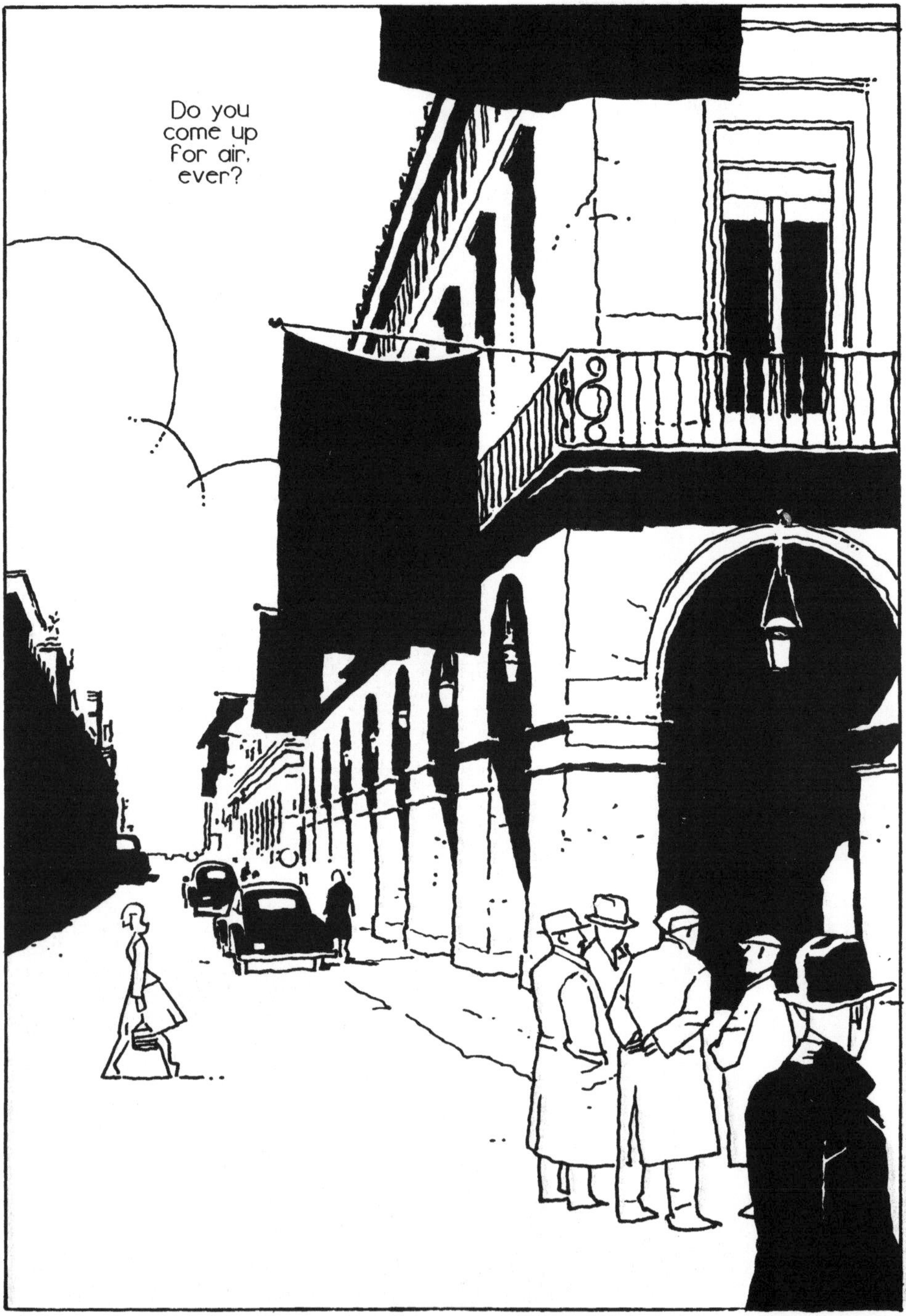
Do you come up for air, ever?

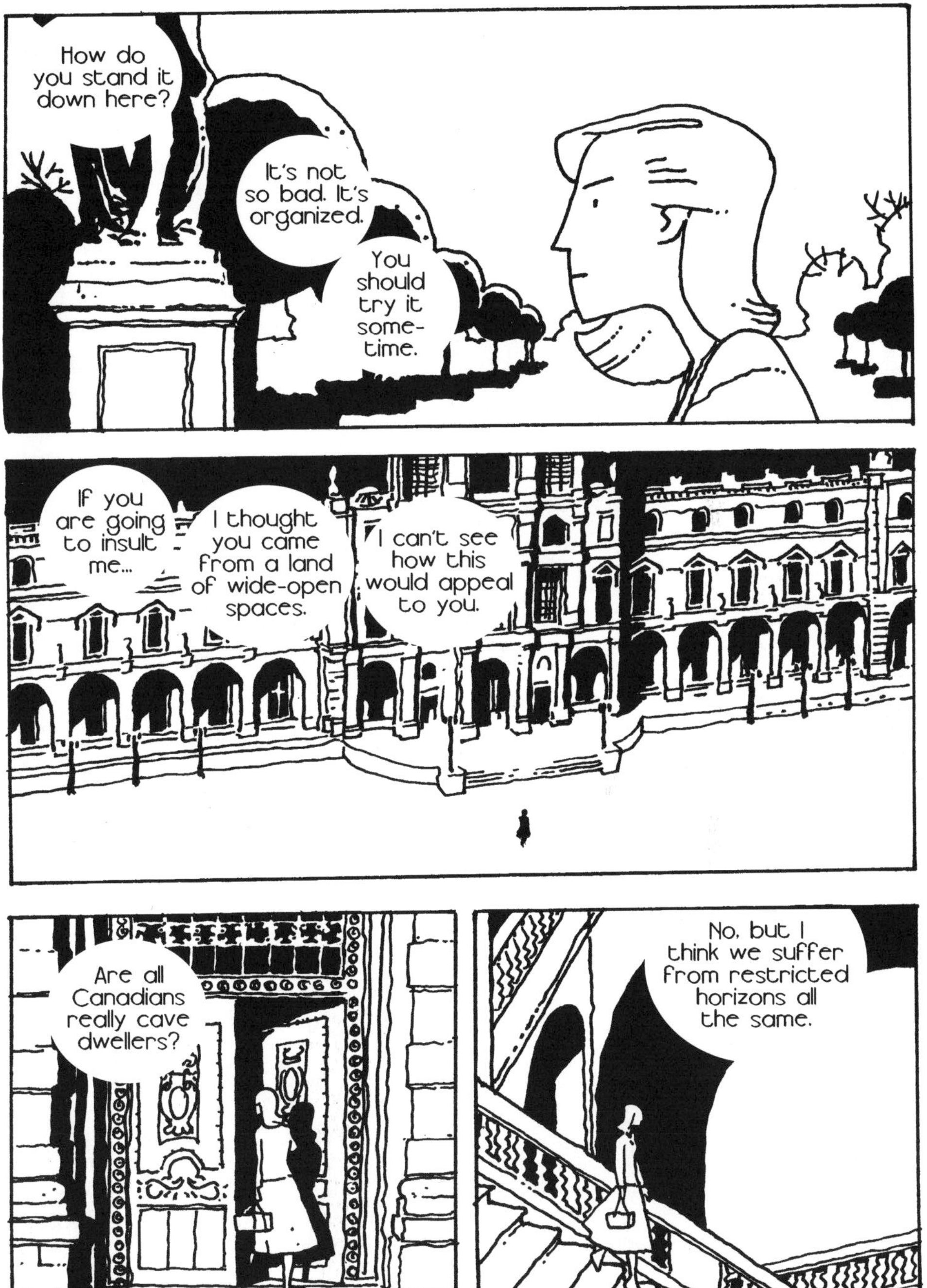
How do you stand it down here?
It's not so bad. It's organized.
You should try it some-time.
If you are going to insult me...
I thought you came from a land of wide-open spaces.
I can't see how this would appeal to you.
Are all Canadians really cave dwellers?
No, but I think we suffer from restricted horizons all the same.

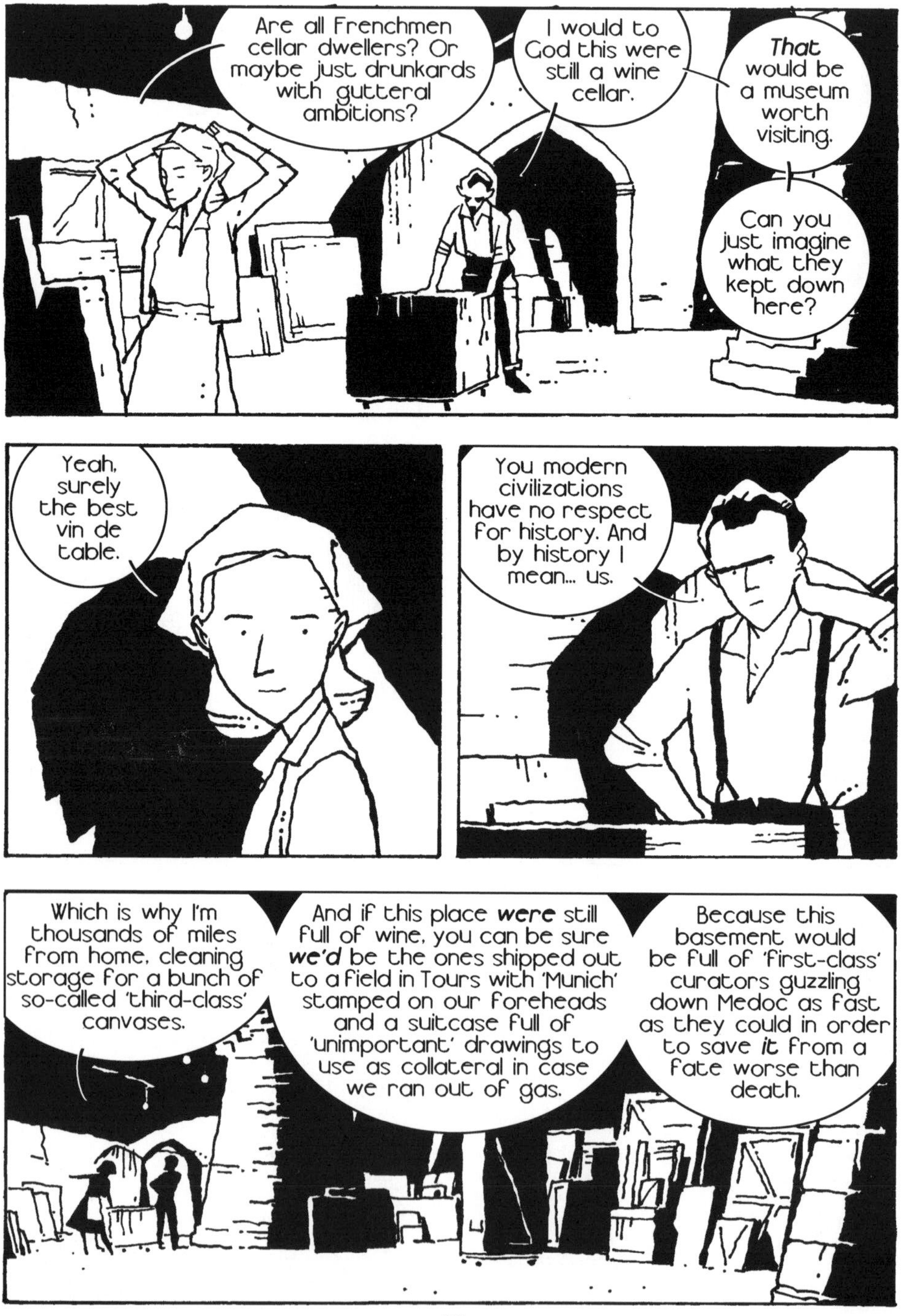
Are all Frenchmen cellar dwellers? Or maybe just drunkards with gutteral ambitions?
I would to God this were still a wine cellar.
That would be a museum worth visiting.
Can you just imagine what they kept down here?
Yeah, surely the best vin de table.
You modern civilizations have no respect for history. And by history I mean... us.
Which is why I'm thousands of miles from home, cleaning storage for a bunch of so-called 'third-class' canvases.
And if this place ***were*** still full of wine, you can be sure ***we'd*** be the ones shipped out to a field in Tours with 'Munich' stamped on our foreheads and a suitcase full of 'unimportant' drawings to use as collateral in case we ran out of gas.
Because this basement would be full of 'first-class' curators guzzling down Medoc as fast as they could in order to save ***it*** from a fate worse than death.

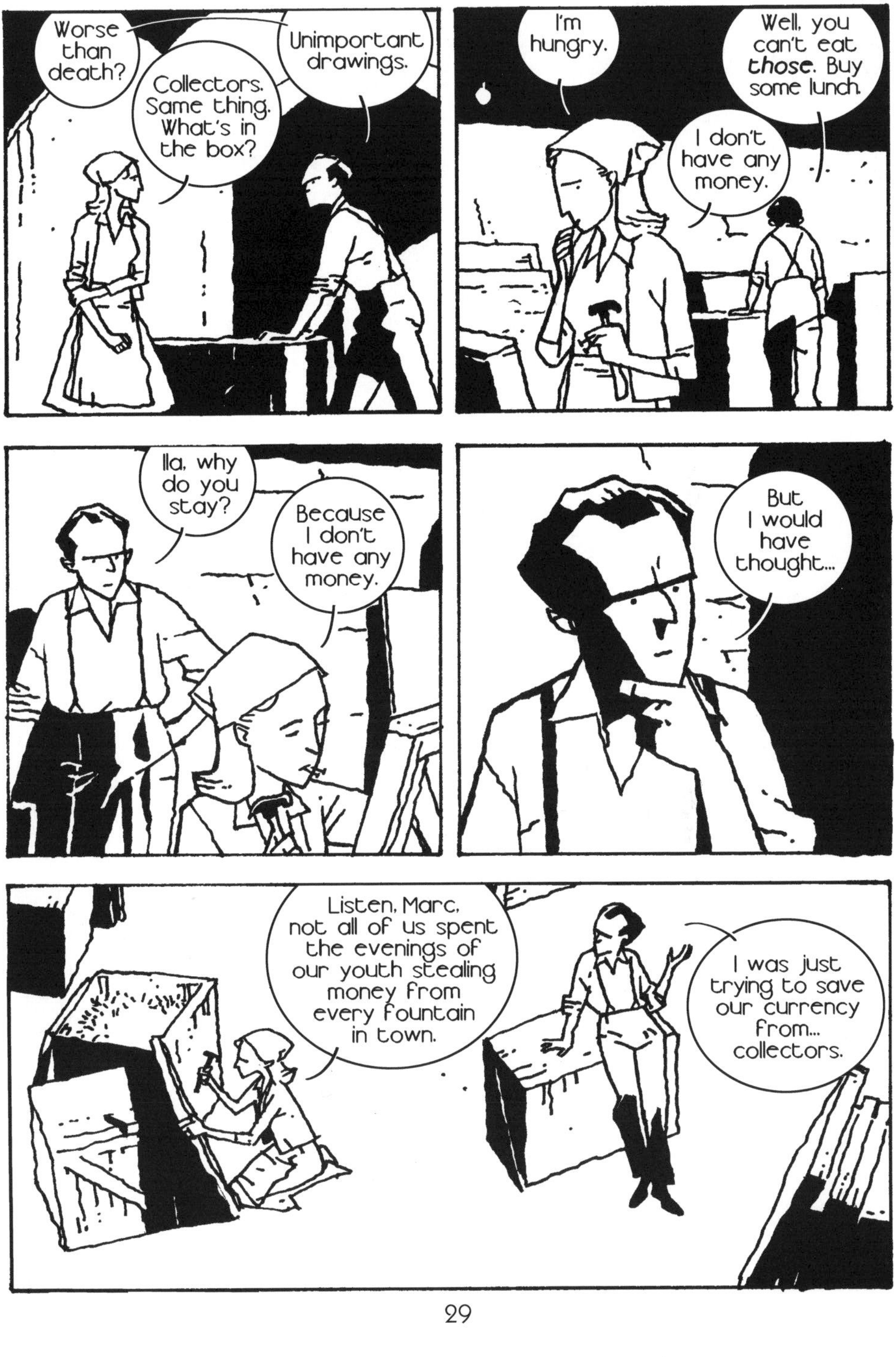
Worse than death?
Unimportant drawings.
Collectors. Same thing. What's in the box?
I'm hungry.
Well, you can't eat *those*. Buy some lunch.
I don't have any money.
Ila, why do you stay?
Because I don't have any money.
But I would have thought...
Listen, Marc, not all of us spent the evenings of our youth stealing money from every fountain in town.
I was just trying to save our currency from... collectors.

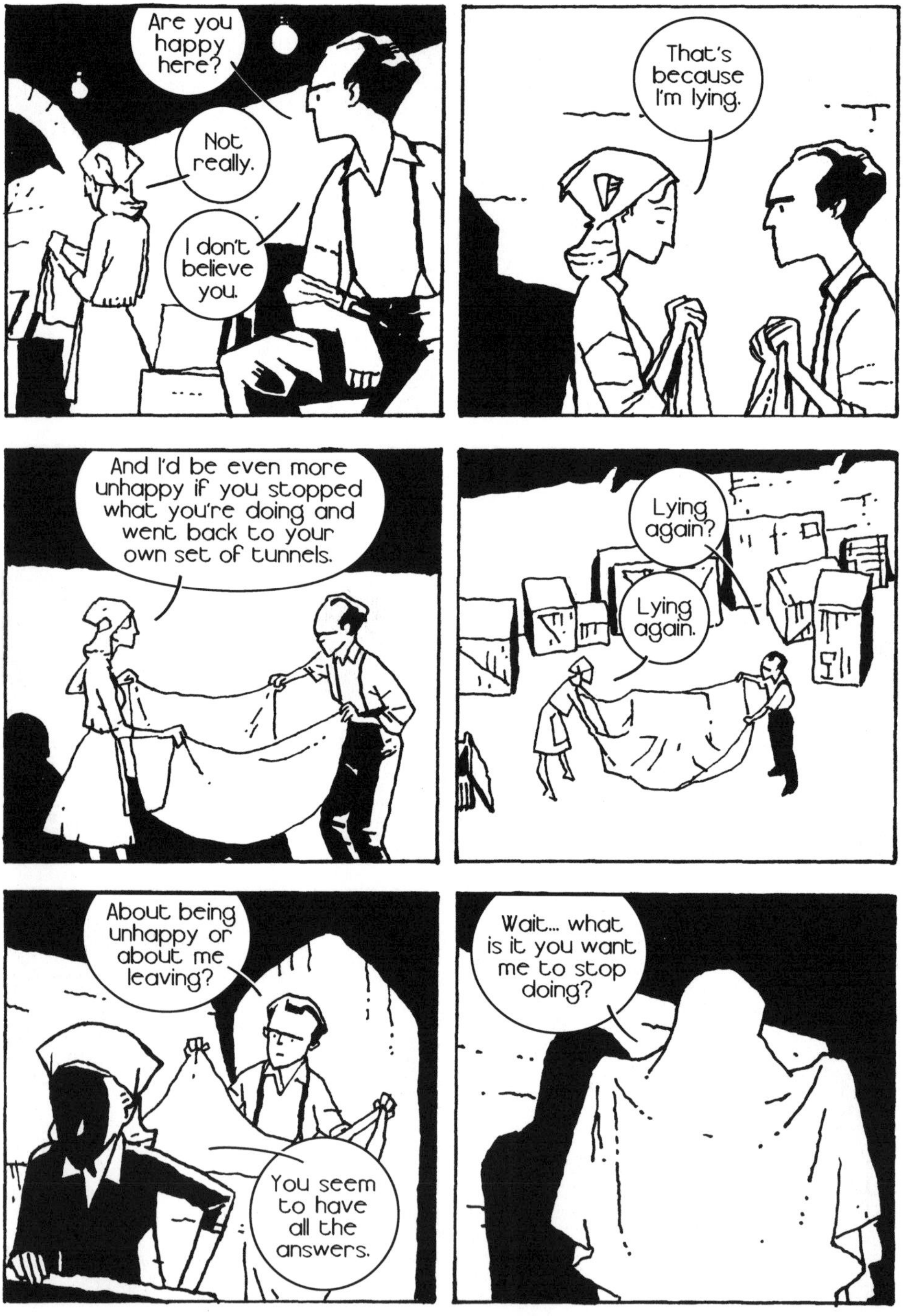
Are you happy here?
Not really.
I don't believe you.
That's because I'm lying.
And I'd be even more unhappy if you stopped what you're doing and went back to your own set of tunnels.
Lying again?
Lying again.
About being unhappy or about me leaving?
You seem to have all the answers.
Wait... what is it you want me to stop doing?

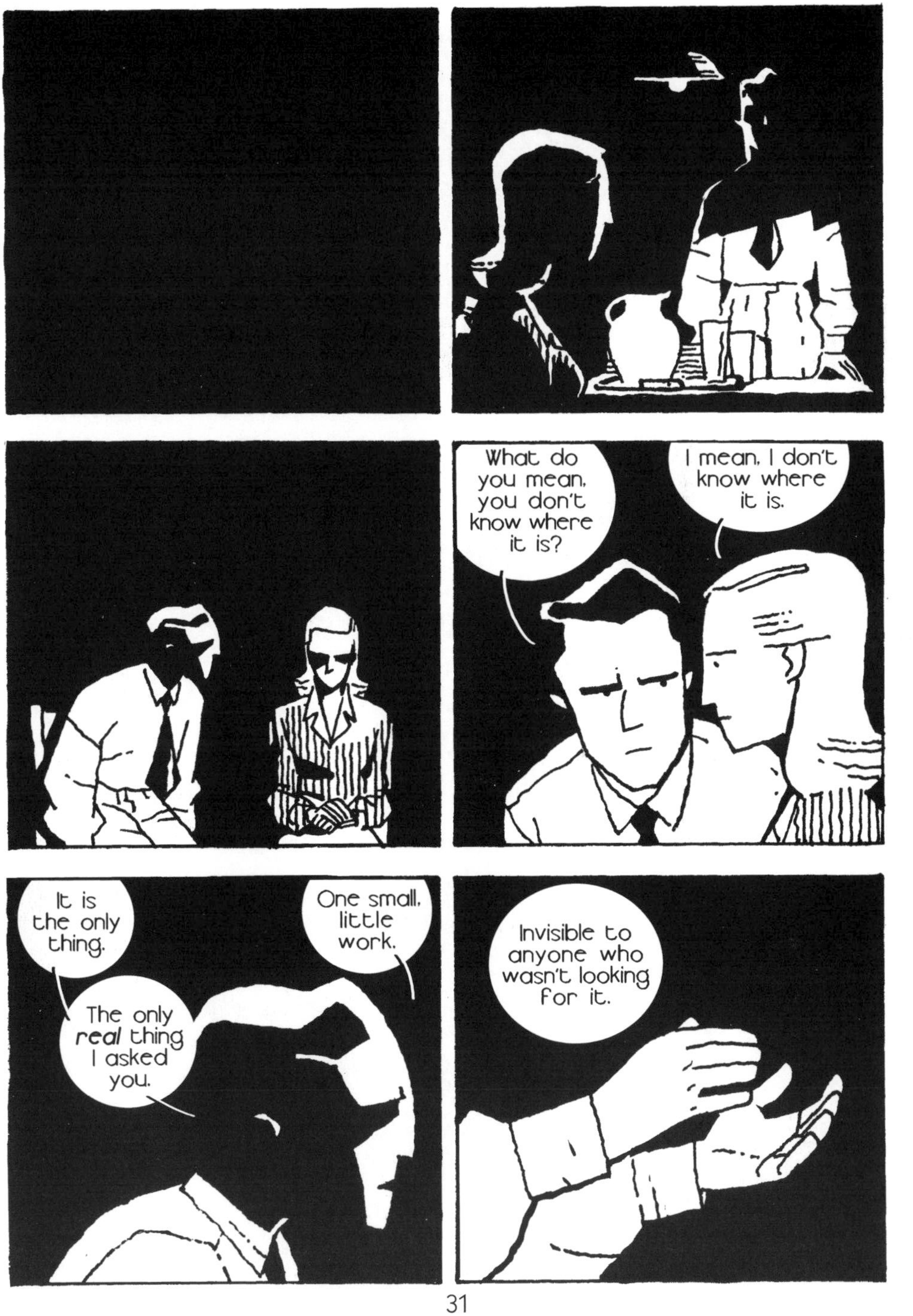
What do you mean, you don't know where it is?
I mean, I don't know where it is.
It is the only thing.
One small, little work.
The only *real* thing I asked you.
Invisible to anyone who wasn't looking for it.

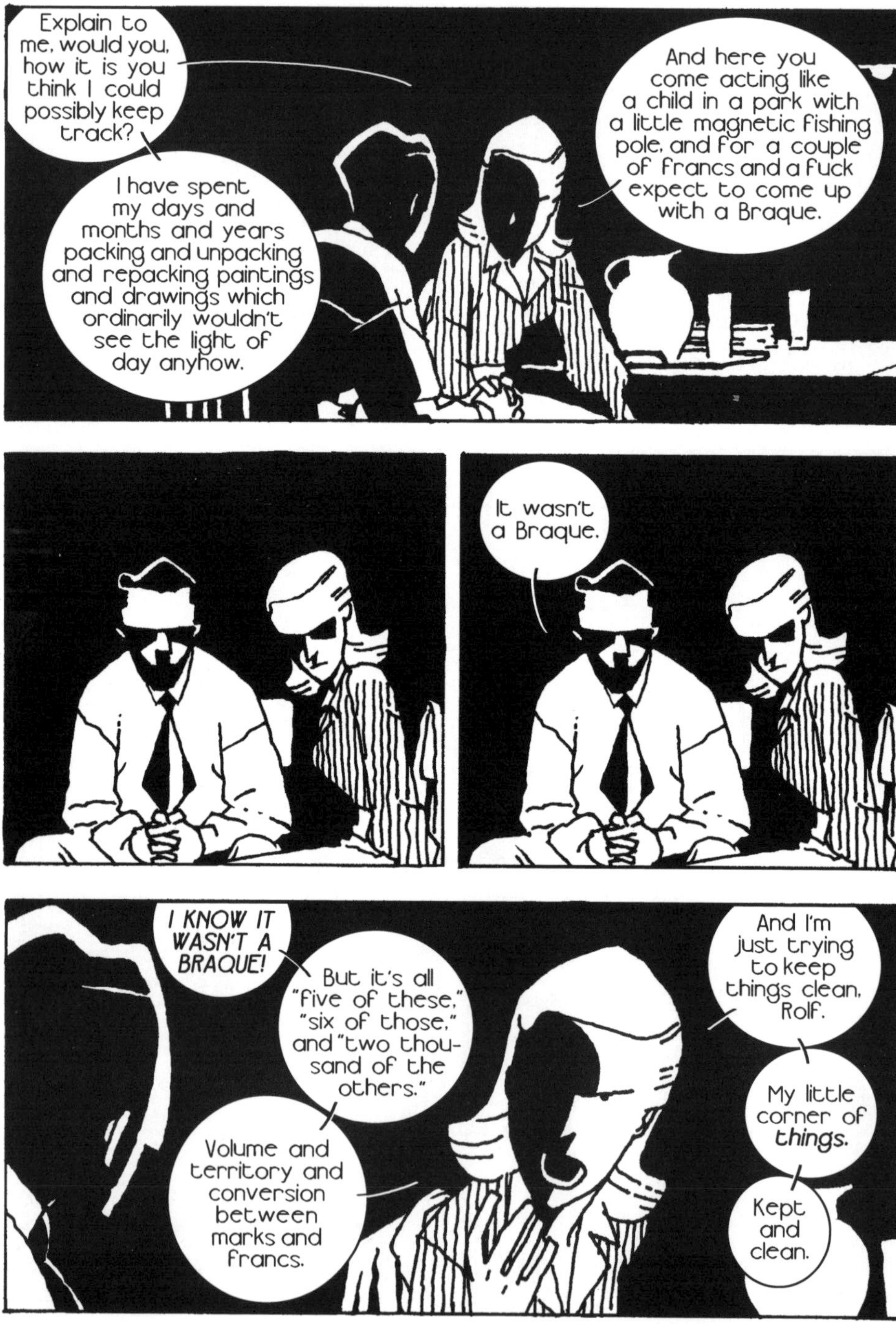
Explain to me, would you, how it is you think I could possibly keep track?
I have spent my days and months and years packing and unpacking and repacking paintings and drawings which ordinarily wouldn't see the light of day anyhow.
And here you come acting like a child in a park with a little magnetic fishing pole, and for a couple of francs and a fuck expect to come up with a Braque.
It wasn't a Braque.
I KNOW IT WASN'T A BRAQUE!
But it's all "five of these," "six of those," and "two thousand of the others."
Volume and territory and conversion between marks and francs.
And I'm just trying to keep things clean, Rolf.
My little corner of *things.*
Kept and clean.

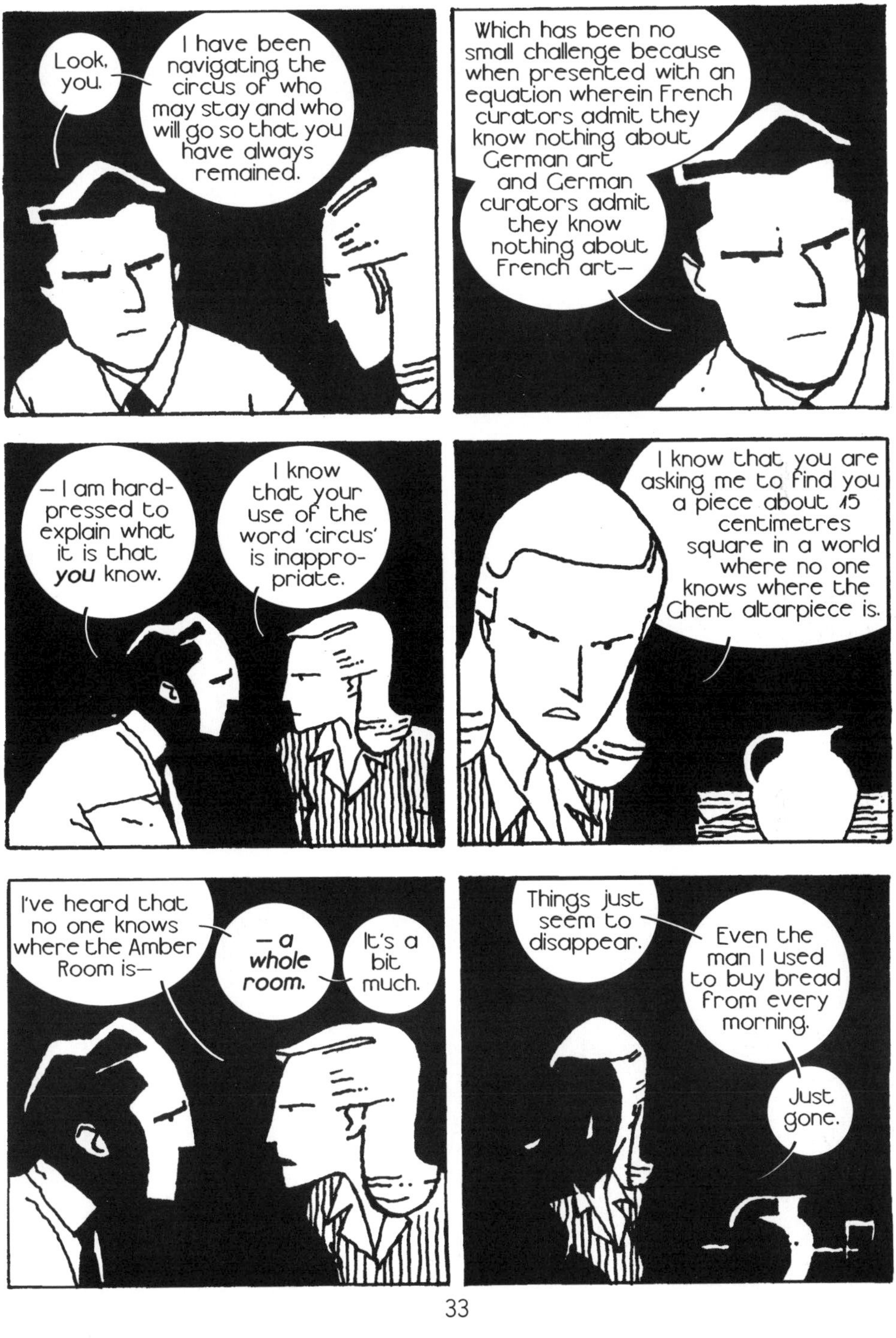
Look, you.
I have been navigating the circus of who may stay and who will go so that you have always remained.
Which has been no small challenge because when presented with an equation wherein French curators admit they know nothing about German art and German curators admit they know nothing about French art—
—I am hard-pressed to explain what it is that *you* know.
I know that your use of the word 'circus' is inappropriate.
I know that you are asking me to find you a piece about 15 centimetres square in a world where no one knows where the Ghent altarpiece is.
I've heard that no one knows where the Amber Room is—
—*a whole room.*
It's a bit much.
Things just seem to disappear.
Even the man I used to buy bread from every morning.
Just gone.

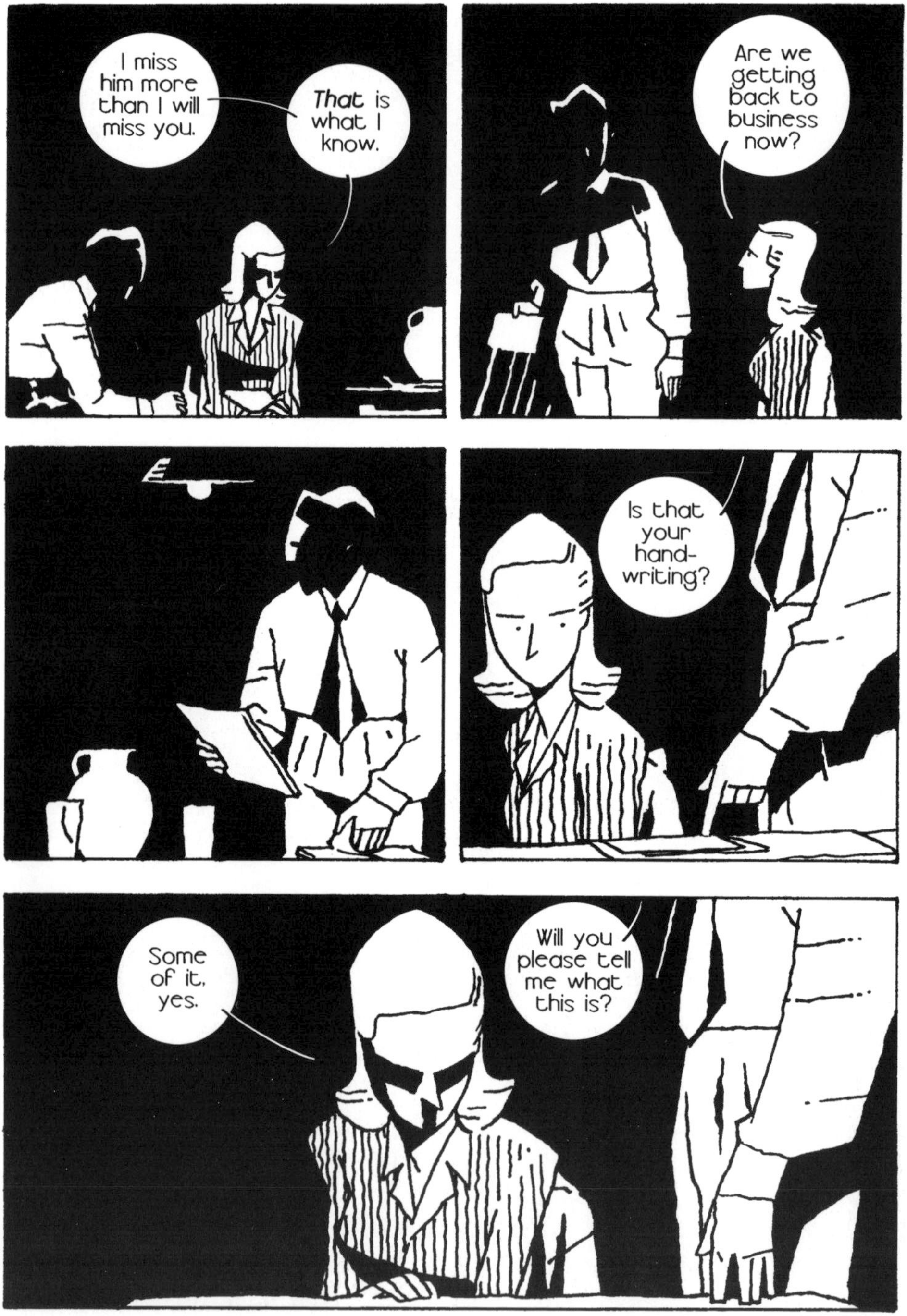
I miss him more than I will miss you.
That is what I know.
Are we getting back to business now?
Is that your hand-writing?
Some of it, yes.
Will you please tell me what this is?

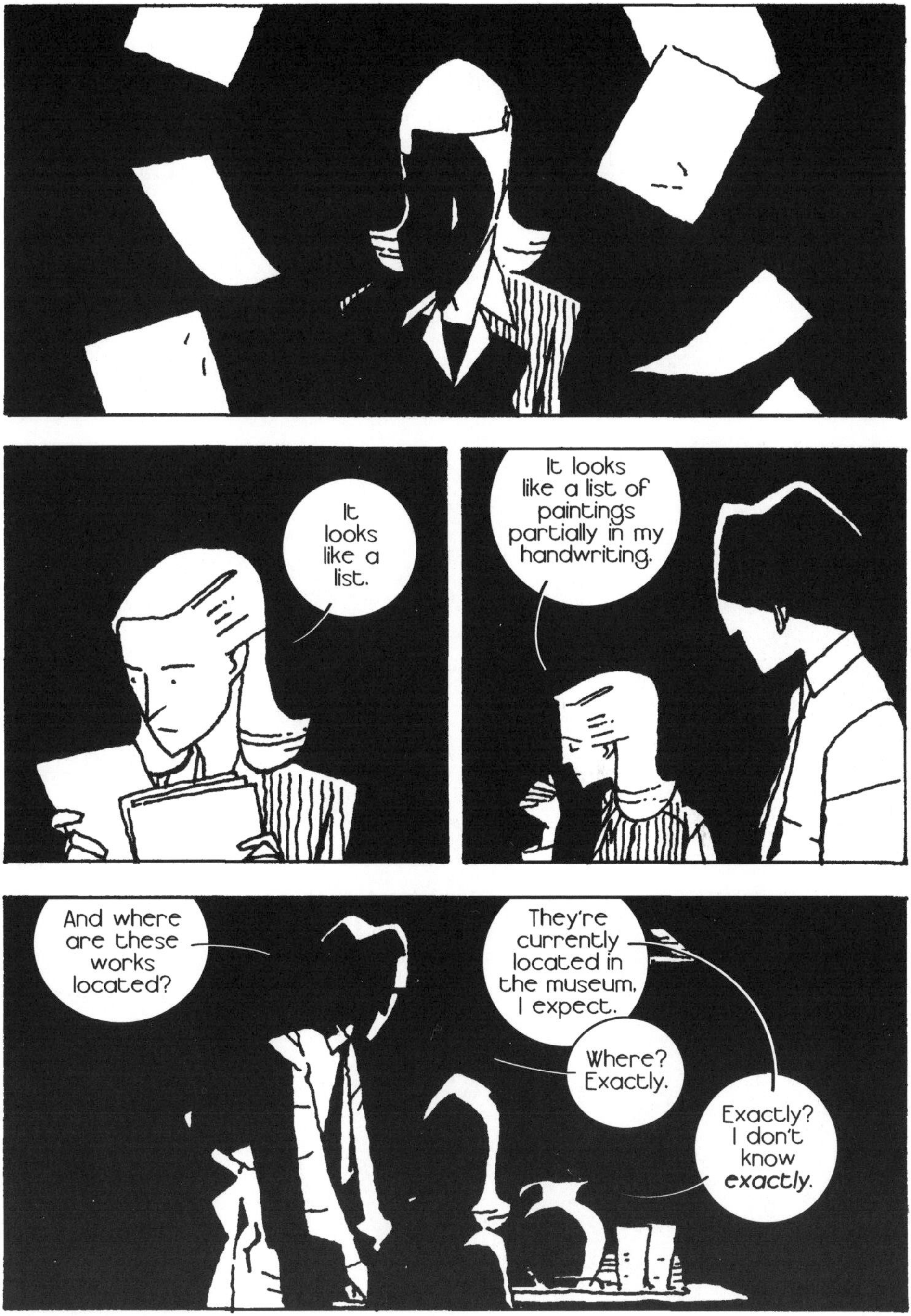
It looks like a list.
It looks like a list of paintings partially in my handwriting.
And where are these works located?
They're currently located in the museum, I expect.
Where? Exactly.
Exactly? I don't know *exactly*.

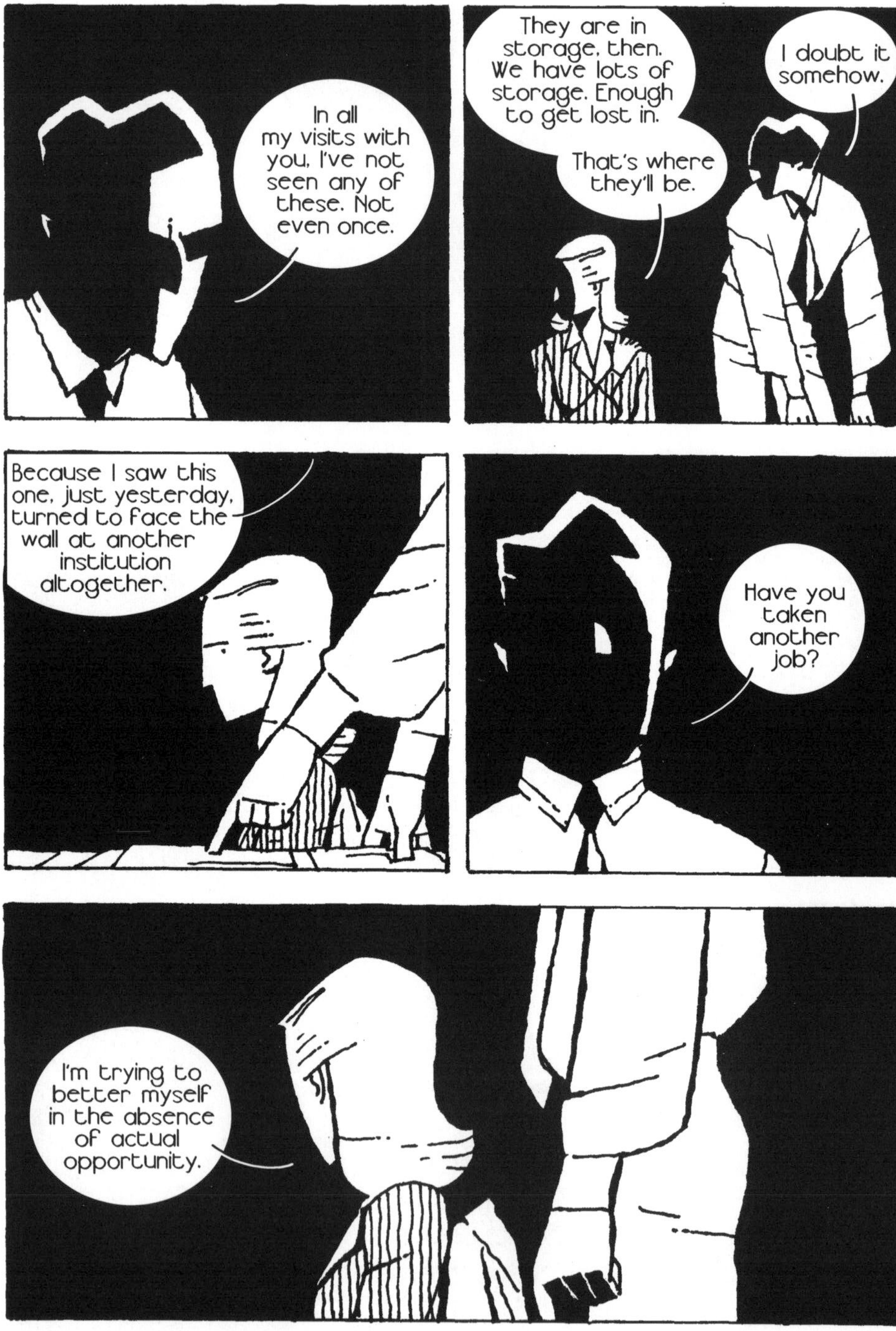
In all my visits with you, I've not seen any of these. Not even once.
They are in storage, then. We have lots of storage. Enough to get lost in.
That's where they'll be.
I doubt it somehow.
Because I saw this one, just yesterday, turned to face the wall at another institution altogether.
Have you taken another job?
I'm trying to better myself in the absence of actual opportunity.

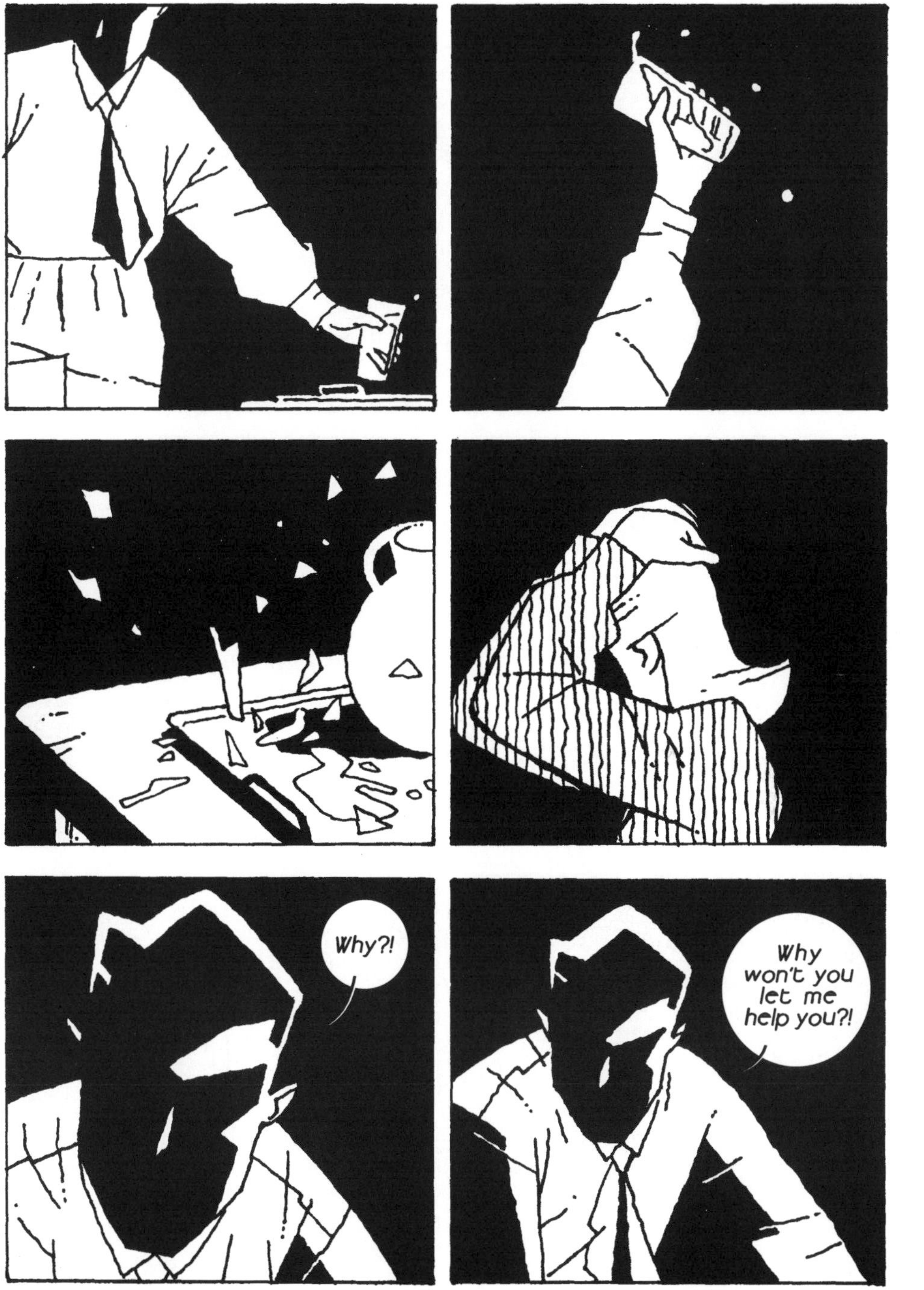
Why?!
Why won't you let me help you?!

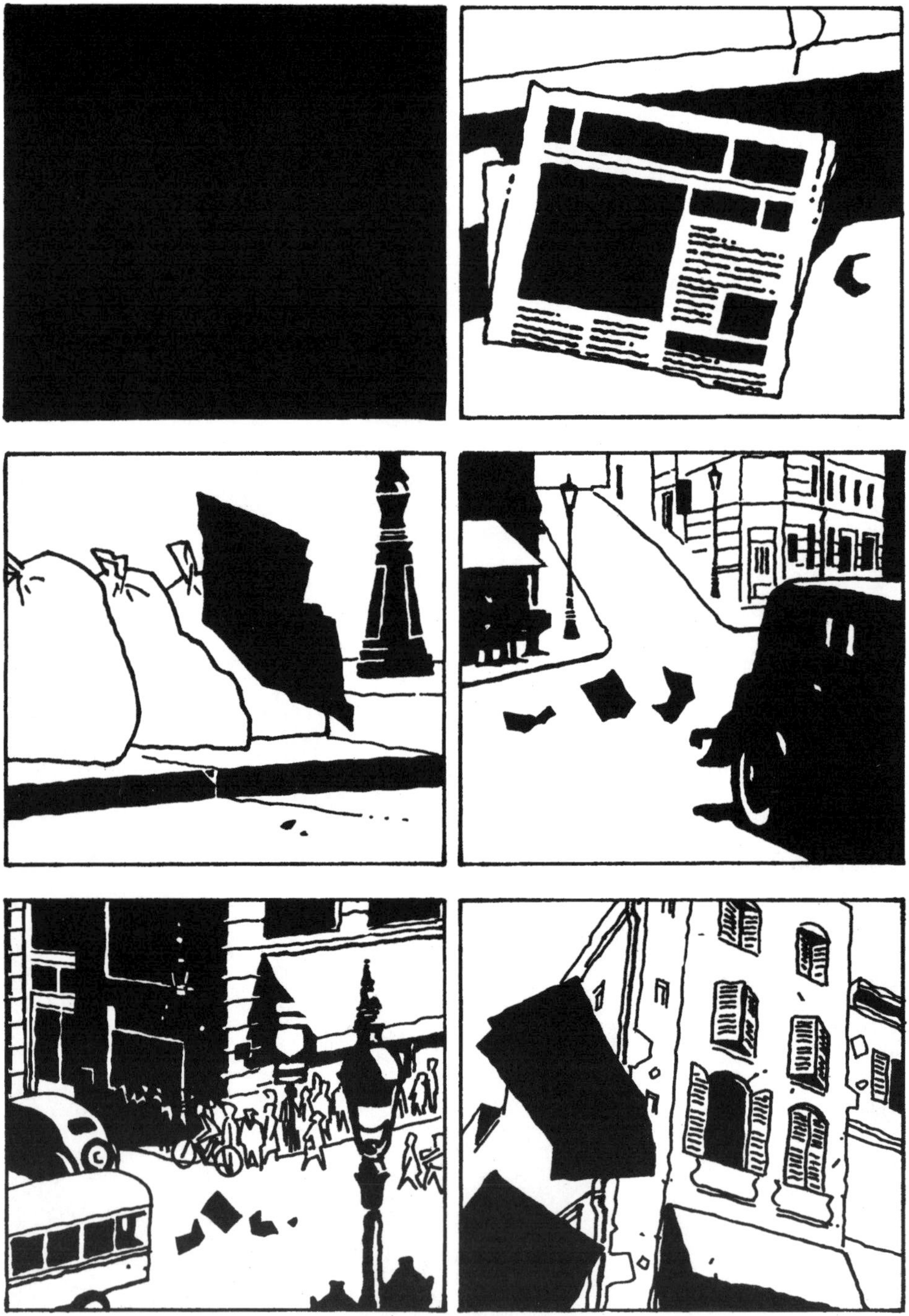

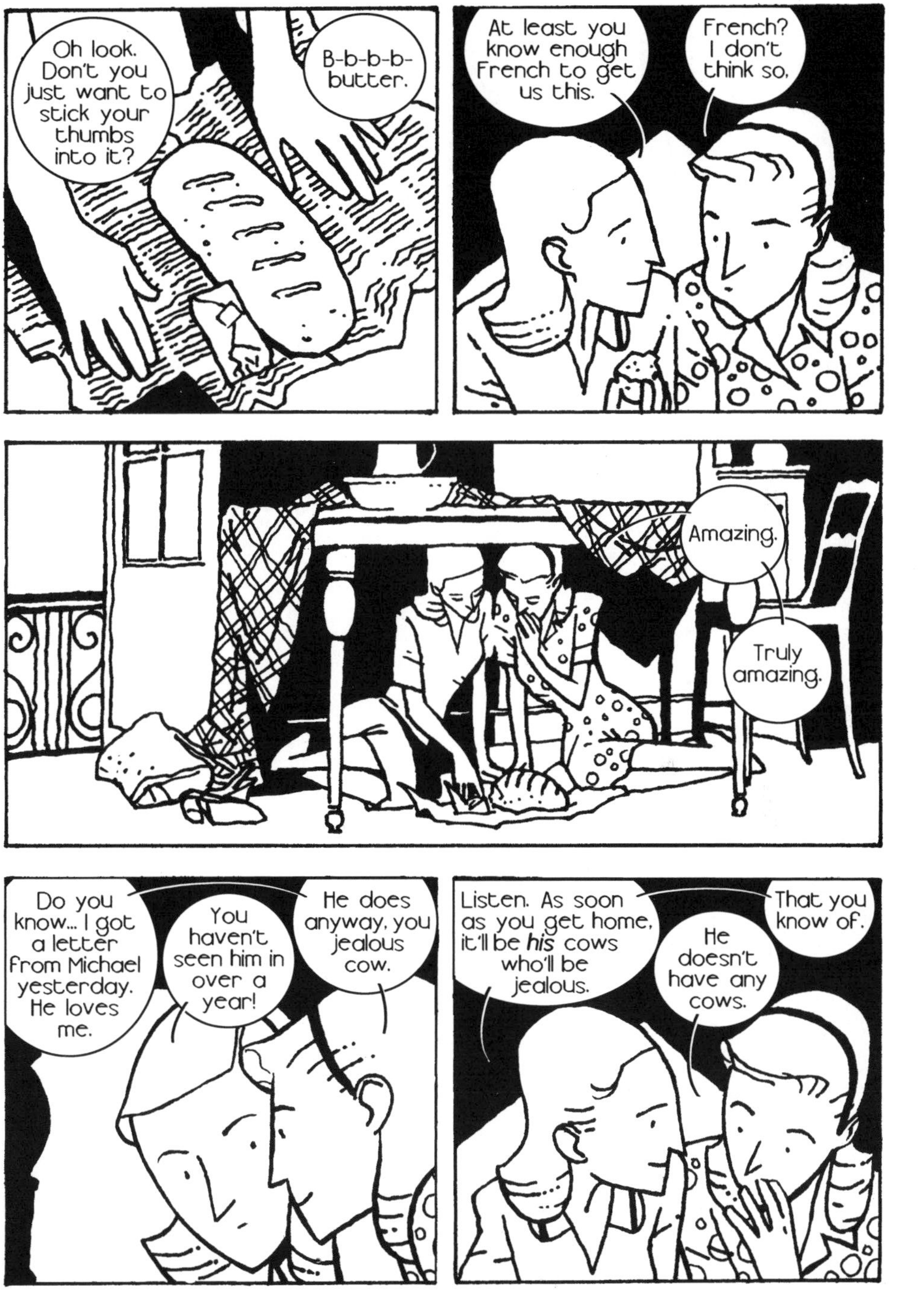
Oh look. Don't you just want to stick your thumbs into it?
B-b-b-b-butter.
At least you know enough French to get us this.
French? I don't think so.
Amazing.
Truly amazing.
Do you know... I got a letter from Michael yesterday. He loves me.
You haven't seen him in over a year!
He does anyway, you jealous cow.
Listen. As soon as you get home, it'll be *his* cows who'll be jealous.
That you know of.
He doesn't have any cows.

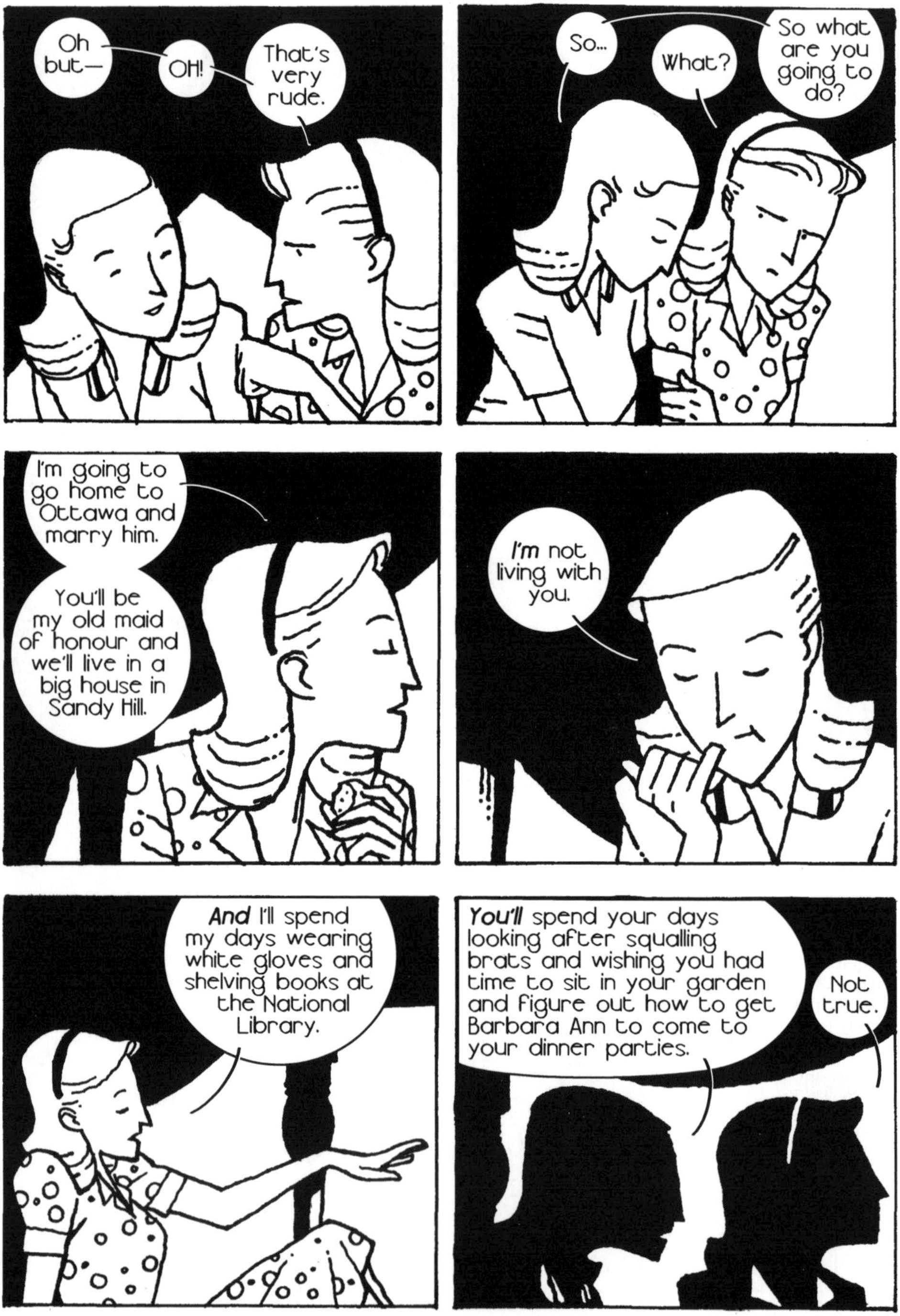
Oh but—
OH!
That's very rude.
So...
What?
So what are you going to do?
I'm going to go home to Ottawa and marry him.
You'll be my old maid of honour and we'll live in a big house in Sandy Hill.
I'm not living with you.
And I'll spend my days wearing white gloves and shelving books at the National Library.
You'll spend your days looking after squalling brats and wishing you had time to sit in your garden and figure out how to get Barbara Ann to come to your dinner parties.
Not true.

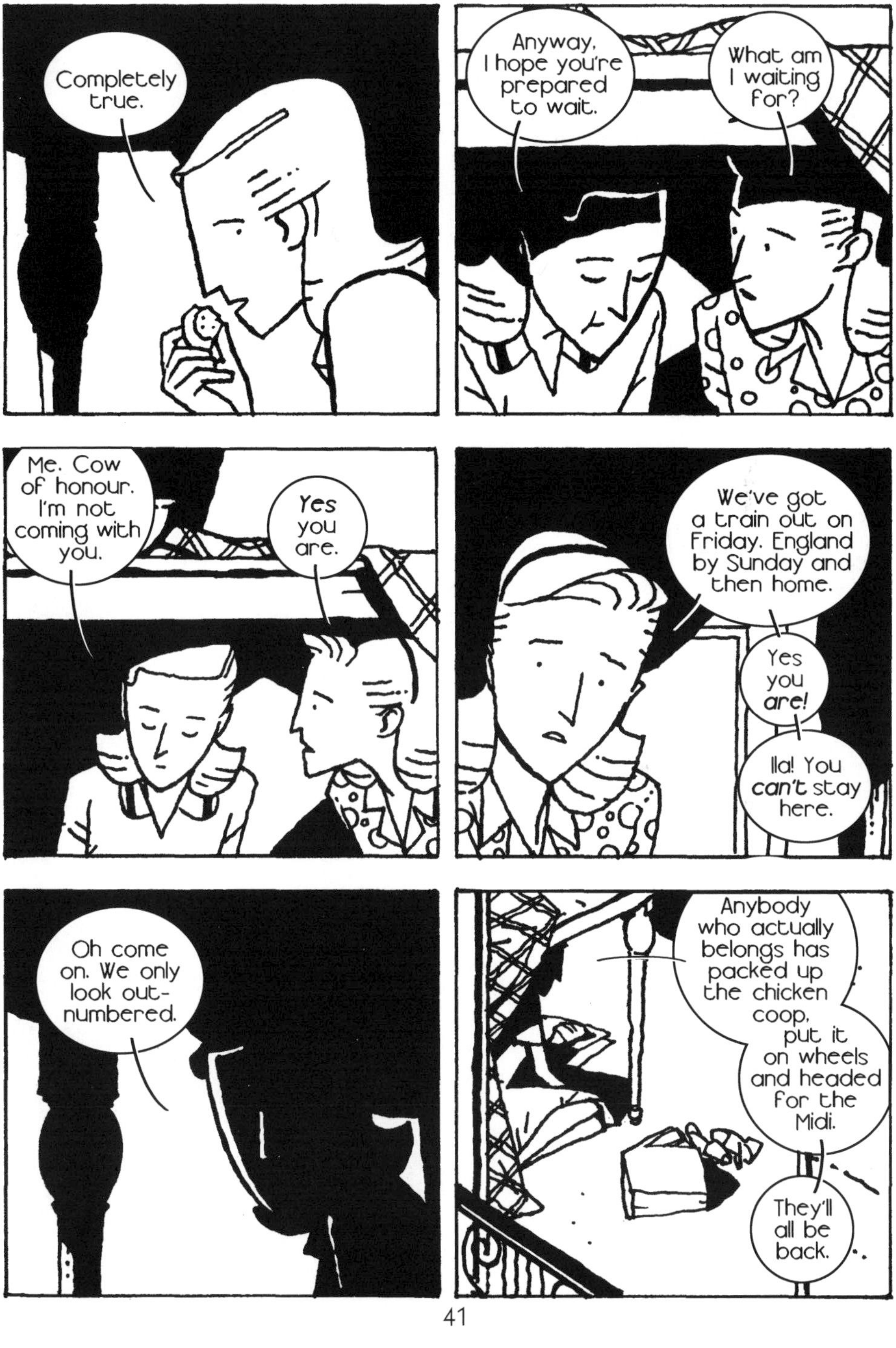
Completely true.
Anyway, I hope you're prepared to wait.
What am I waiting for?
Me. Cow of honour. I'm not coming with you.
Yes you are.
We've got a train out on Friday. England by Sunday and then home.
Yes you *are!*
Ila! You *can't* stay here.
Oh come on. We only look out-numbered.
Anybody who actually belongs has packed up the chicken coop,
put it on wheels and headed for the Midi.
They'll all be back.

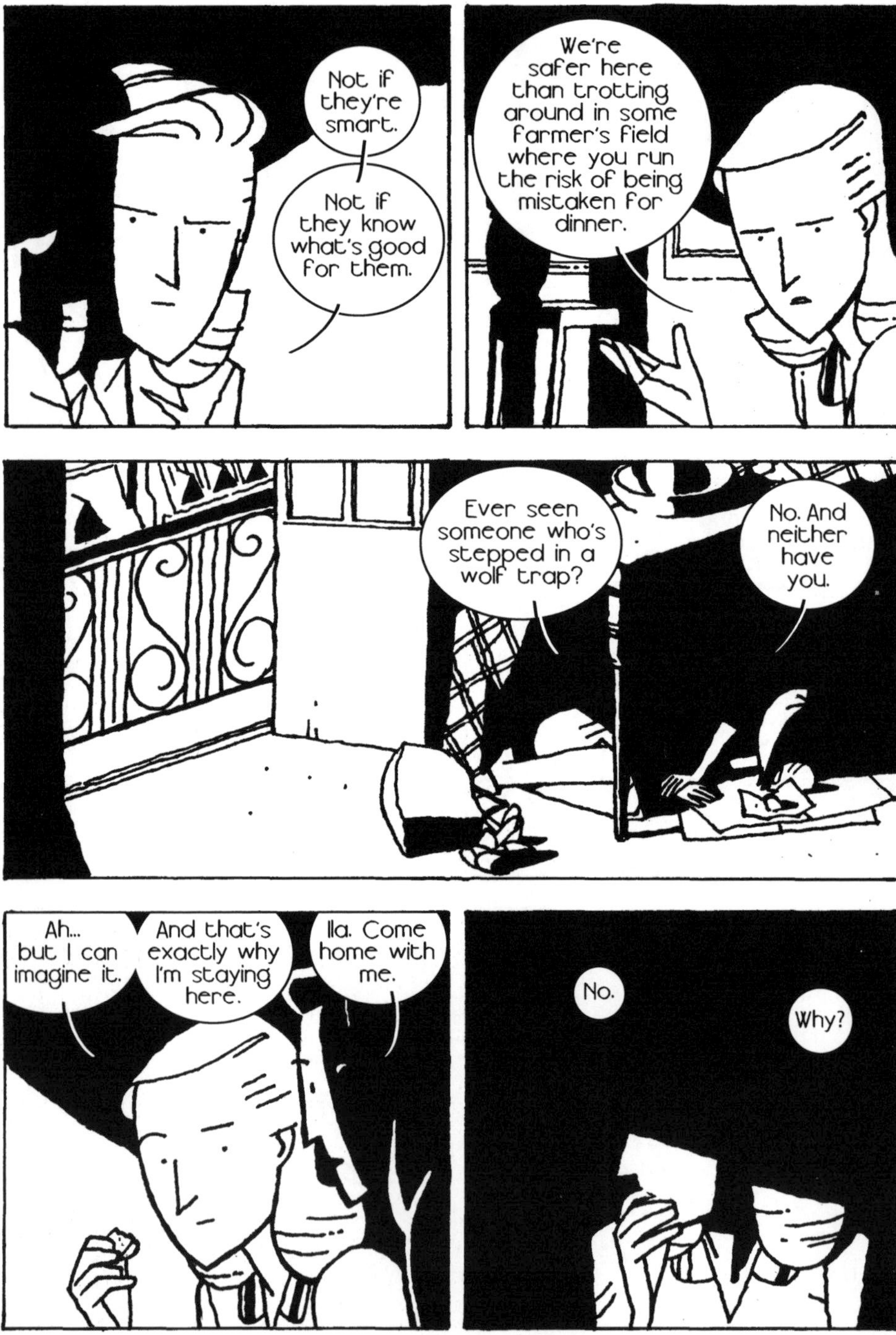
Not if they're smart.
Not if they know what's good for them.
We're safer here than trotting around in some farmer's field where you run the risk of being mistaken for dinner.
Ever seen someone who's stepped in a wolf trap?
No. And neither have you.
Ah... but I can imagine it.
And that's exactly why I'm staying here.
Ila. Come home with me.
No.
Why?

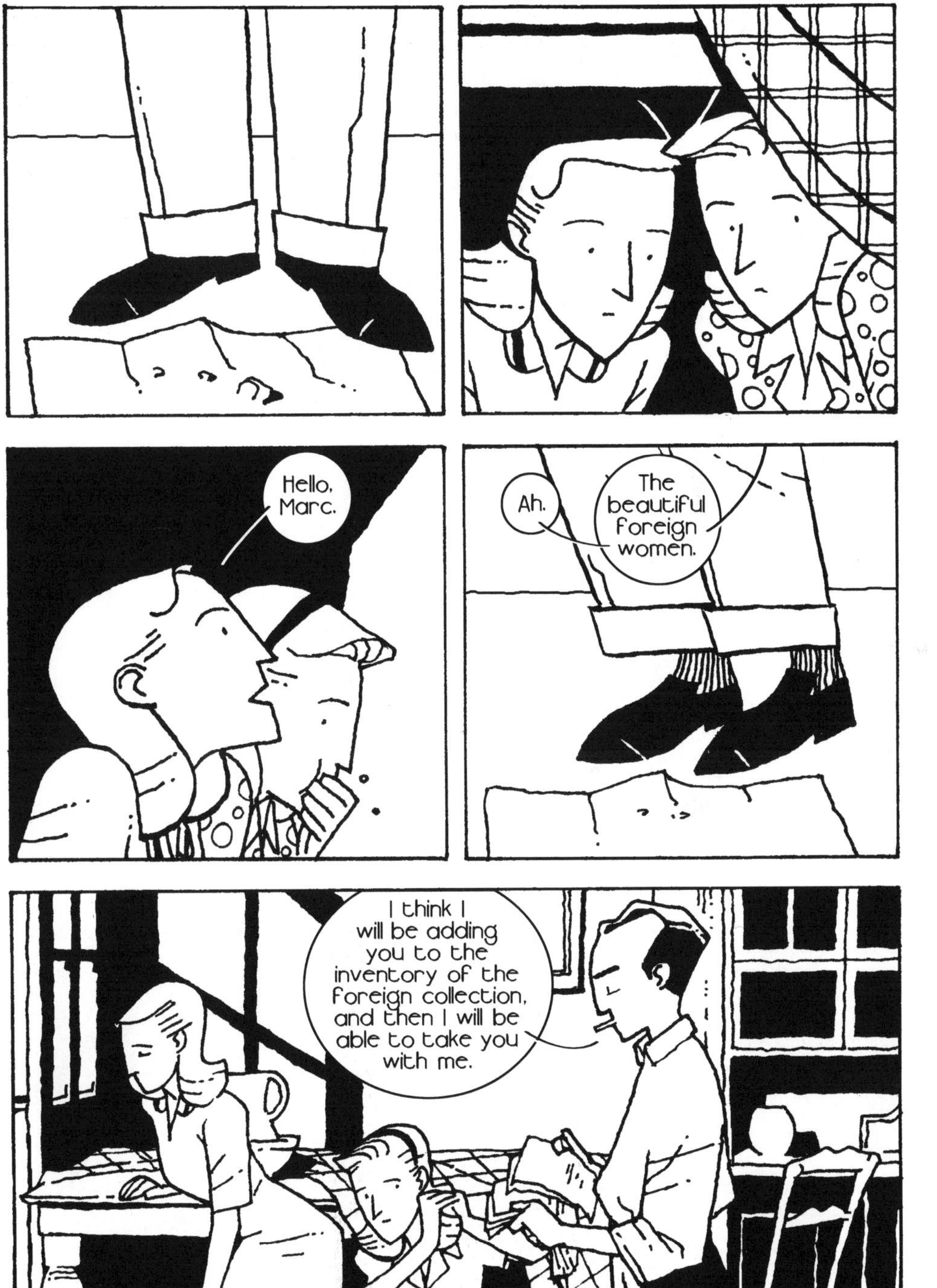
Hello, Marc.
Ah.
The beautiful foreign women.
I think I will be adding you to the inventory of the foreign collection, and then I will be able to take you with me.

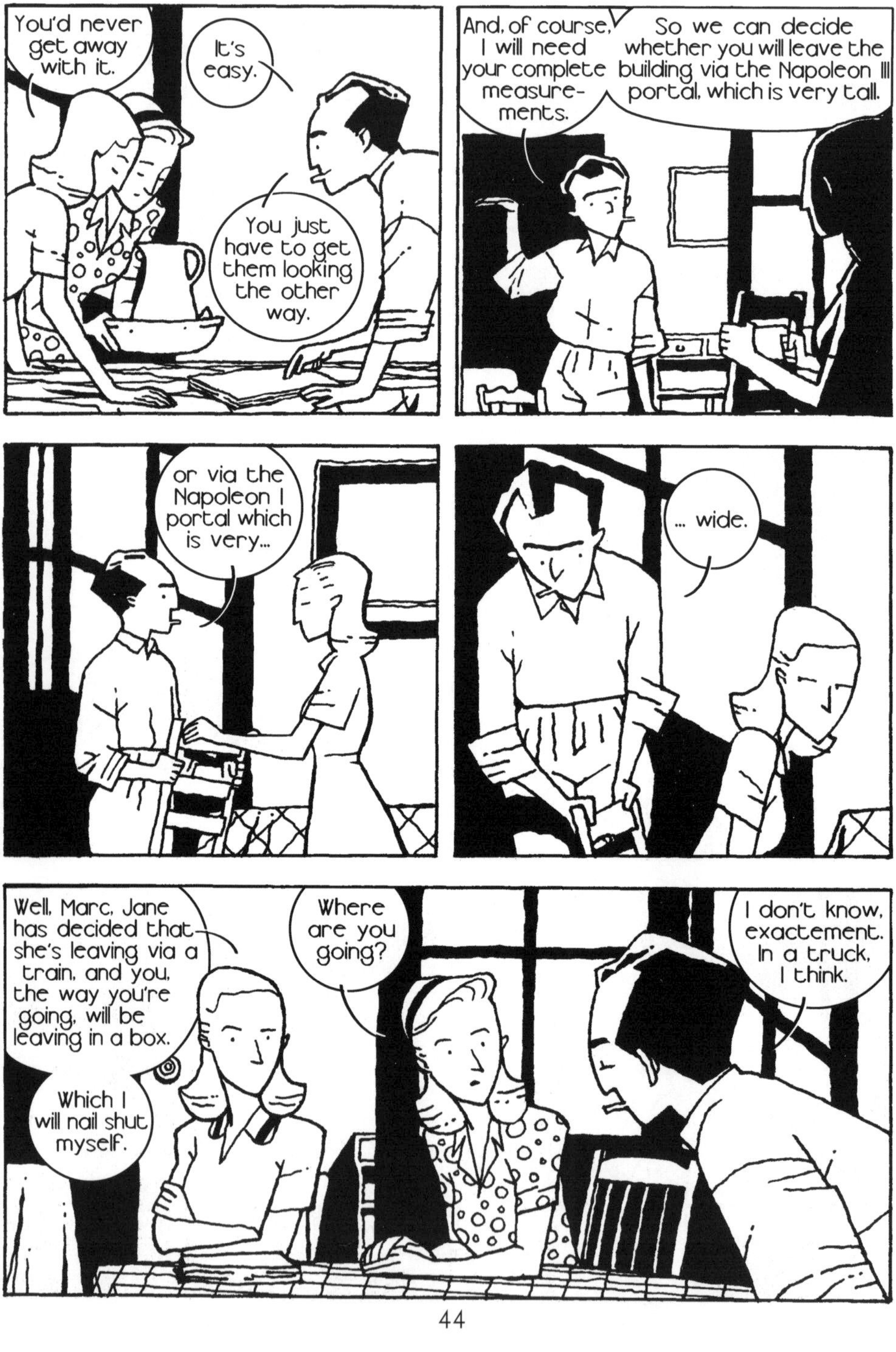
You'd never get away with it.
It's easy.
You just have to get them looking the other way.
And, of course, I will need your complete measurements.
So we can decide whether you will leave the building via the Napoleon III portal, which is very tall.
or via the Napoleon I portal which is very...
... wide.
Well, Marc, Jane has decided that she's leaving via a train, and you, the way you're going, will be leaving in a box.
Which I will nail shut myself.
Where are you going?
I don't know, exactement. In a truck, I think.

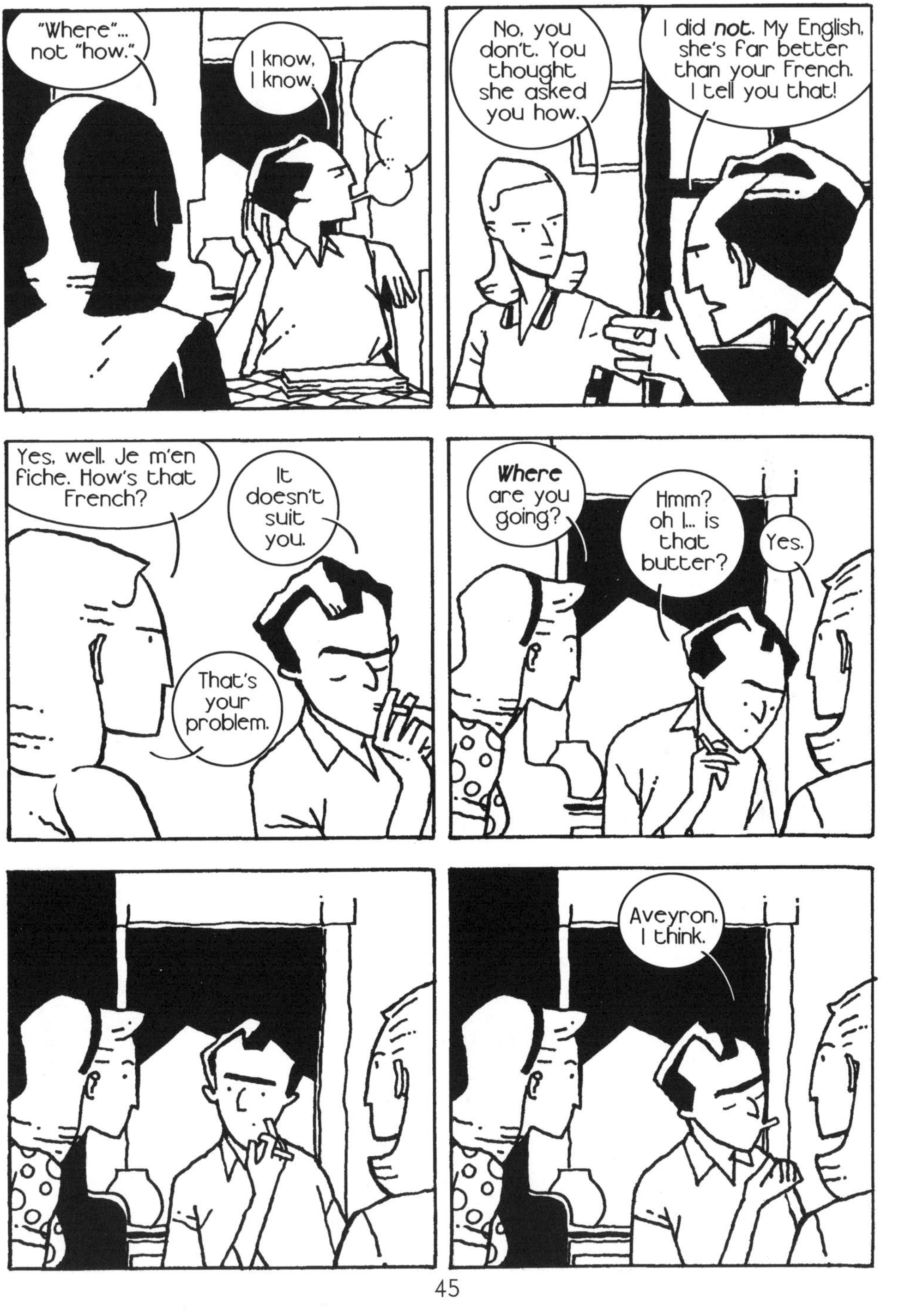
"Where"... not "how."
I know, I know.
No, you don't. You thought she asked you how.
I did **not**. My English, she's far better than your French. I tell you that!
Yes, well. Je m'en fiche. How's that French?
It doesn't suit you.
That's your problem.
Where are you going?
Hmm? oh I... is that butter?
Yes.
Aveyron, I think.

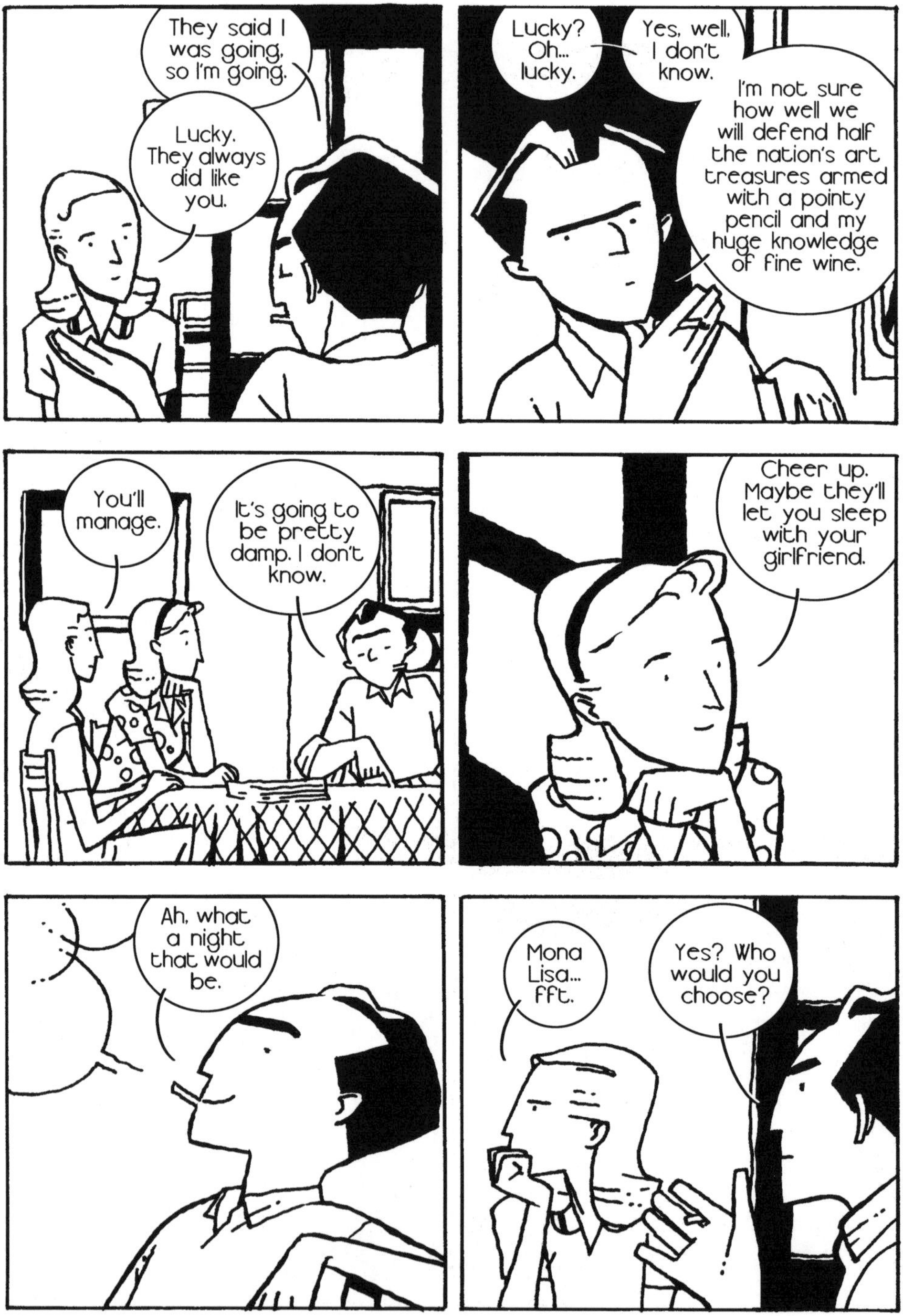
They said I was going, so I'm going.
Lucky. They always did like you.
Lucky? Oh... lucky.
Yes, well, I don't know.
I'm not sure how well we will defend half the nation's art treasures armed with a pointy pencil and my huge knowledge of fine wine.
You'll manage.
It's going to be pretty damp. I don't know.
Cheer up. Maybe they'll let you sleep with your girlfriend.
Ah, what a night that would be.
Mona Lisa... fft.
Yes? Who would you choose?

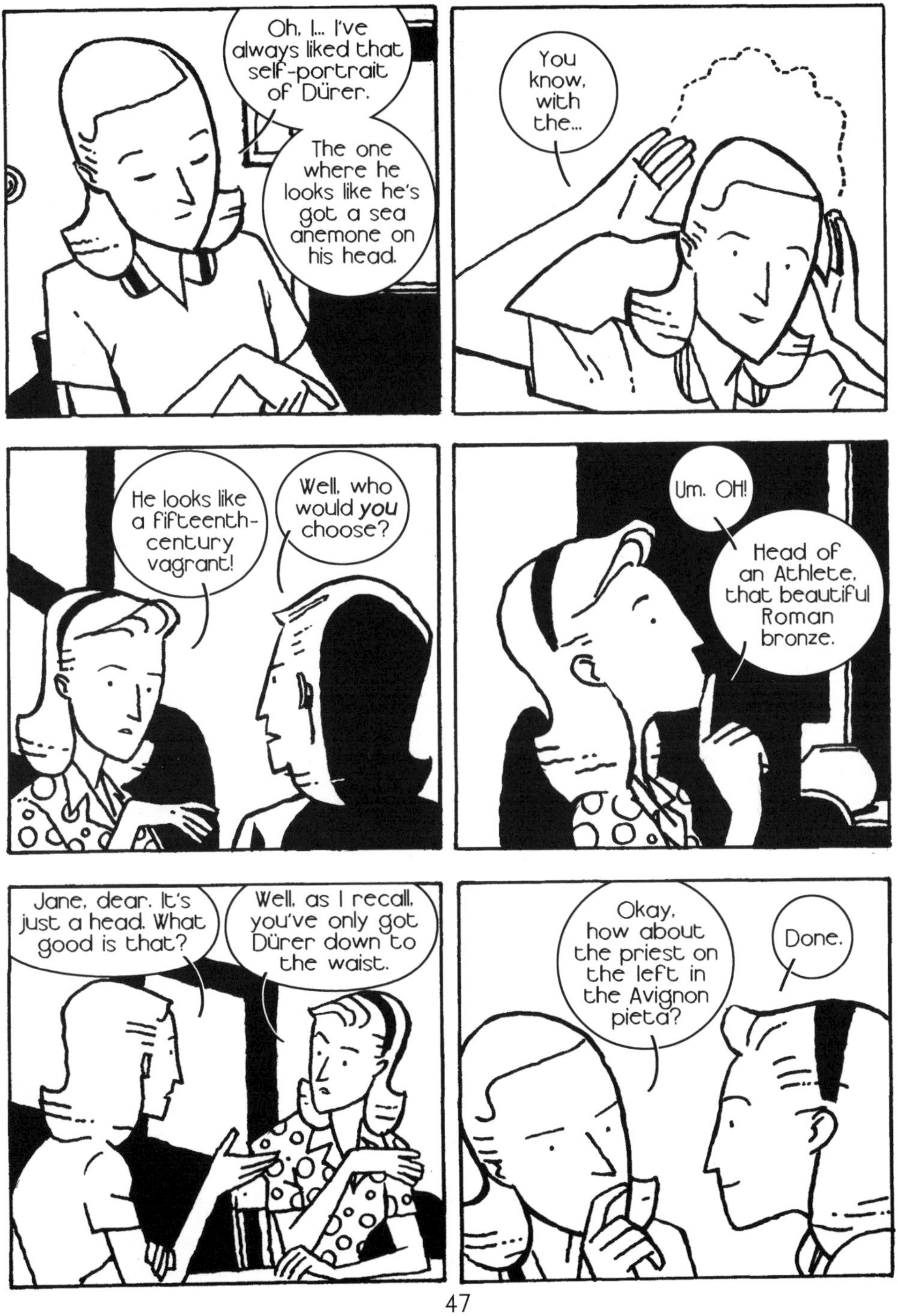
Oh, I... I've always liked that self-portrait of Dürer.
The one where he looks like he's got a sea anemone on his head.
You know, with the...
He looks like a fifteenth-century vagrant!
Well, who would *you* choose?
Um. OH!
Head of an Athlete, that beautiful Roman bronze.
Jane, dear. It's just a head. What good is that?
Well, as I recall, you've only got Dürer down to the waist.
Okay, how about the priest on the left in the Avignon pieta?
Done.

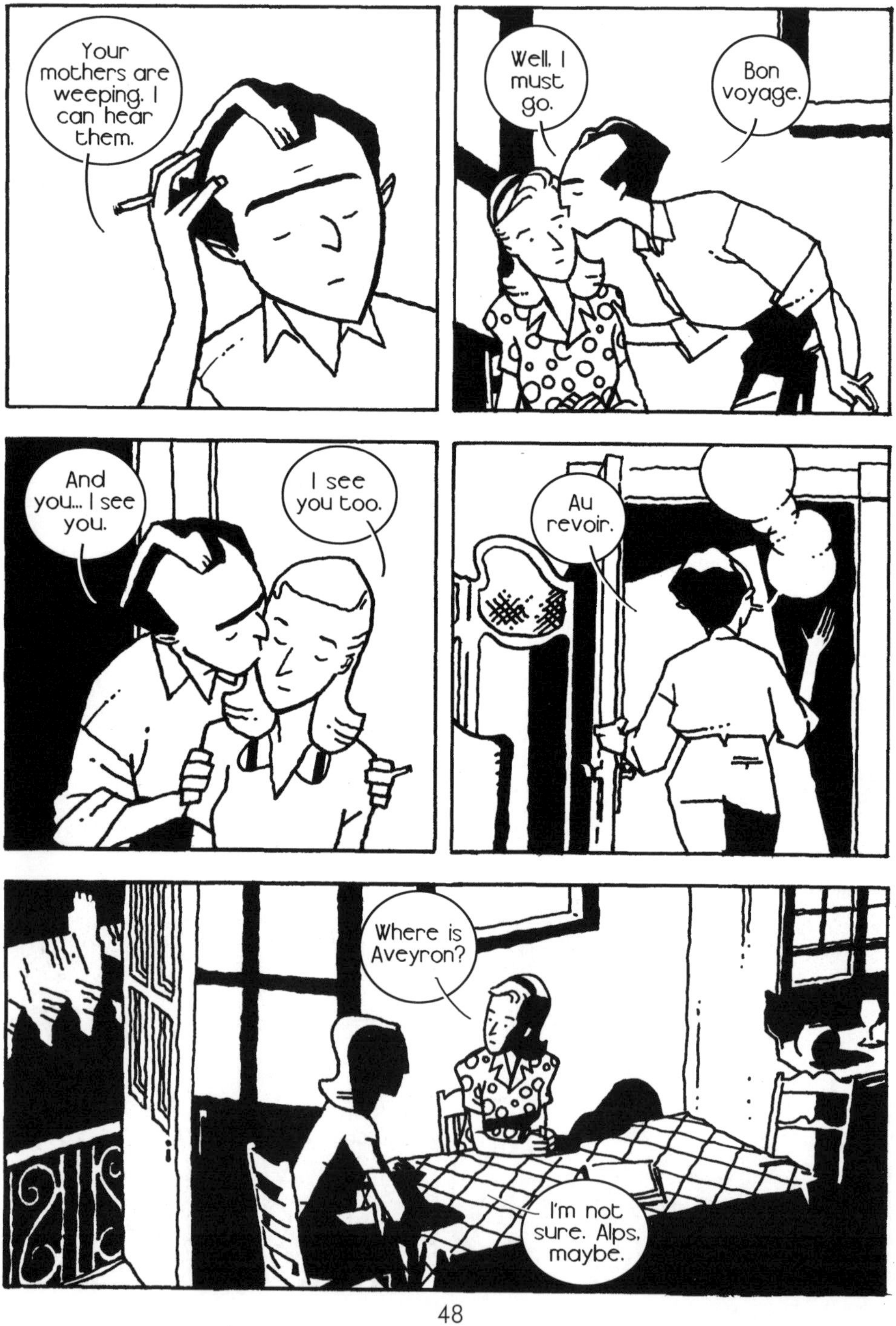
Your mothers are weeping. I can hear them.
Well, I must go.
Bon voyage.
And you... I see you.
I see you too.
Au revoir.
Where is Aveyron?
I'm not sure. Alps, maybe.

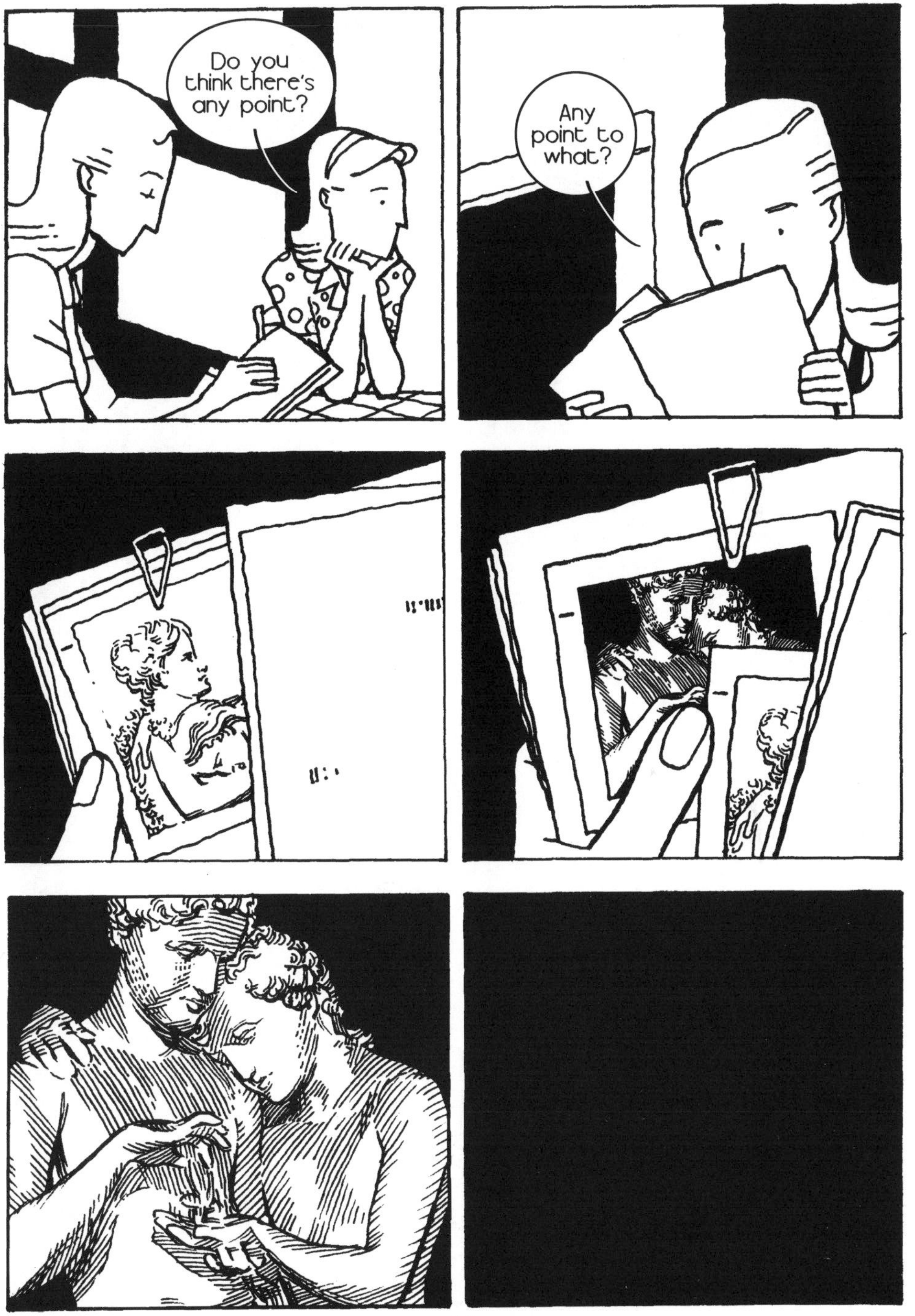
Do you think there's any point?
Any point to what?

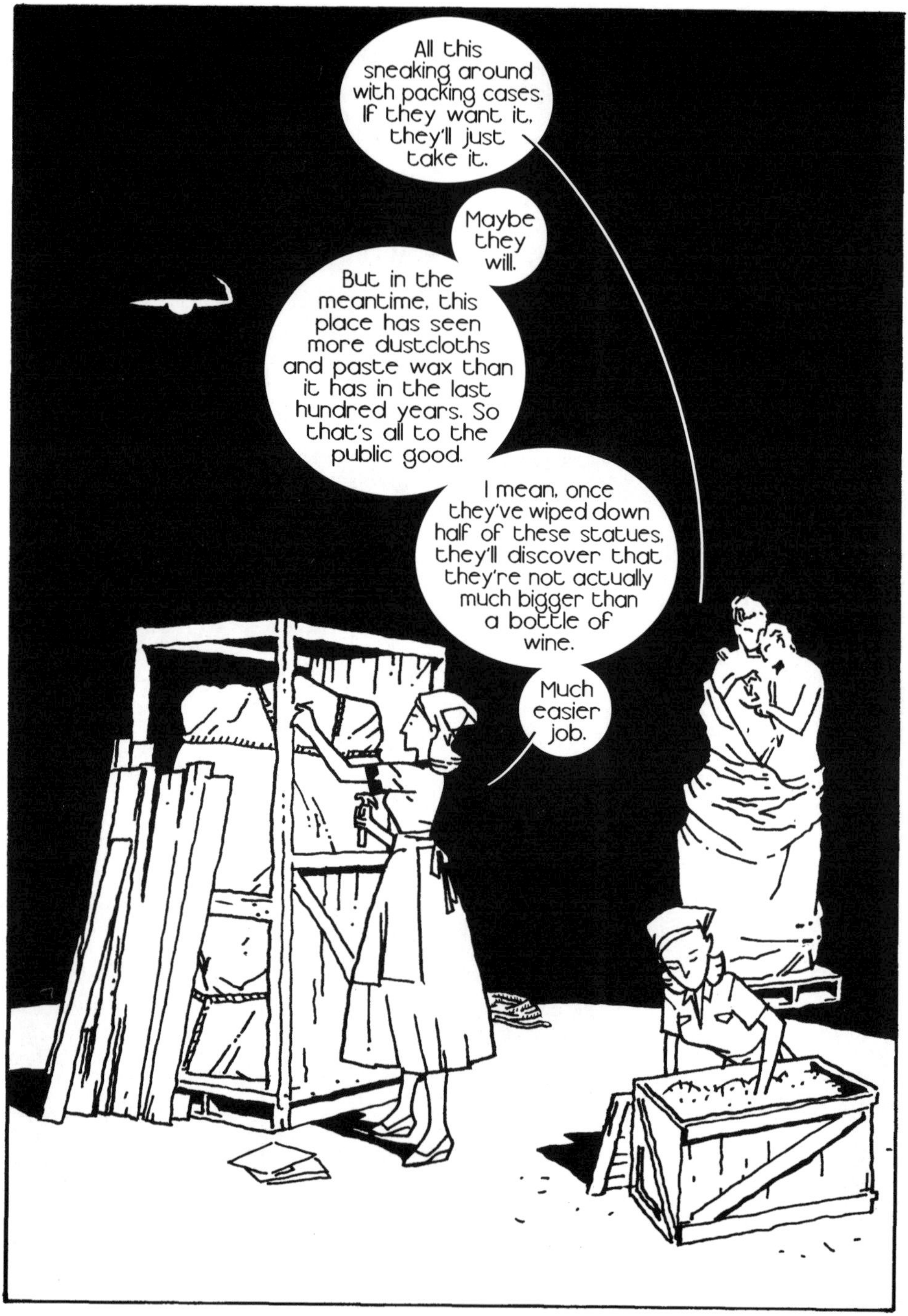
All this sneaking around with packing cases. If they want it, they'll just take it.
Maybe they will.
But in the meantime, this place has seen more dustcloths and paste wax than it has in the last hundred years. So that's all to the public good.
I mean, once they've wiped down half of these statues, they'll discover that they're not actually much bigger than a bottle of wine.
Much easier job.

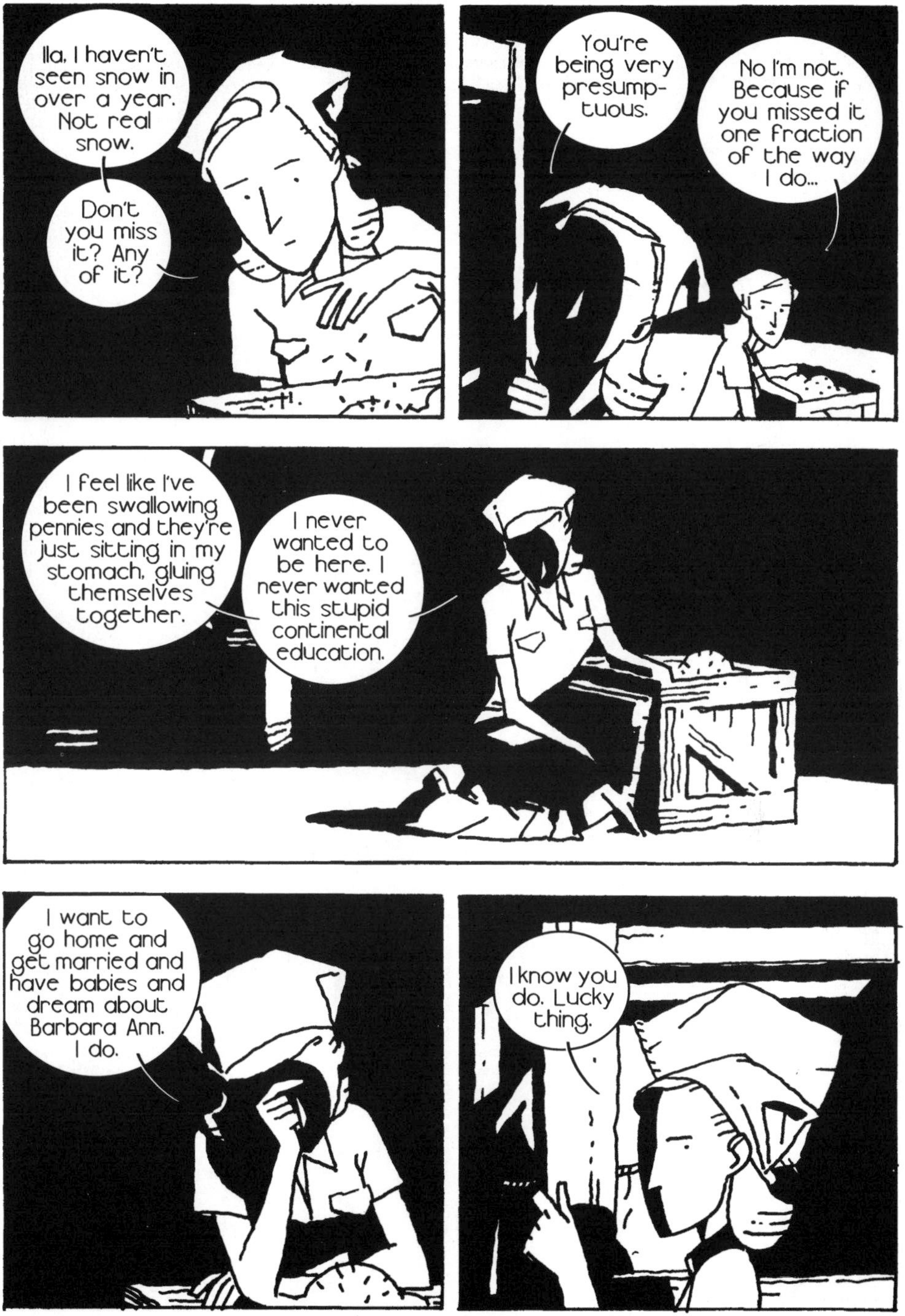
Ila, I haven't seen snow in over a year. Not real snow.
Don't you miss it? Any of it?
You're being very presump-tuous.
No I'm not. Because if you missed it one fraction of the way I do...
I feel like I've been swallowing pennies and they're just sitting in my stomach, gluing themselves together.
I never wanted to be here. I never wanted this stupid continental education.
I want to go home and get married and have babies and dream about Barbara Ann. I do.
I know you do. Lucky thing.

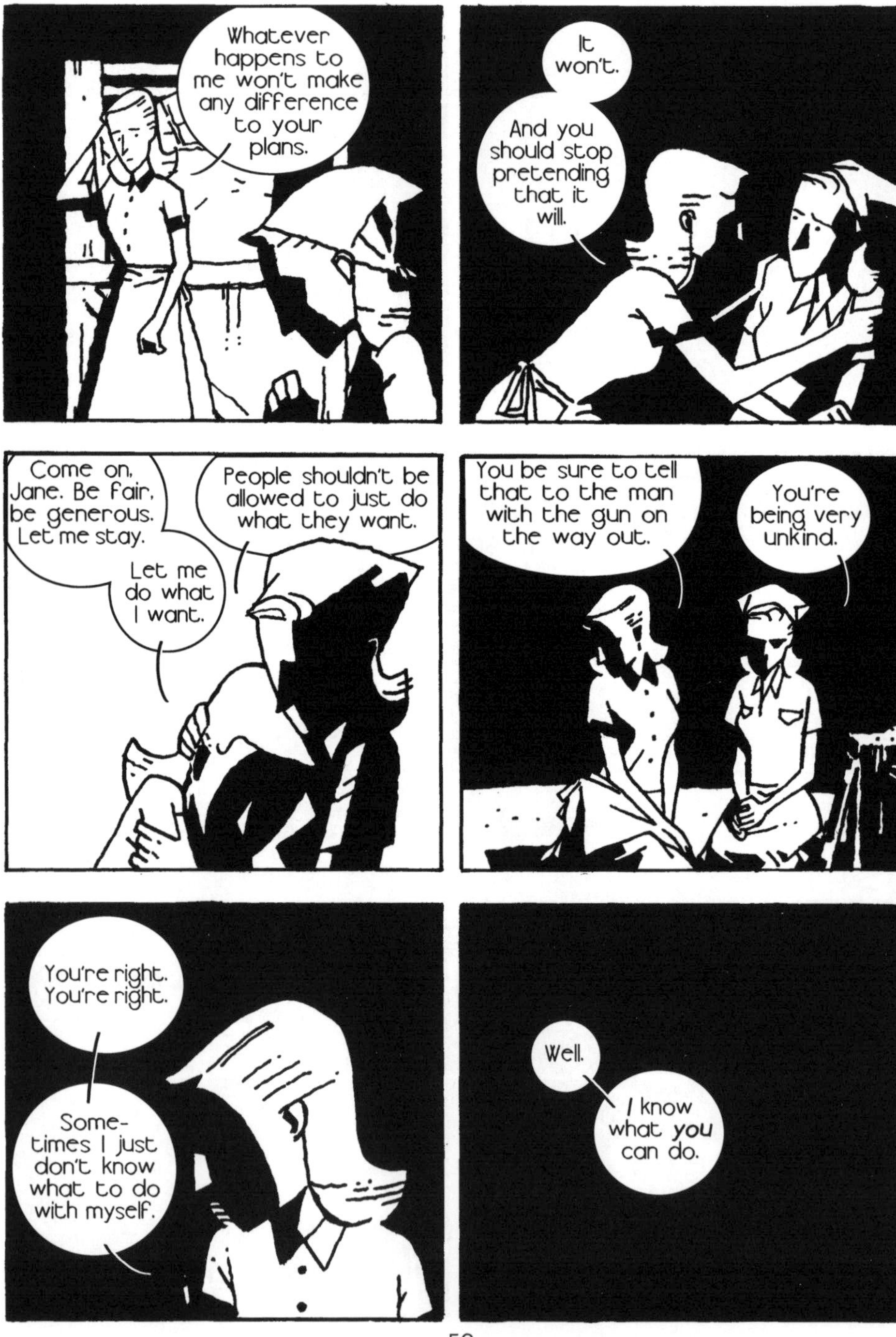
Whatever happens to me won't make any difference to your plans.
It won't.
And you should stop pretending that it will.
Come on, Jane. Be fair, be generous. Let me stay.
Let me do what I want.
People shouldn't be allowed to just do what they want.
You be sure to tell that to the man with the gun on the way out.
You're being very unkind.
You're right. You're right.
Some-times I just don't know what to do with myself.
Well.
I know what *you* can do.

Merde.

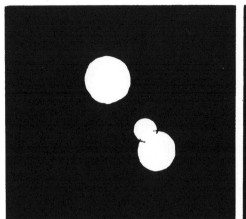

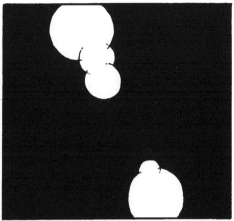

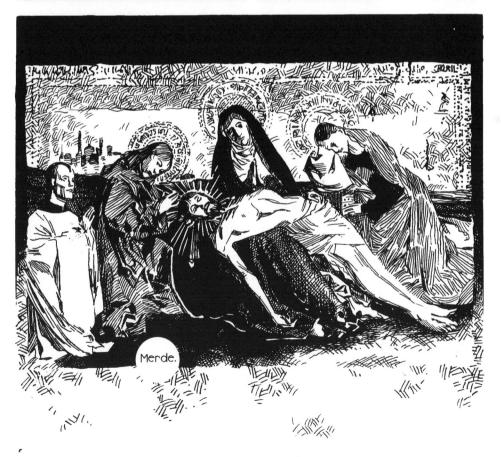

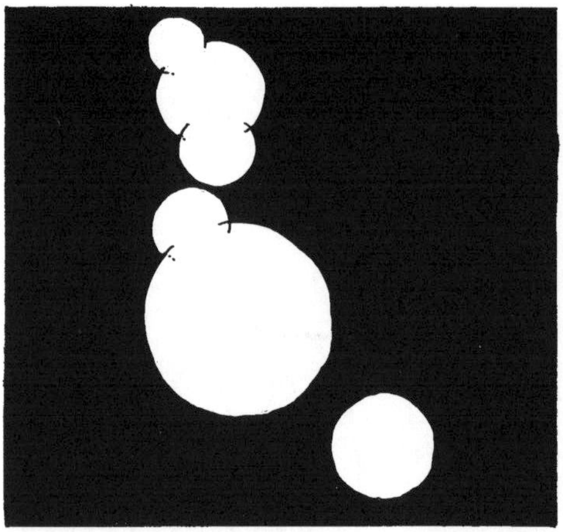
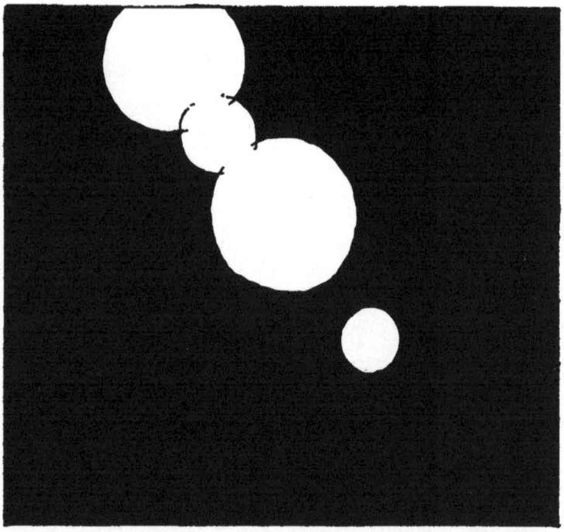
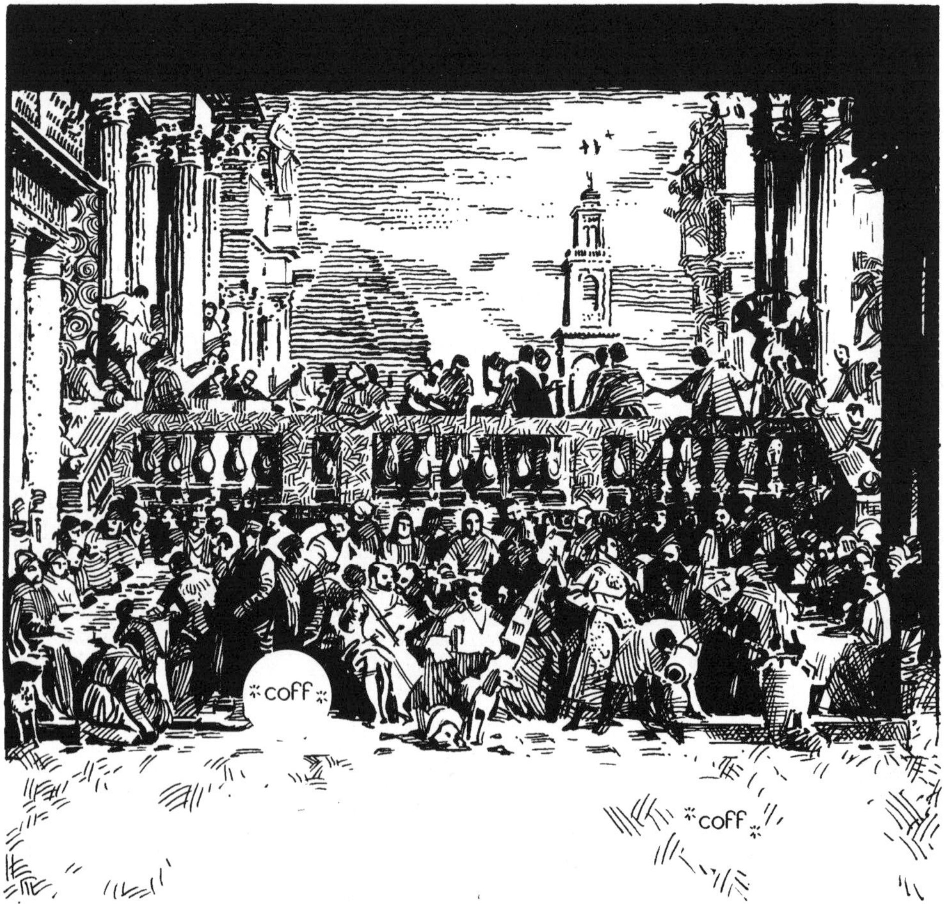
coff
coff

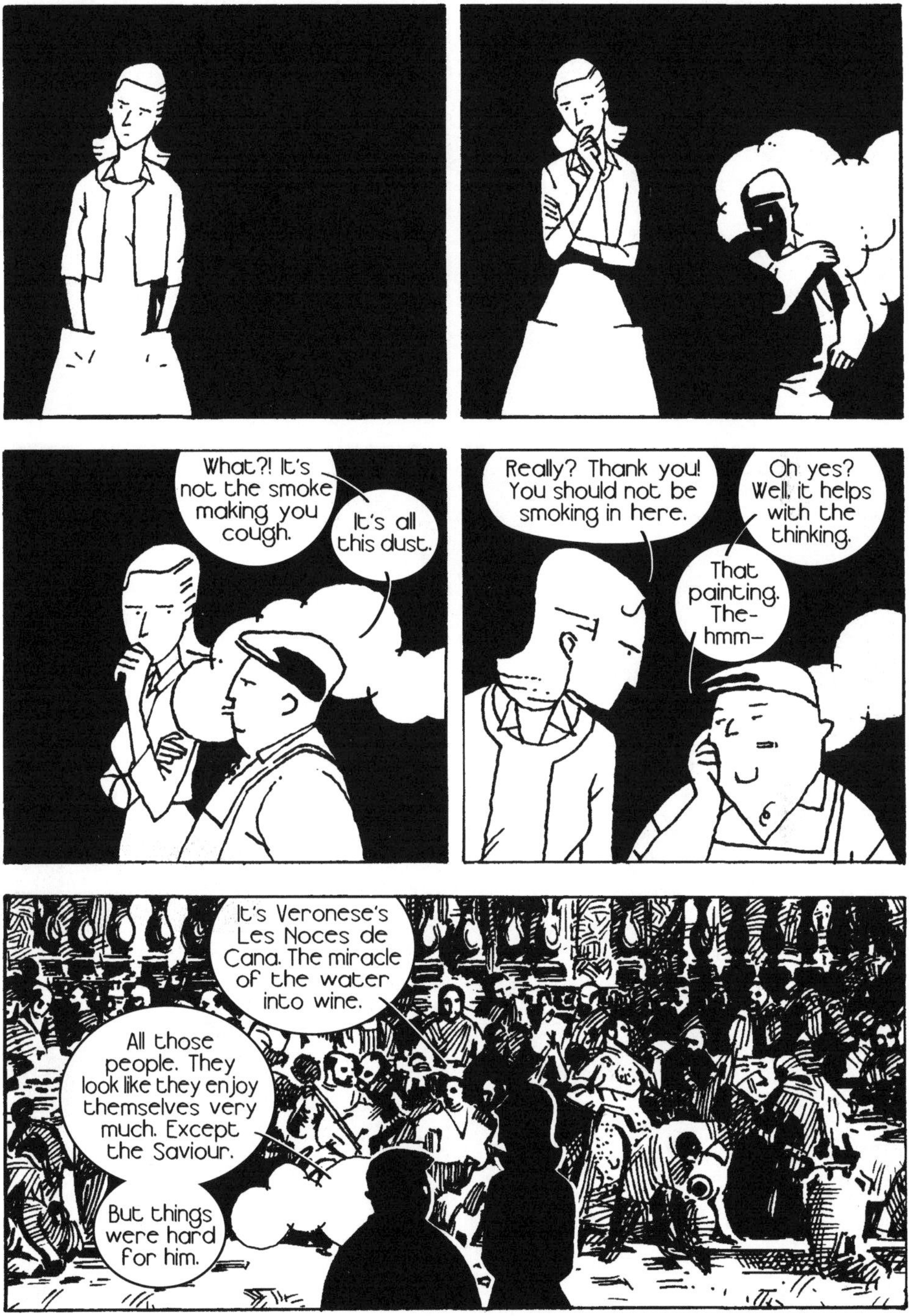
What?! It's not the smoke making you cough.
It's all this dust.
Really? Thank you! You should not be smoking in here.
Oh yes? Well, it helps with the thinking.
That painting. The- hmm-
It's Veronese's Les Noces de Cana. The miracle of the water into wine.
All those people. They look like they enjoy themselves very much. Except the Saviour.
But things were hard for him.

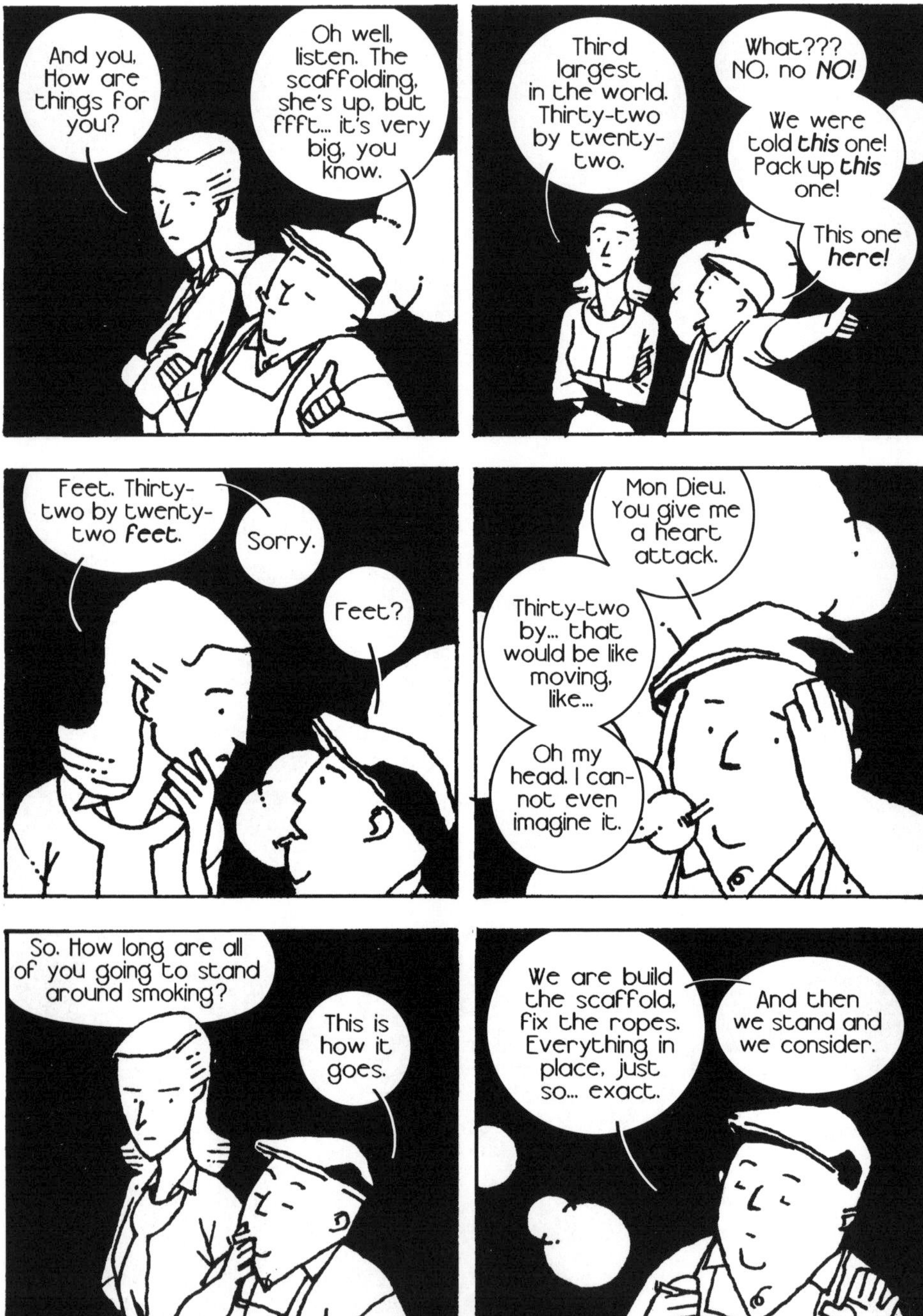
And you, How are things for you?
Oh well, listen. The scaffolding, she's up, but ffft... it's very big, you know.
Third largest in the world. Thirty-two by twenty-two.
What??? NO, no *NO!*
We were told *this* one! Pack up *this* one!
This one *here!*
Feet. Thirty-two by twenty-two **feet**.
Sorry.
Feet?
Mon Dieu. You give me a heart attack.
Thirty-two by... that would be like moving, like...
Oh my head. I cannot even imagine it.
So. How long are all of you going to stand around smoking?
This is how it goes.
We are build the scaffold, fix the ropes. Everything in place, just so... exact.
And then we stand and we consider.

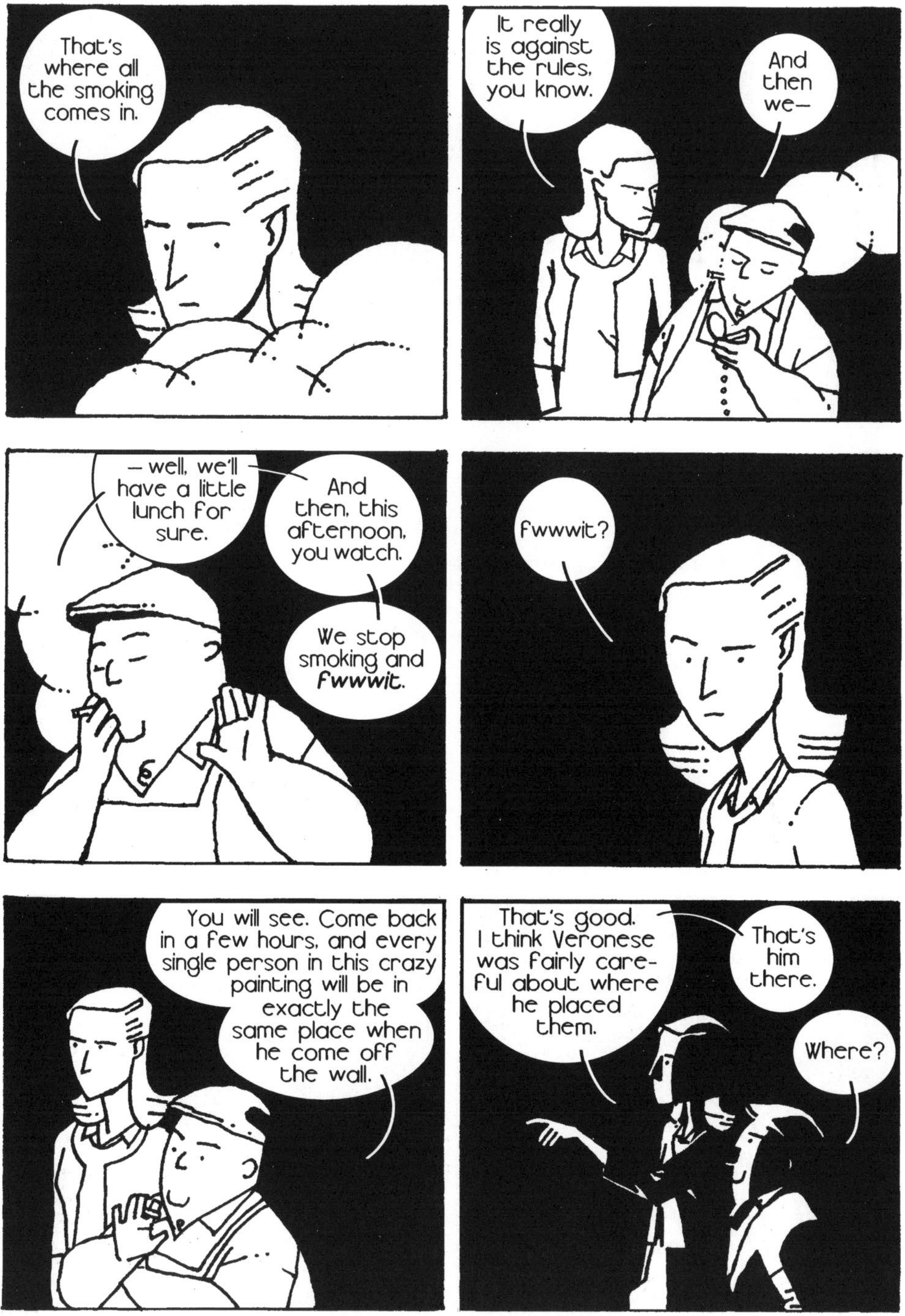
That's where all the smoking comes in.
It really is against the rules, you know.
And then we—
—well, we'll have a little lunch for sure.
And then, this afternoon, you watch.
We stop smoking and **fwwwit**.
fwwwit?
You will see. Come back in a few hours, and every single person in this crazy painting will be in exactly the same place when he come off the wall.
That's good. I think Veronese was fairly careful about where he placed them.
That's him there.
Where?

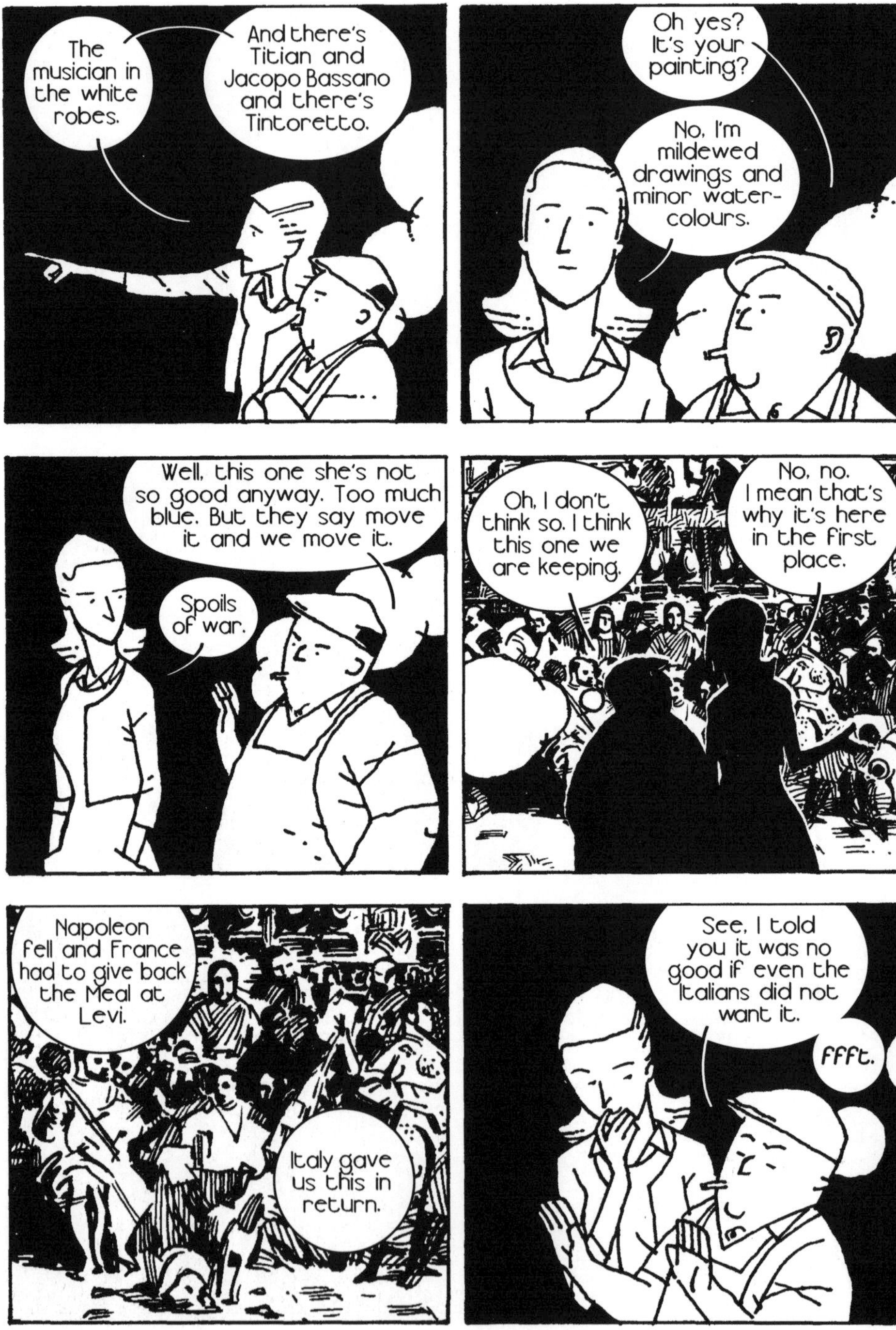
The musician in the white robes.
And there's Titian and Jacopo Bassano and there's Tintoretto.
Oh yes? It's your painting?
No, I'm mildewed drawings and minor water-colours.
Well, this one she's not so good anyway. Too much blue. But they say move it and we move it.
Spoils of war.
Oh, I don't think so. I think this one we are keeping.
No, no. I mean that's why it's here in the first place.
Napoleon fell and France had to give back the Meal at Levi.
Italy gave us this in return.
See, I told you it was no good if even the Italians did not want it.
ffft.

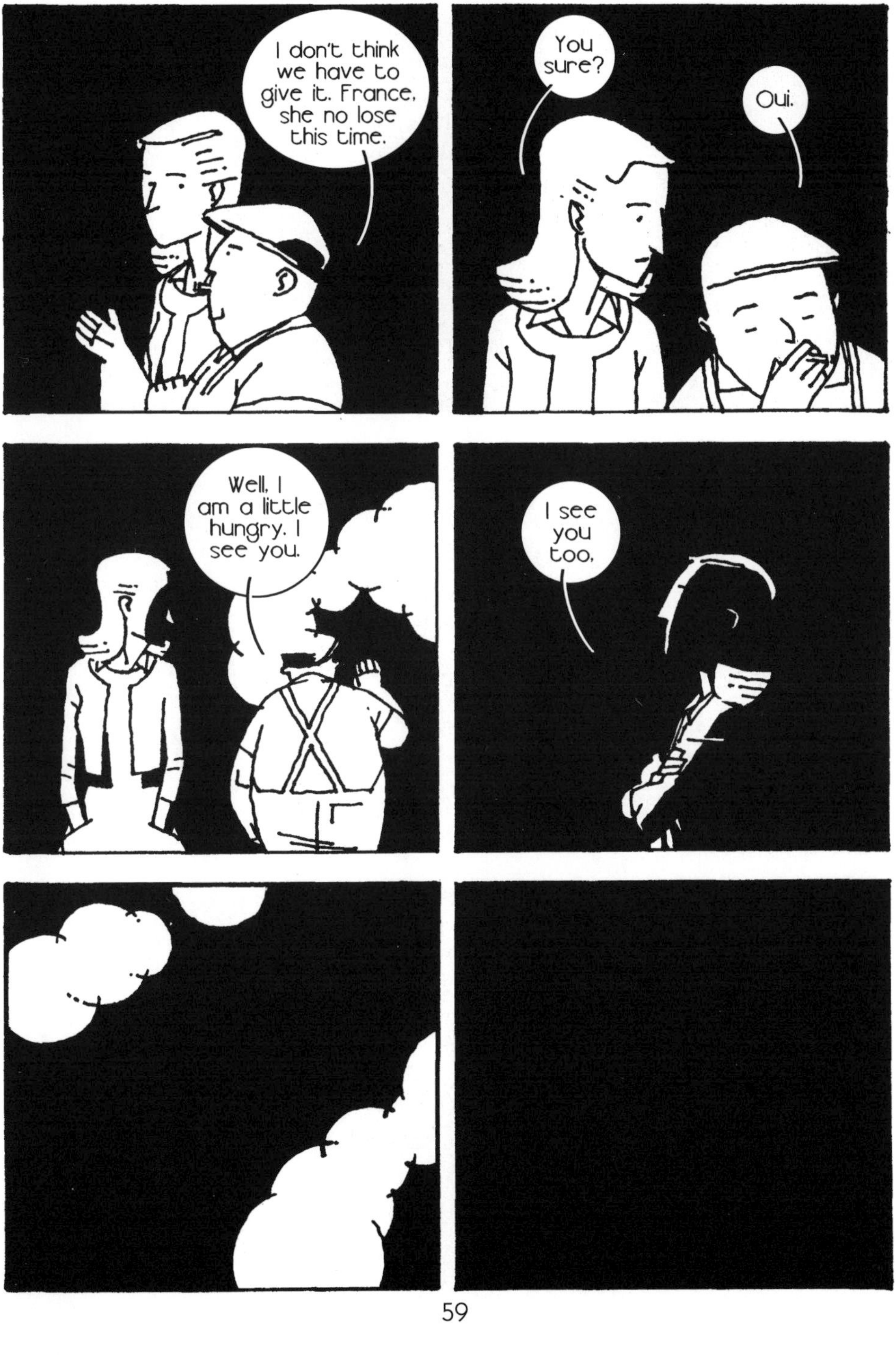

I don't think we have to give it. France, she no lose this time.
You sure?
Oui.
Well, I am a little hungry. I see you.
I see you too,

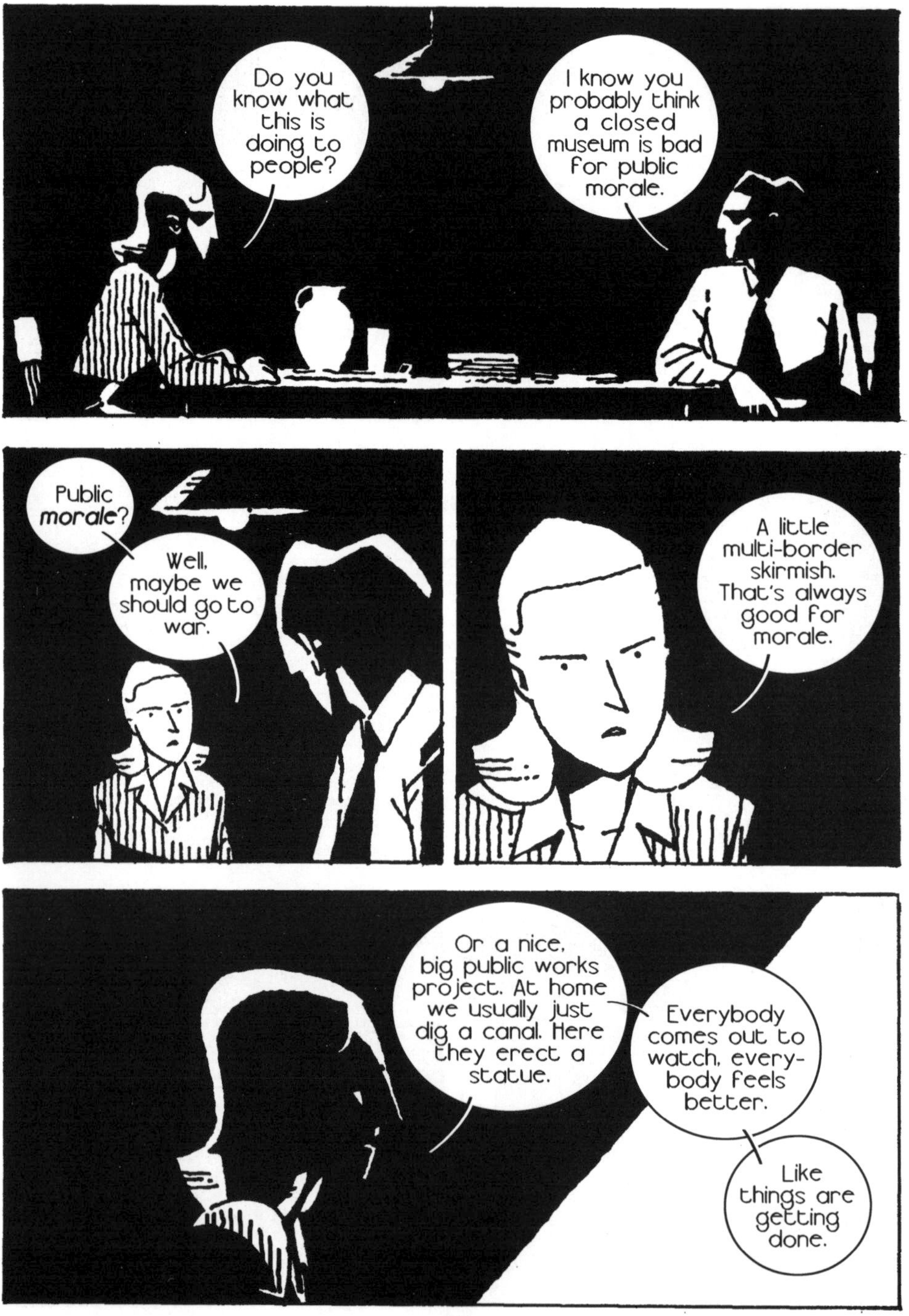
Do you know what this is doing to people?
I know you probably think a closed museum is bad for public morale.
Public *morale*?
Well, maybe we should go to war.
A little multi-border skirmish. That's always good for morale.
Or a nice, big public works project. At home we usually just dig a canal. Here they erect a statue.
Everybody comes out to watch, every-body feels better.
Like things are getting done.

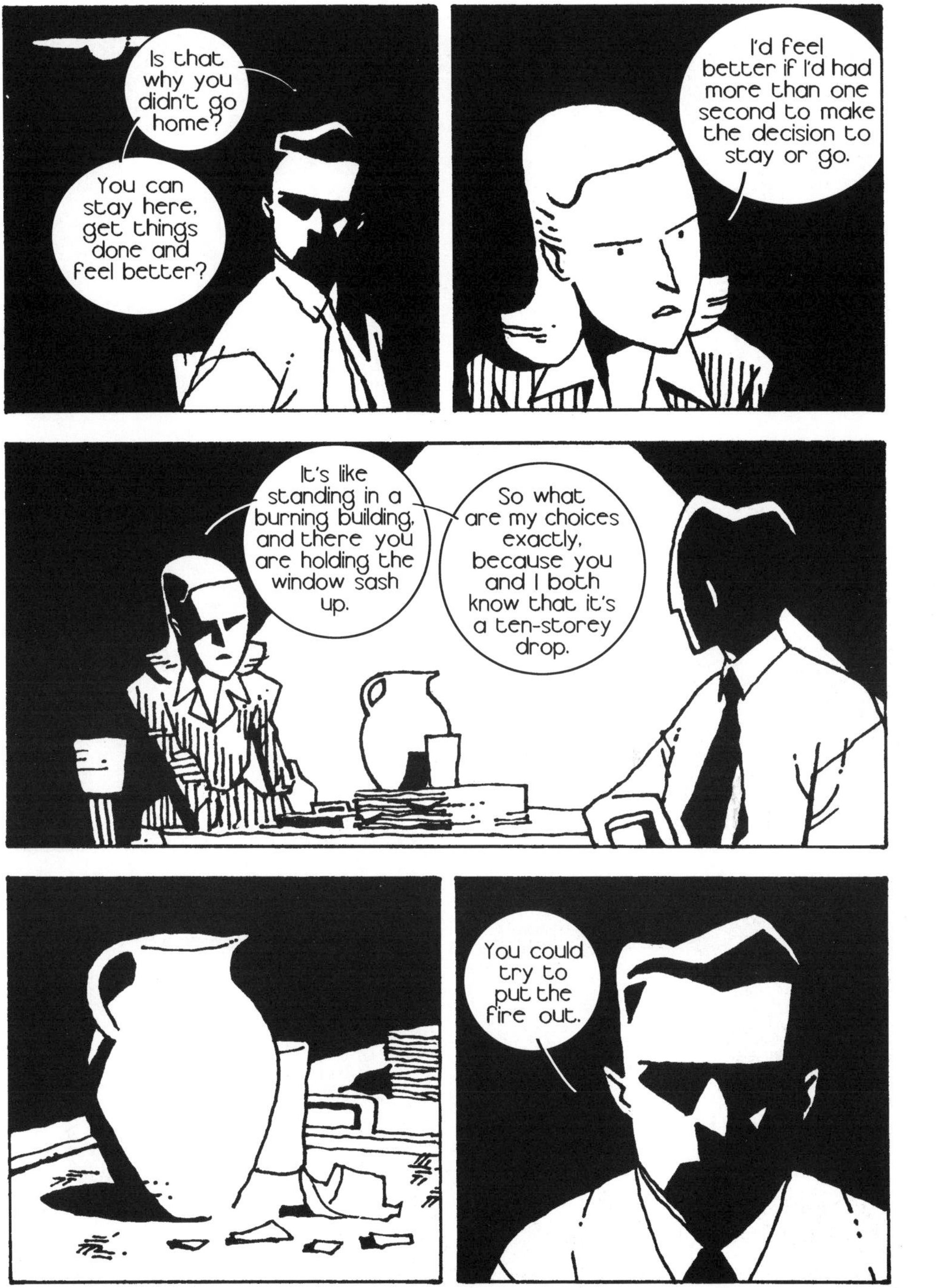
Is that why you didn't go home?
You can stay here, get things done and feel better?
I'd feel better if I'd had more than one second to make the decision to stay or go.
It's like standing in a burning building, and there you are holding the window sash up.
So what are my choices exactly, because you and I both know that it's a ten-storey drop.
You could try to put the fire out.

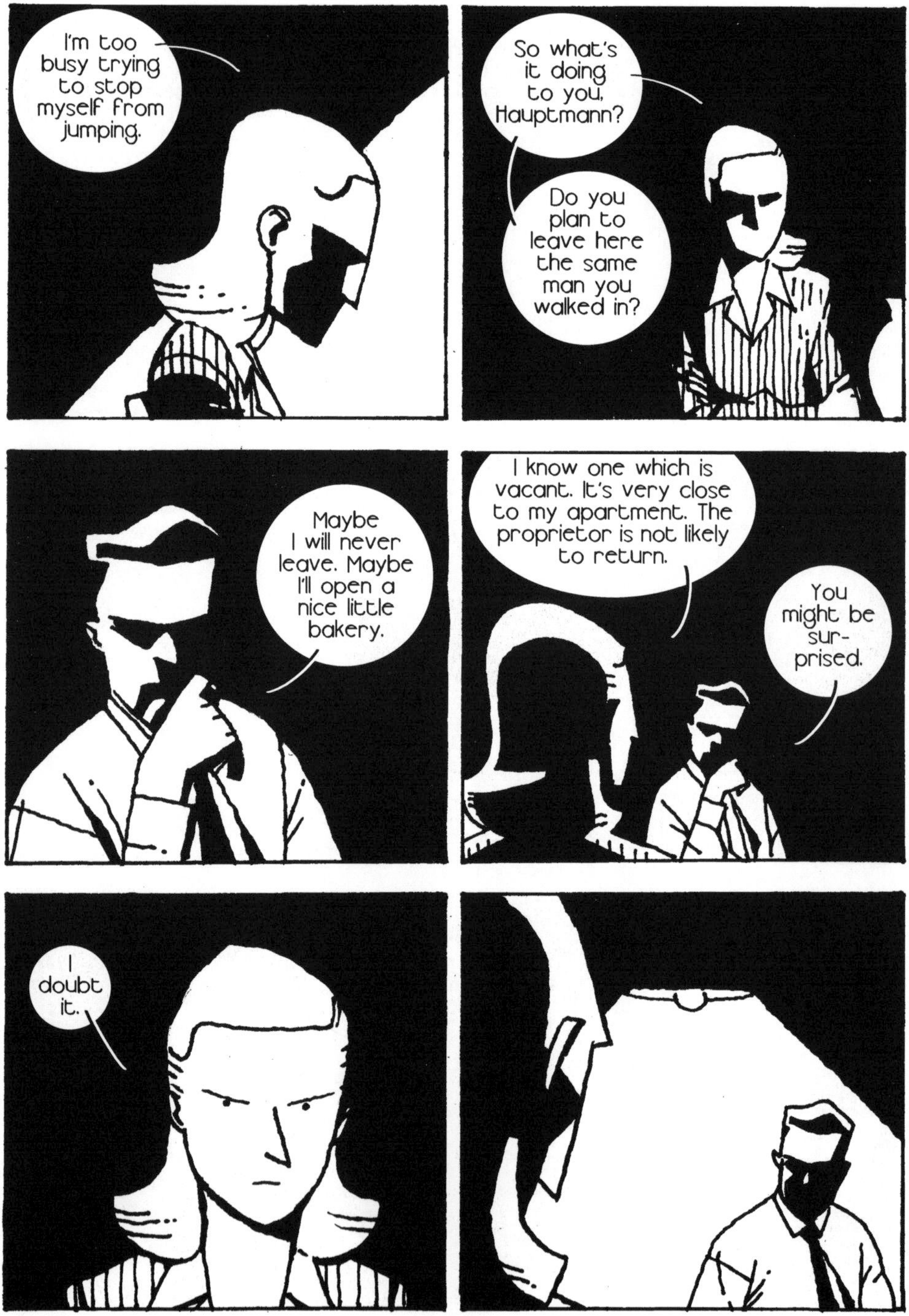
I'm too busy trying to stop myself from jumping.
So what's it doing to you, Hauptmann?
Do you plan to leave here the same man you walked in?
Maybe I will never leave. Maybe I'll open a nice little bakery.
I know one which is vacant. It's very close to my apartment. The proprietor is not likely to return.
You might be sur-prised.
I doubt it.

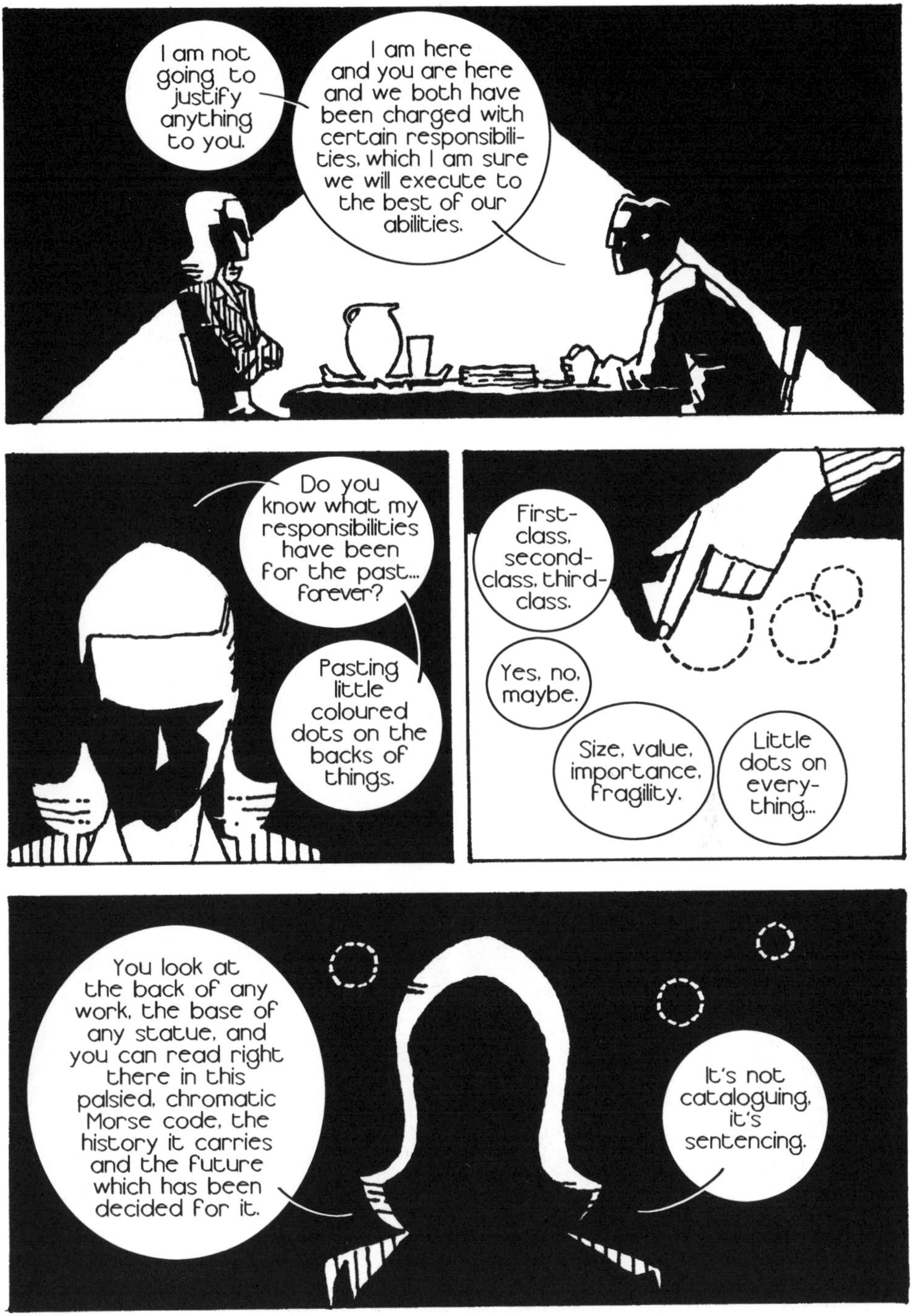
I am not going to justify anything to you.
I am here and you are here and we both have been charged with certain responsibilities, which I am sure we will execute to the best of our abilities.
Do you know what my responsibilities have been for the past... forever?
Pasting little coloured dots on the backs of things.
First-class, second-class, third-class.
Yes, no, maybe.
Size, value, importance, fragility.
Little dots on everything...
You look at the back of any work, the base of any statue, and you can read right there in this palsied, chromatic Morse code, the history it carries and the future which has been decided for it.
It's not cataloguing, it's sentencing.

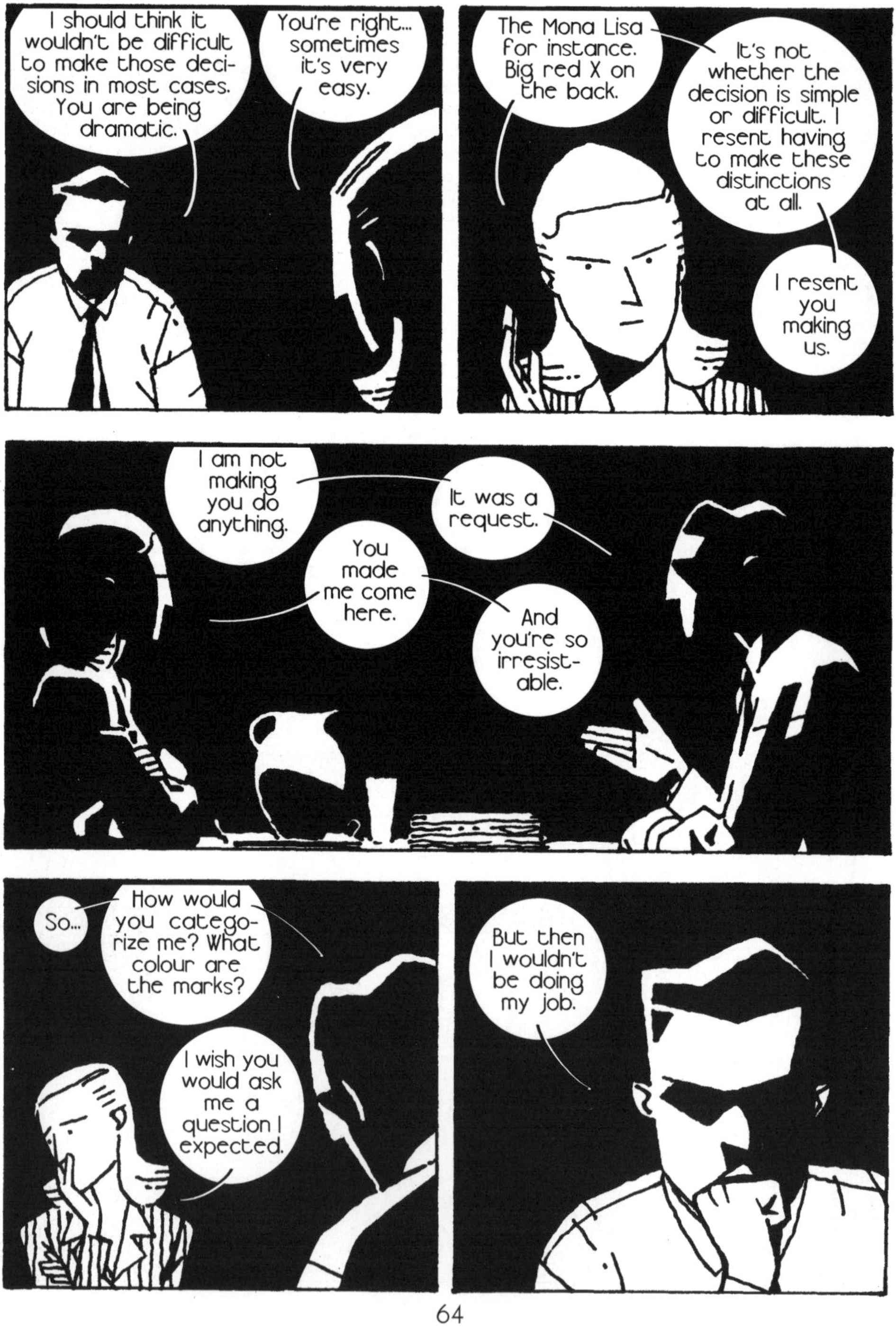
I should think it wouldn't be difficult to make those decisions in most cases. You are being dramatic.
You're right... sometimes it's very easy.
The Mona Lisa for instance. Big red X on the back.
It's not whether the decision is simple or difficult. I resent having to make these distinctions at all.
I resent you making us.
I am not making you do anything.
It was a request.
You made me come here.
And you're so irresistable.
So...
How would you categorize me? What colour are the marks?
I wish you would ask me a question I expected.
But then I wouldn't be doing my job.

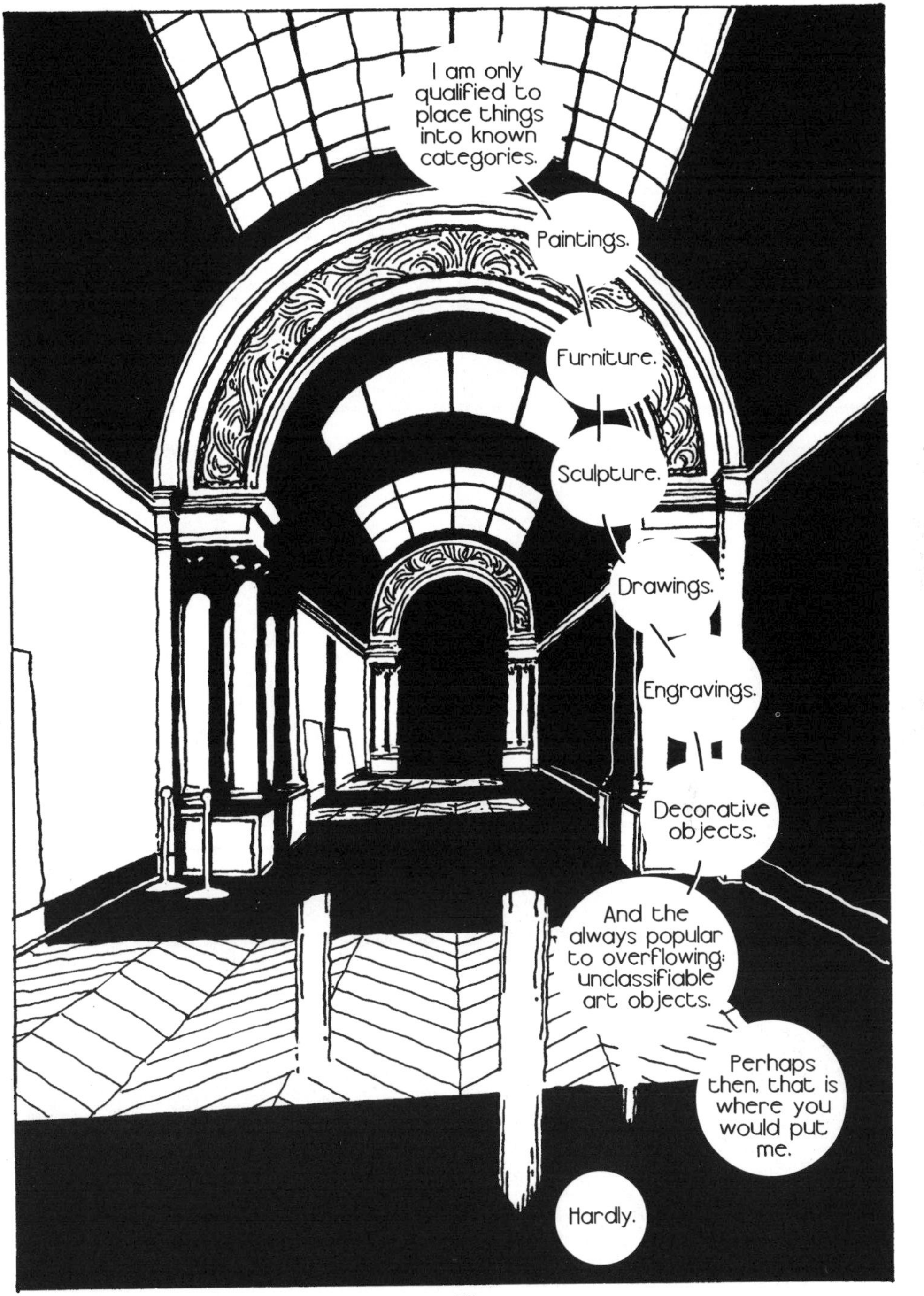
I am only qualified to place things into known categories.
Paintings.
Furniture.
Sculpture.
Drawings.
Engravings.
Decorative objects.
And the always popular to overflowing: unclassifiable art objects.
Perhaps then, that is where you would put me.
Hardly.

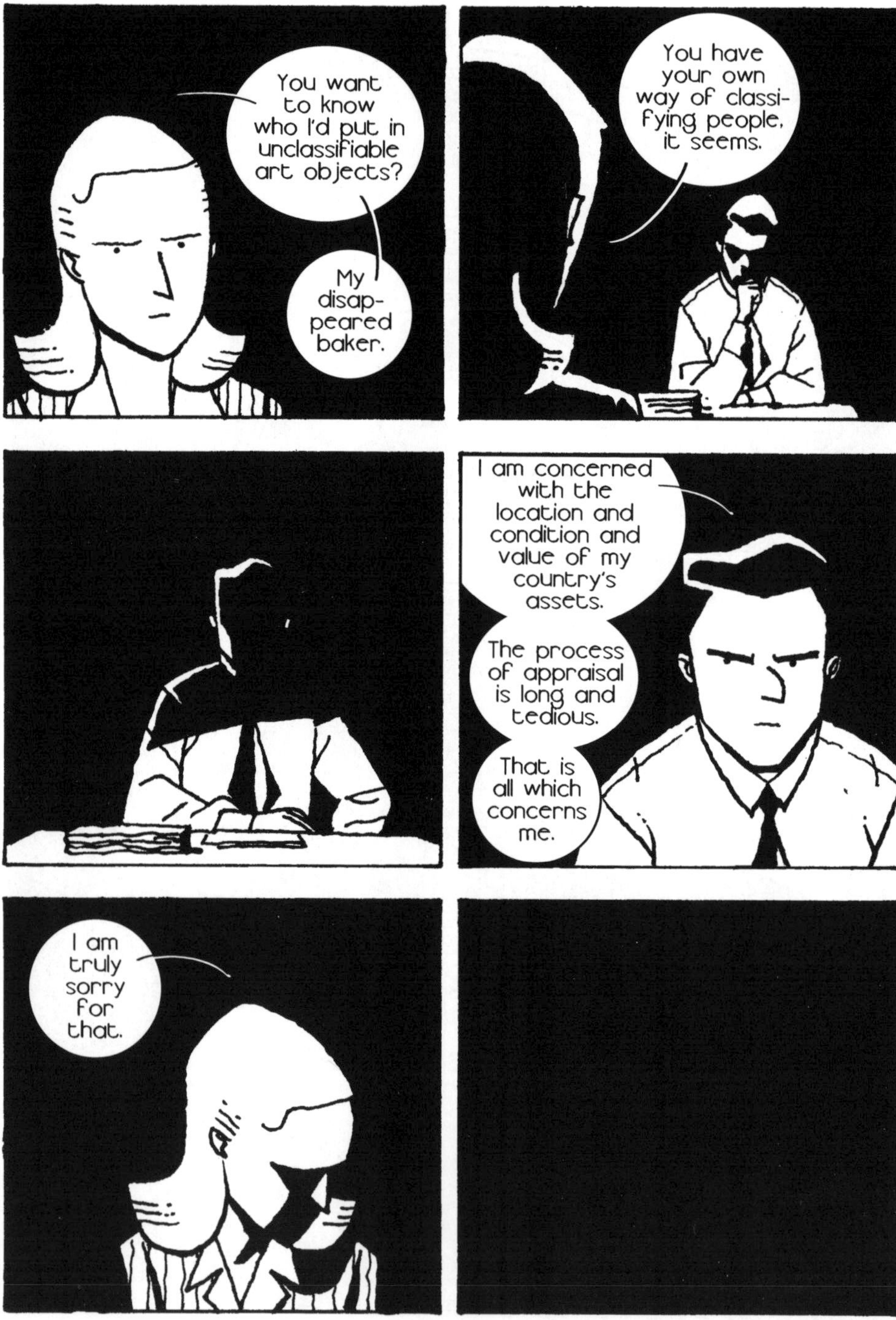
You want to know who I'd put in unclassifiable art objects?
My disap-peared baker.
You have your own way of classi-fying people, it seems.
I am concerned with the location and condition and value of my country's assets.
The process of appraisal is long and tedious.
That is all which concerns me.
I am truly sorry for that.

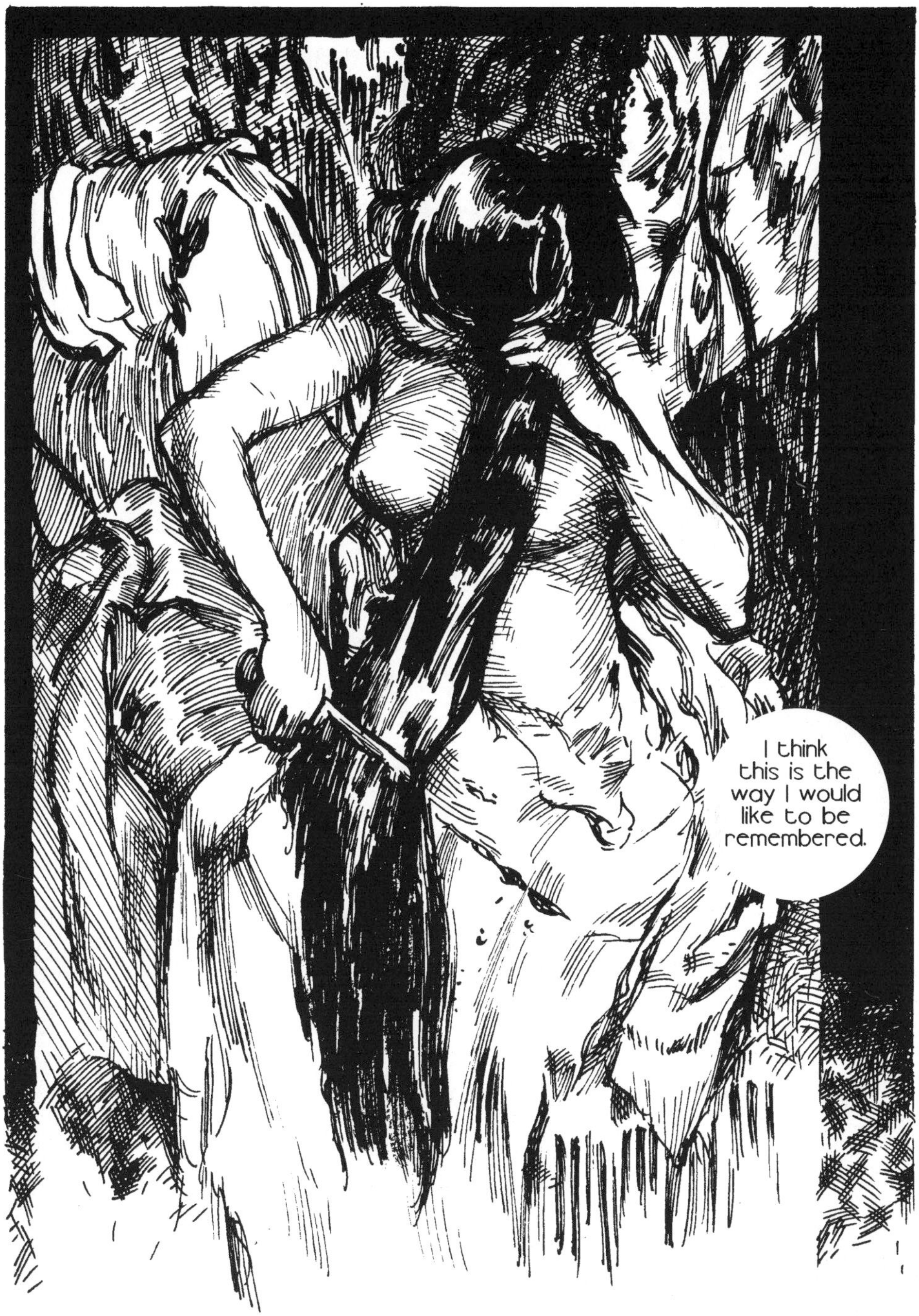
I think this is the way I would like to be remembered.

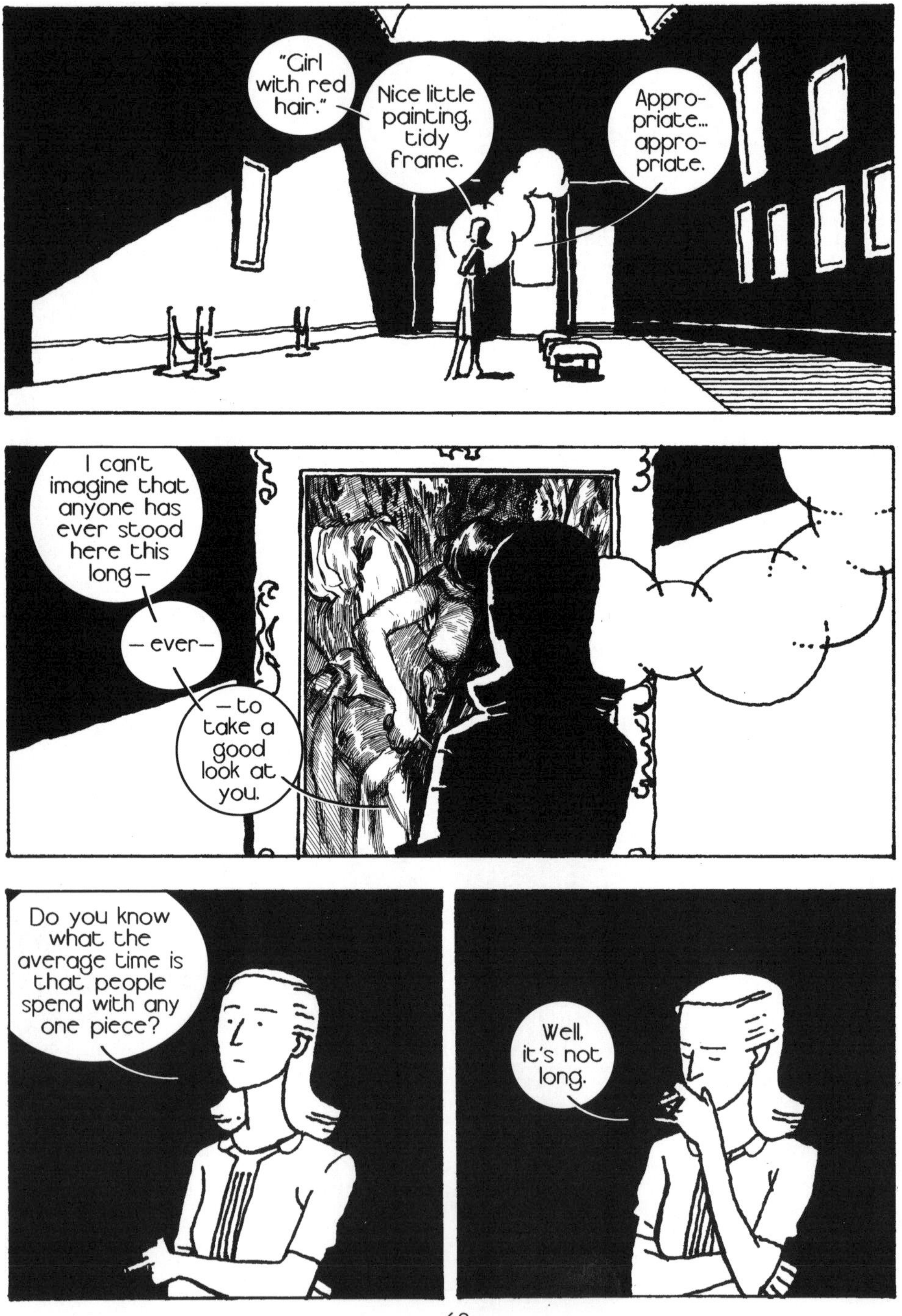
"Girl with red hair."
Nice little painting, tidy frame.
Appro-priate... appro-priate.
I can't imagine that anyone has ever stood here this long—
—ever—
—to take a good look at you.
Do you know what the average time is that people spend with any one piece?
Well, it's not long.

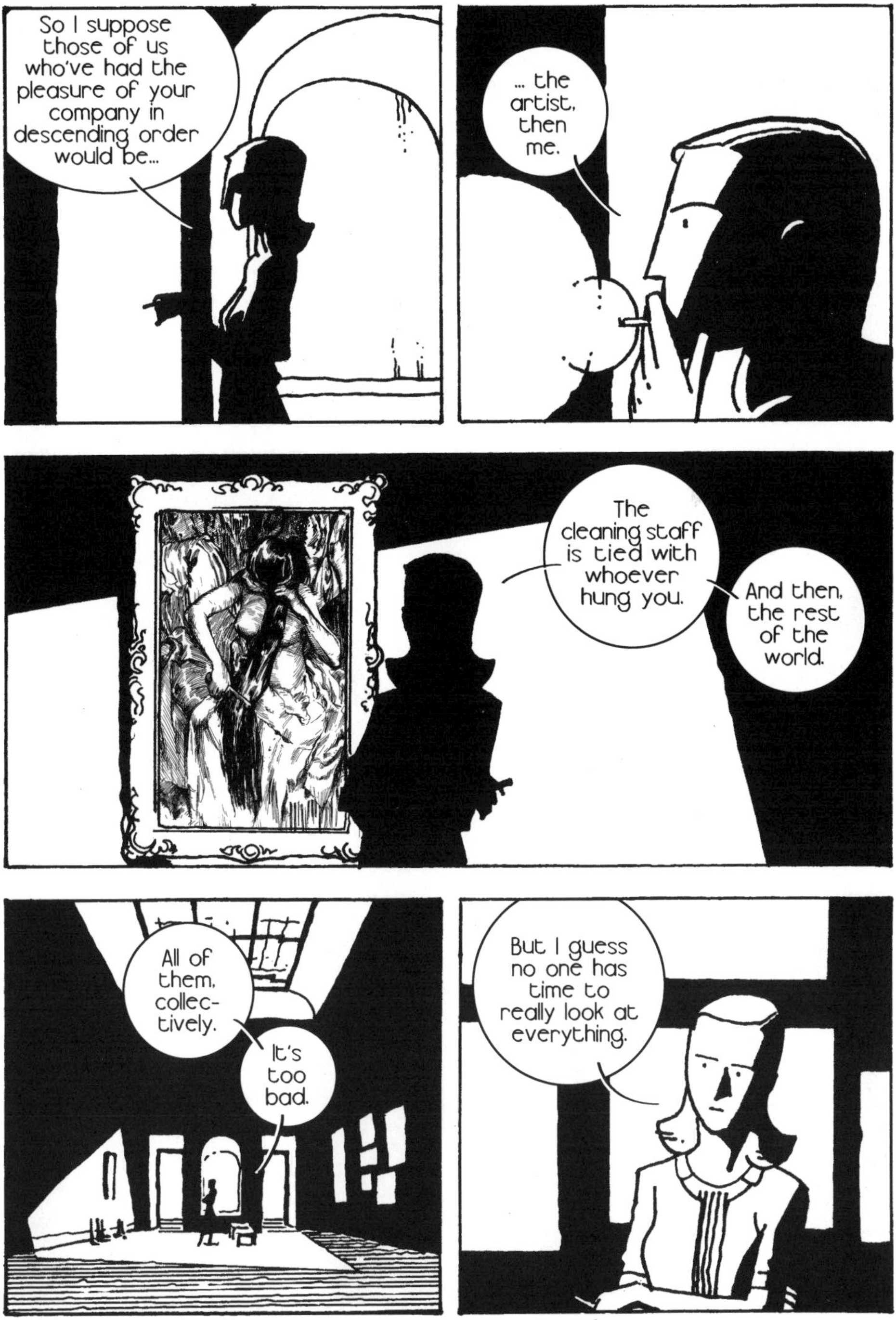
So I suppose those of us who've had the pleasure of your company in descending order would be...
... the artist, then me.
The cleaning staff is tied with whoever hung you.
And then, the rest of the world.
All of them, collectively.
It's too bad.
But I guess no one has time to really look at everything.

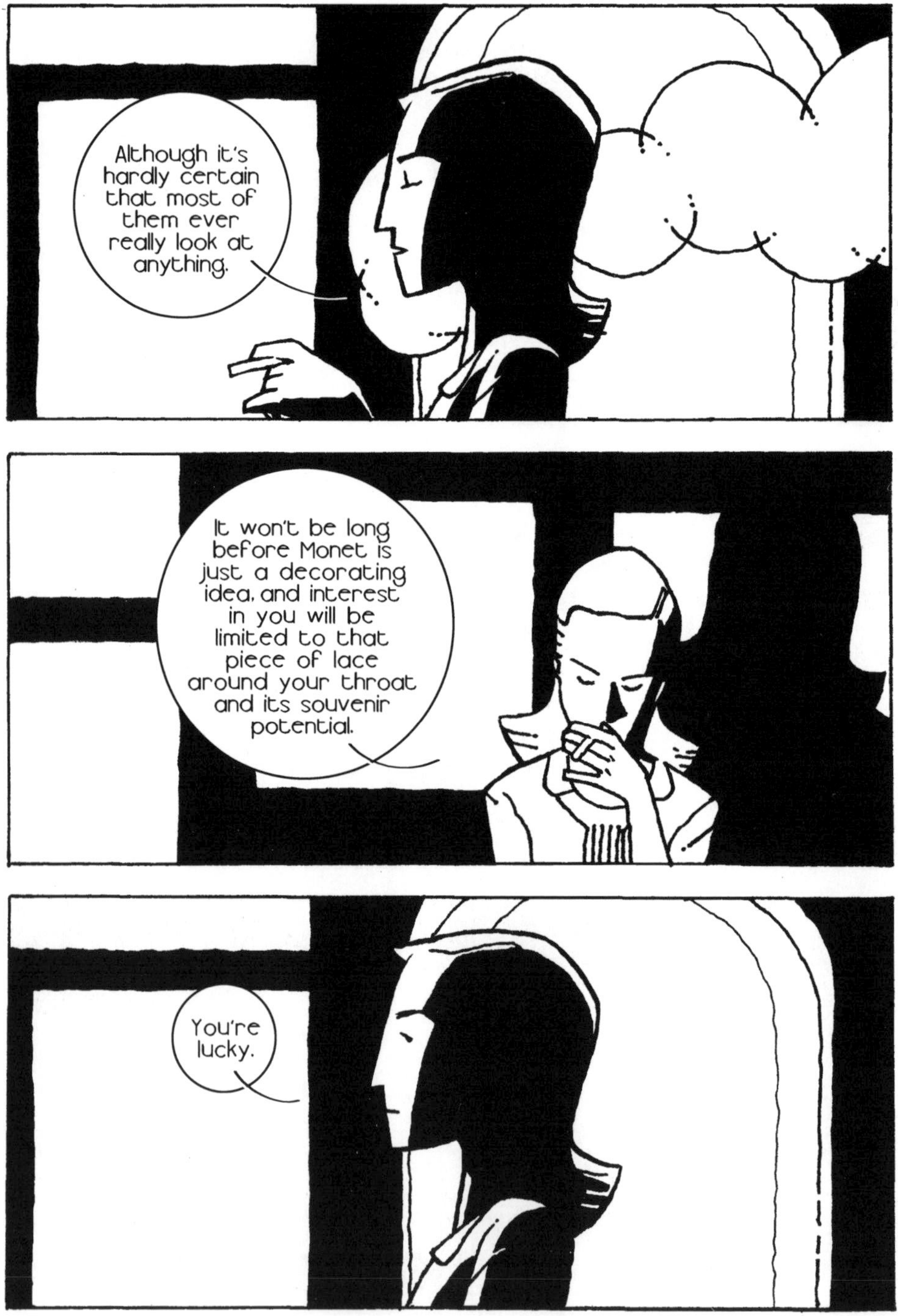
Although it's hardly certain that most of them ever really look at anything.
It won't be long before Monet is just a decorating idea, and interest in you will be limited to that piece of lace around your throat and its souvenir potential.
You're lucky.

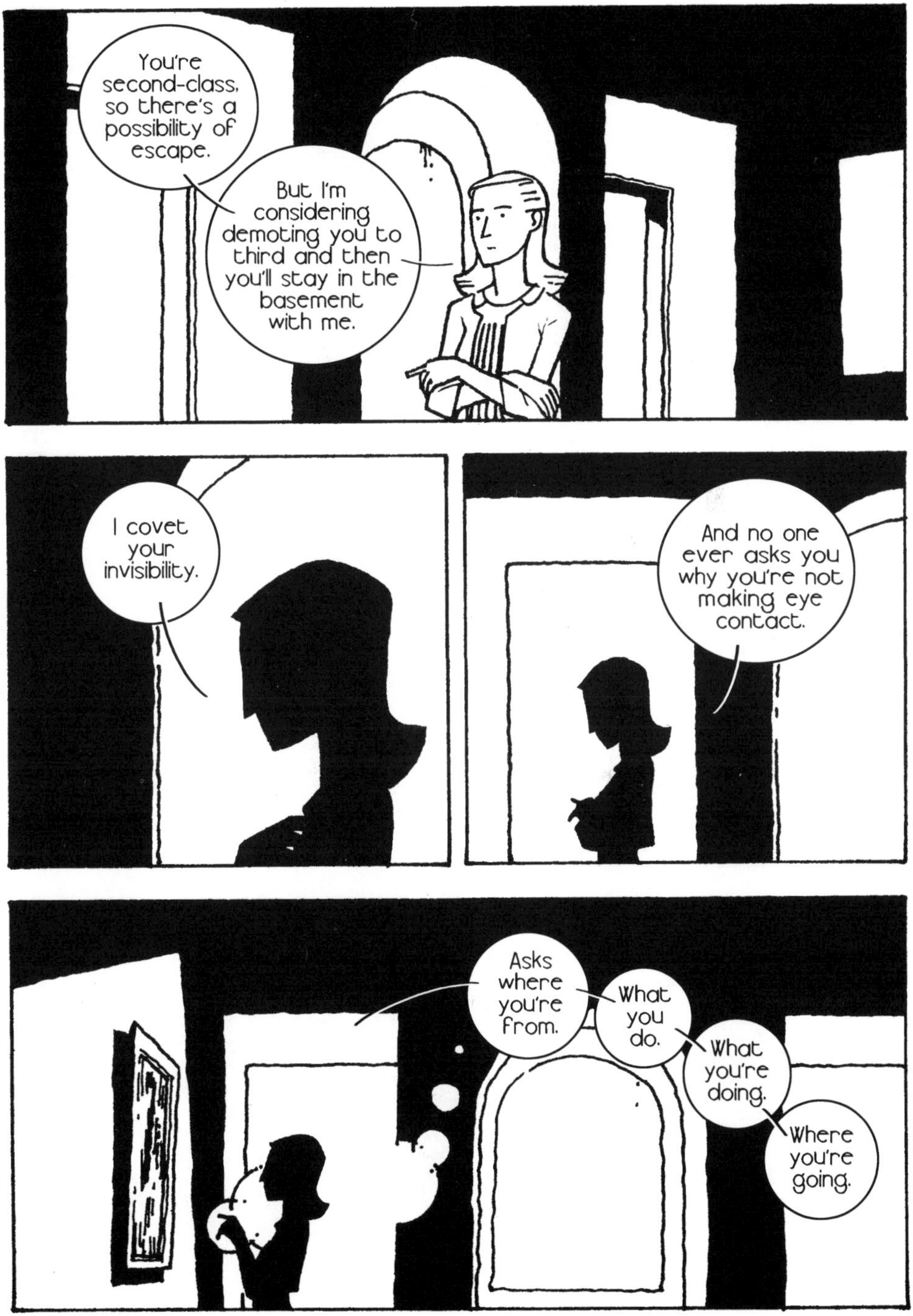
You're second-class, so there's a possibility of escape.
But I'm considering demoting you to third and then you'll stay in the basement with me.
I covet your invisibility.
And no one ever asks you why you're not making eye contact.
Asks where you're from.
What you do.
What you're doing.
Where you're going.

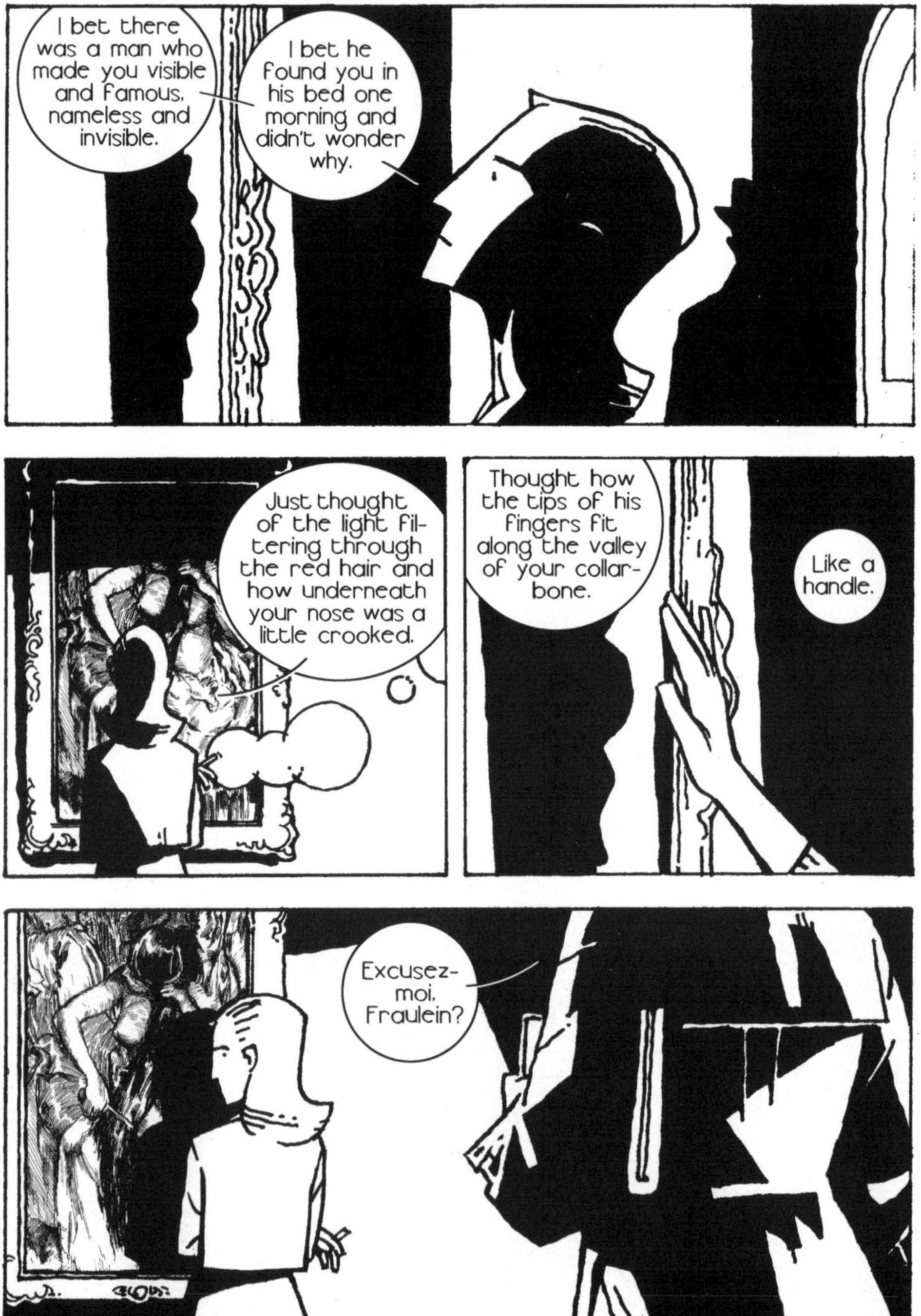
I bet there was a man who made you visible and famous, nameless and invisible.
I bet he found you in his bed one morning and didn't wonder why.
Just thought of the light filtering through the red hair and how underneath your nose was a little crooked.
Thought how the tips of his fingers fit along the valley of your collarbone.
Like a handle.
Excusez-moi, Fraulein?

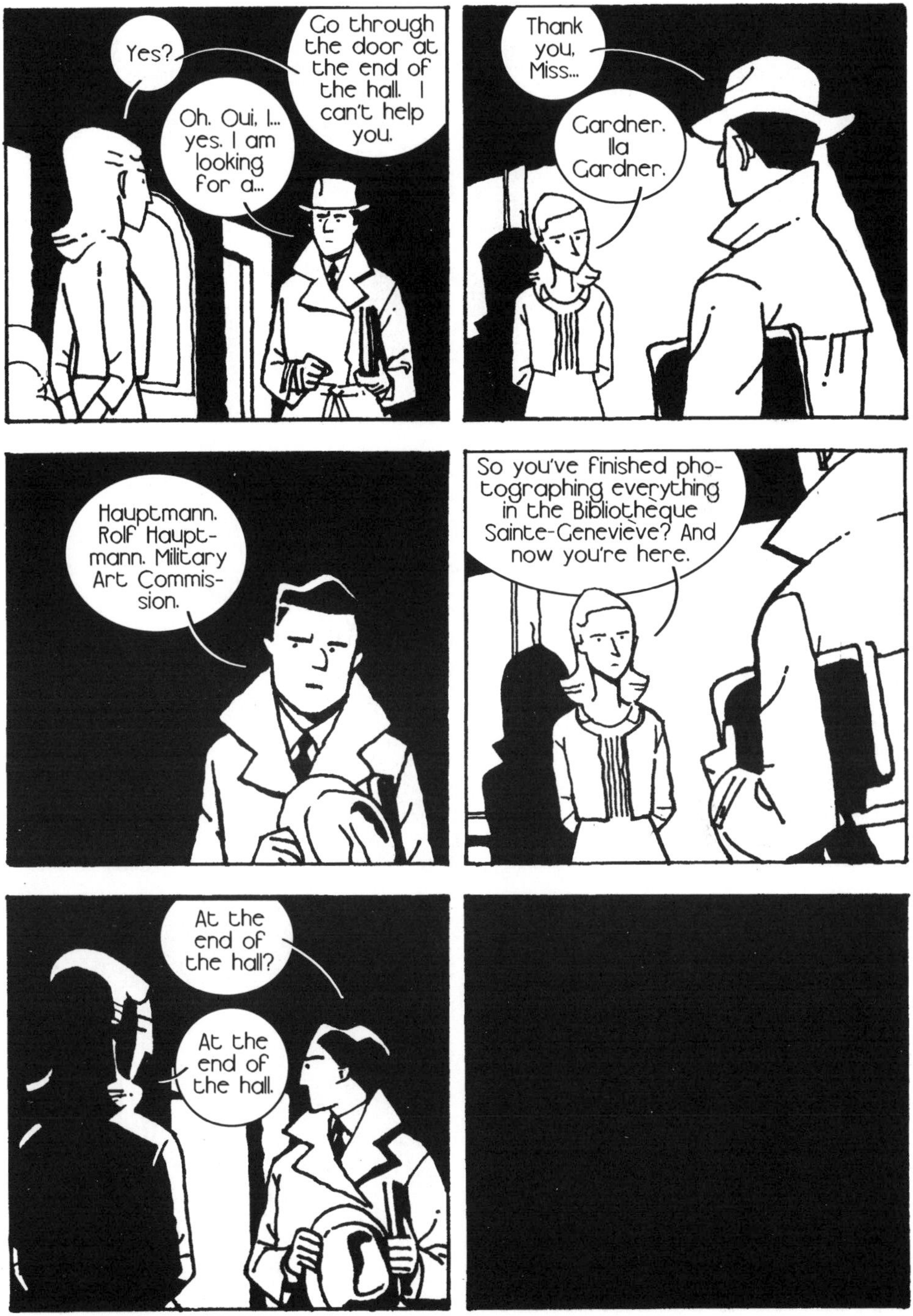
Yes?
Go through the door at the end of the hall. I can't help you.
Oh. Oui, I... yes. I am looking for a...
Thank you, Miss...
Gardner. Ila Gardner.
Hauptmann. Rolf Hauptmann. Military Art Commission.
So you've finished photographing everything in the Bibliothèque Sainte-Geneviève? And now you're here.
At the end of the hall?
At the end of the hall.

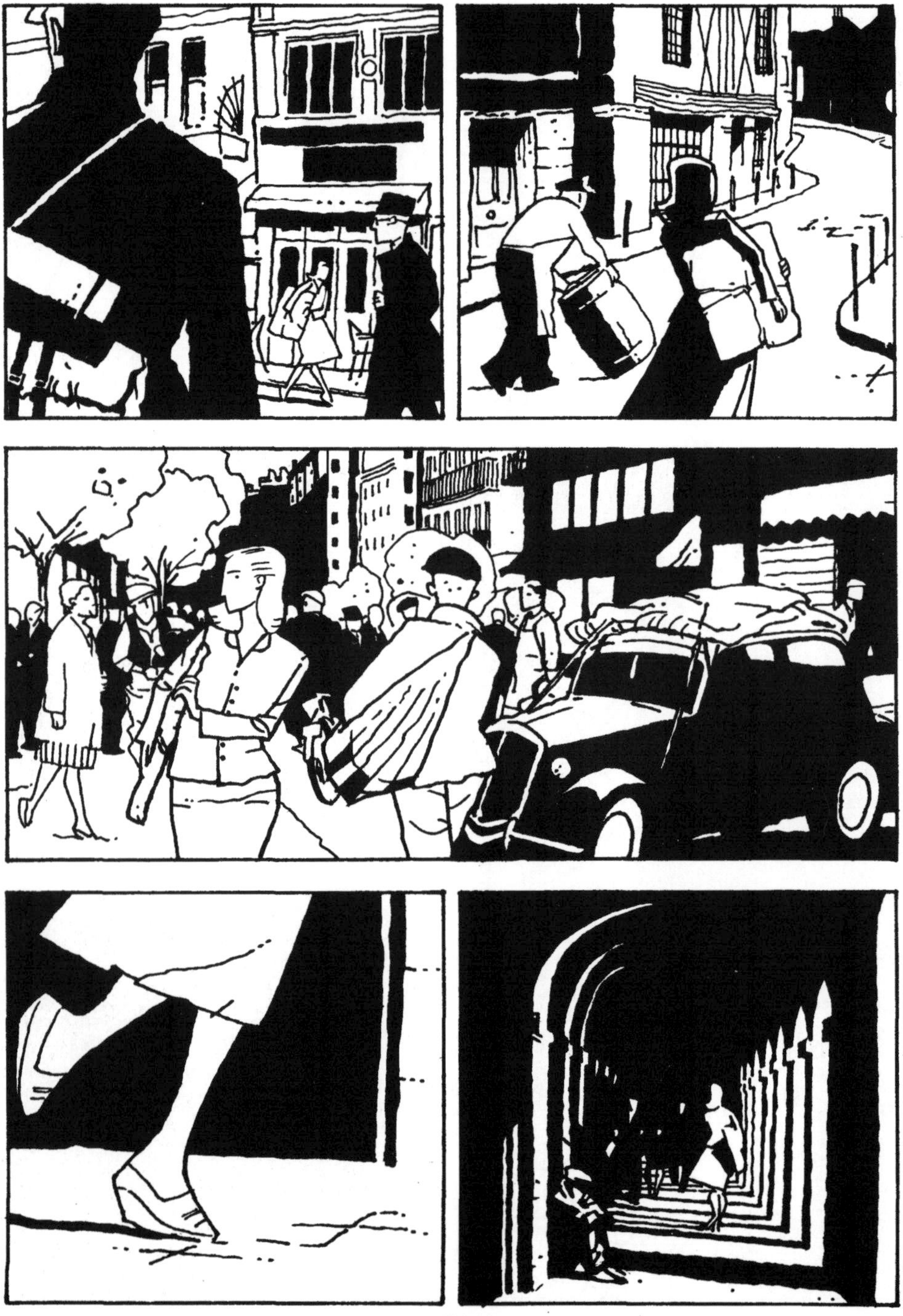

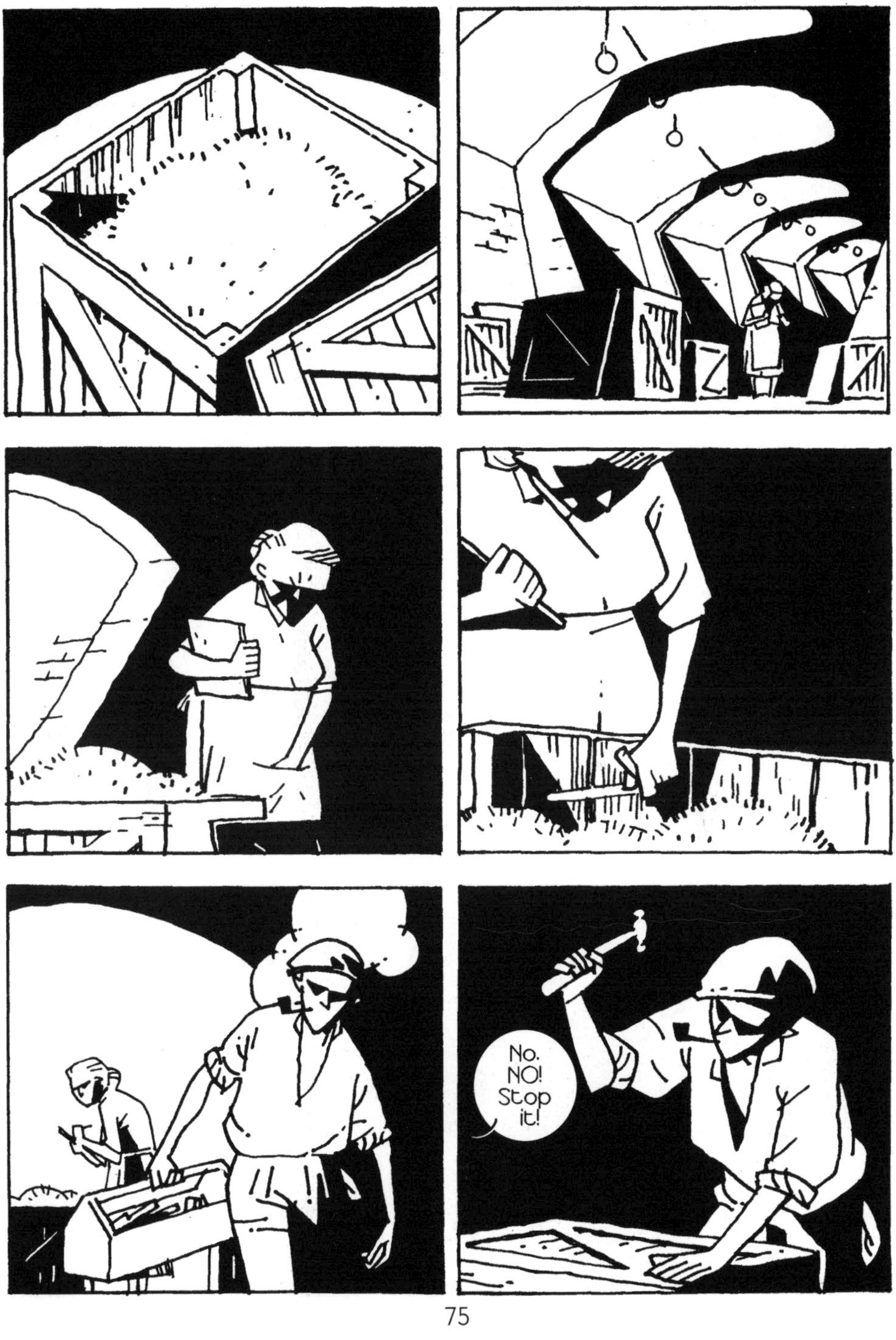
No. NO! Stop it!

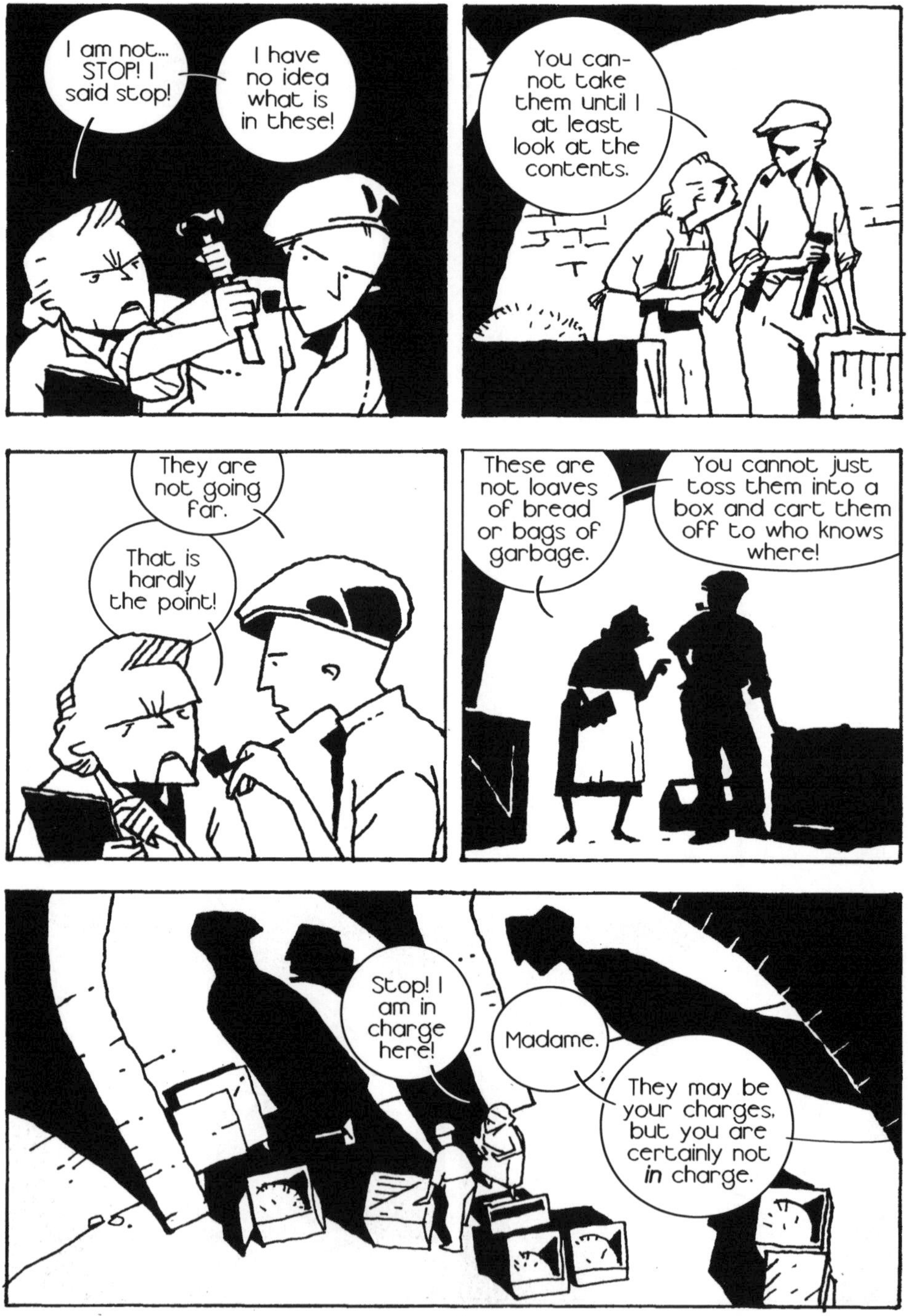
I am not... STOP! I said stop!
I have no idea what is in these!
You can-not take them until I at least look at the contents.
They are not going far.
That is hardly the point!
These are not loaves of bread or bags of garbage.
You cannot just toss them into a box and cart them off to who knows where!
Stop! I am in charge here!
Madame.
They may be your charges, but you are certainly not *in* charge.

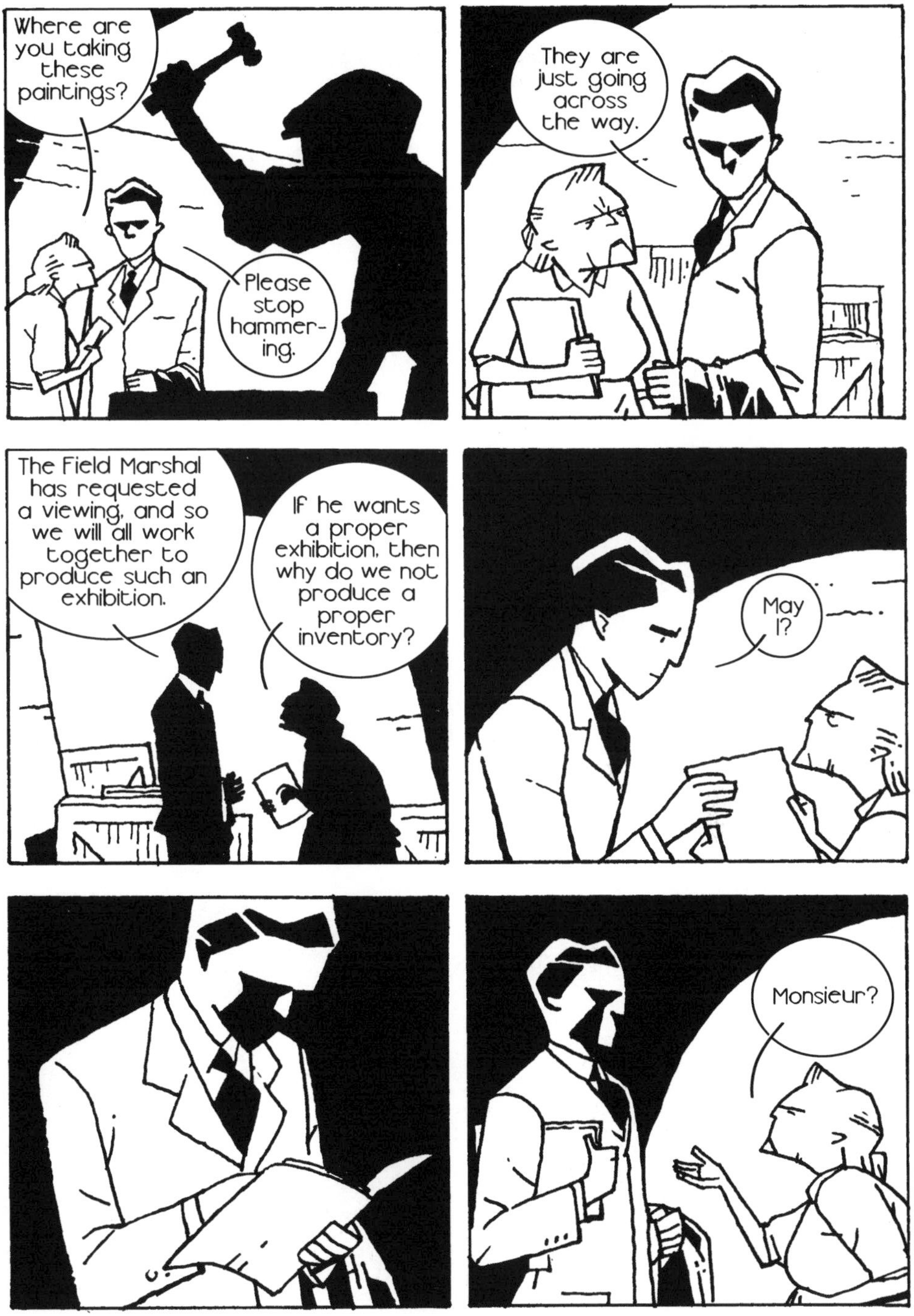
Where are you taking these paintings?
Please stop hammer-ing.
They are just going across the way.
The Field Marshal has requested a viewing, and so we will all work together to produce such an exhibition.
If he wants a proper exhibition, then why do we not produce a proper inventory?
May I?
Monsieur?

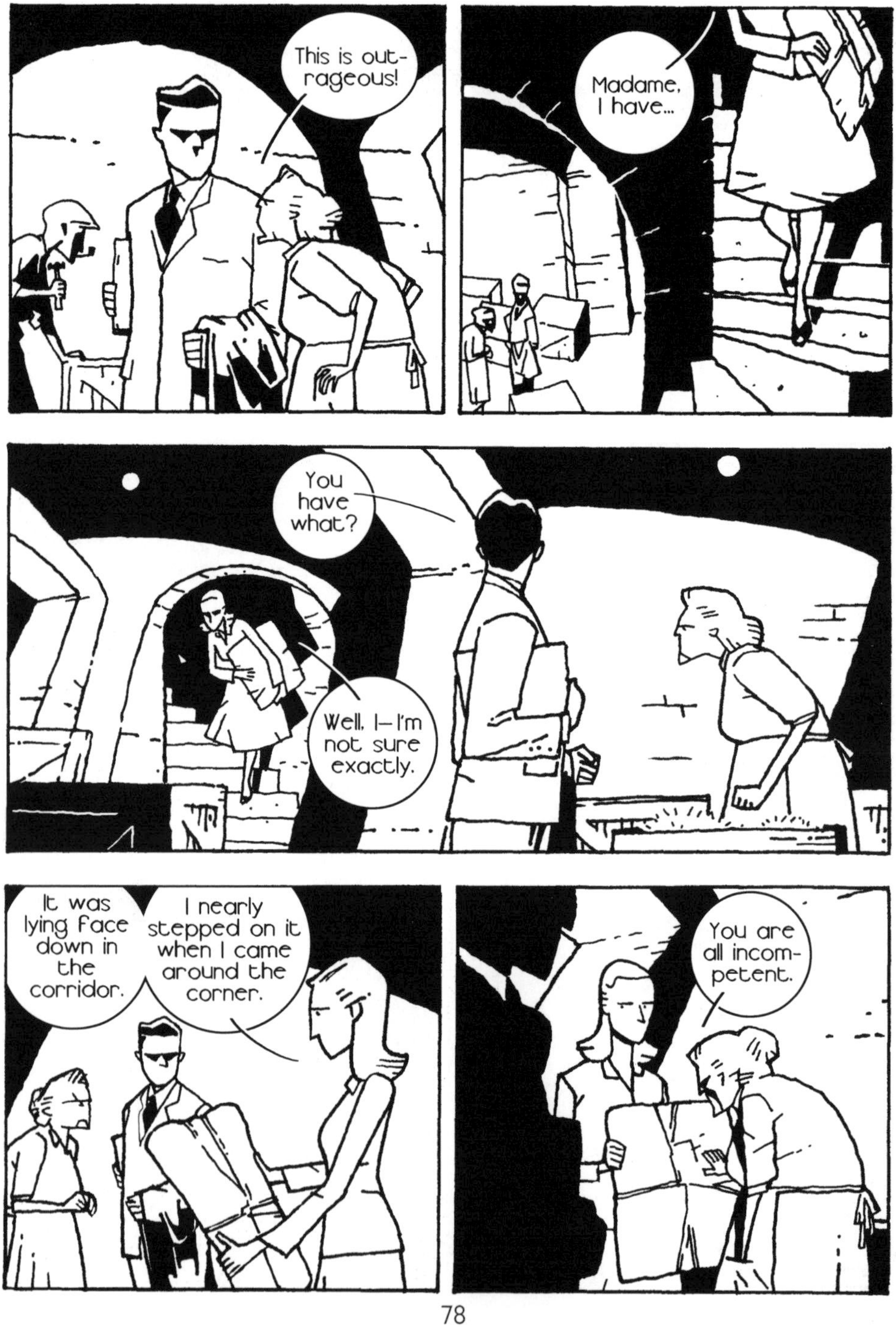
This is outrageous!
Madame, I have...
You have what?
Well, I– I'm not sure exactly.
It was lying face down in the corridor.
I nearly stepped on it when I came around the corner.
You are all incompetent.

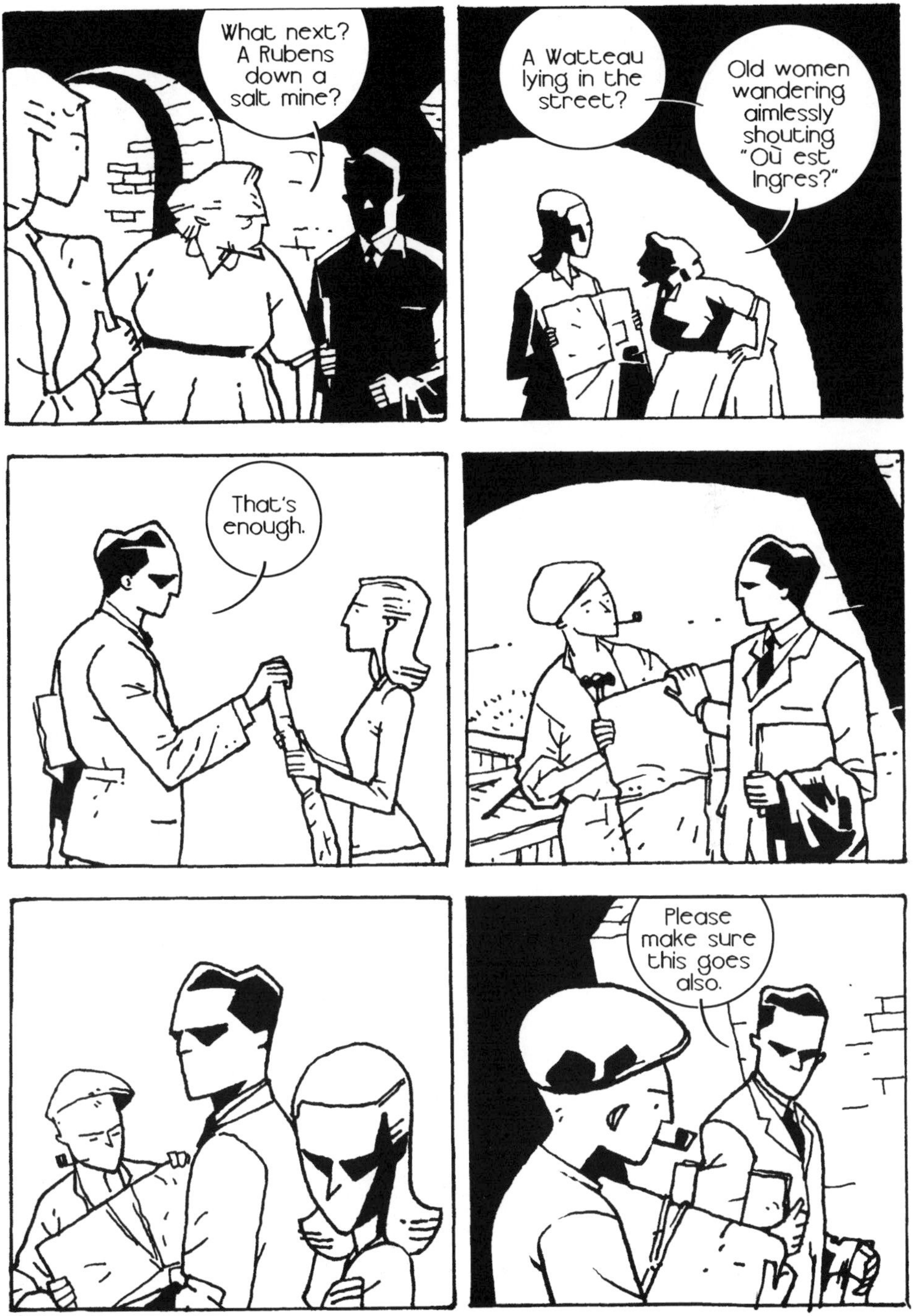
What next? A Rubens down a salt mine?
A Watteau lying in the street?
Old women wandering aimlessly shouting "Où est Ingres?"
That's enough.
Please make sure this goes also.

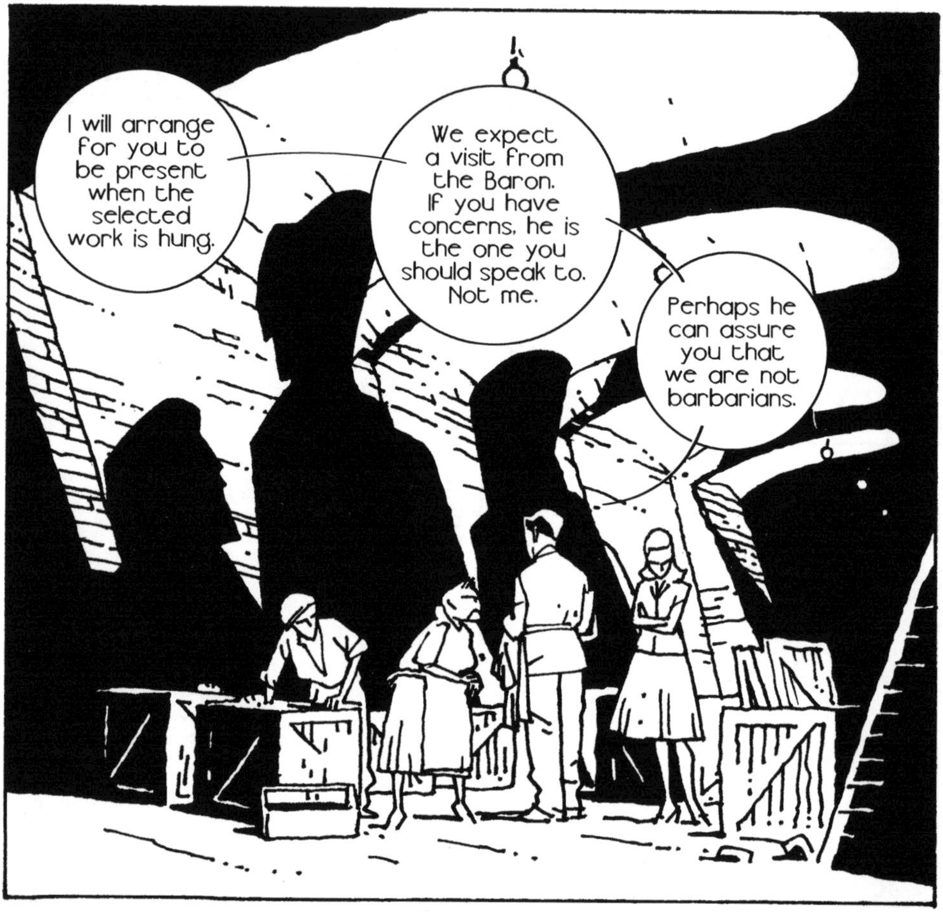
I will arrange for you to be present when the selected work is hung.
We expect a visit from the Baron. If you have concerns, he is the one you should speak to. Not me.
Perhaps he can assure you that we are not barbarians.

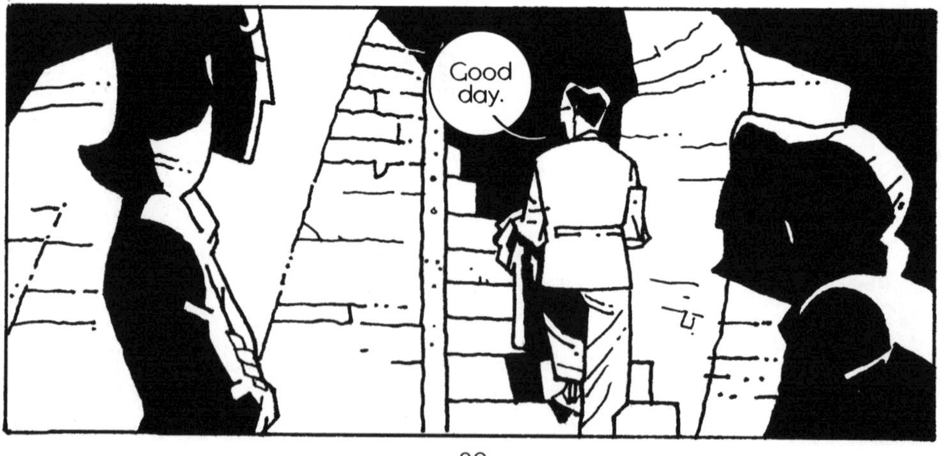
Good day.

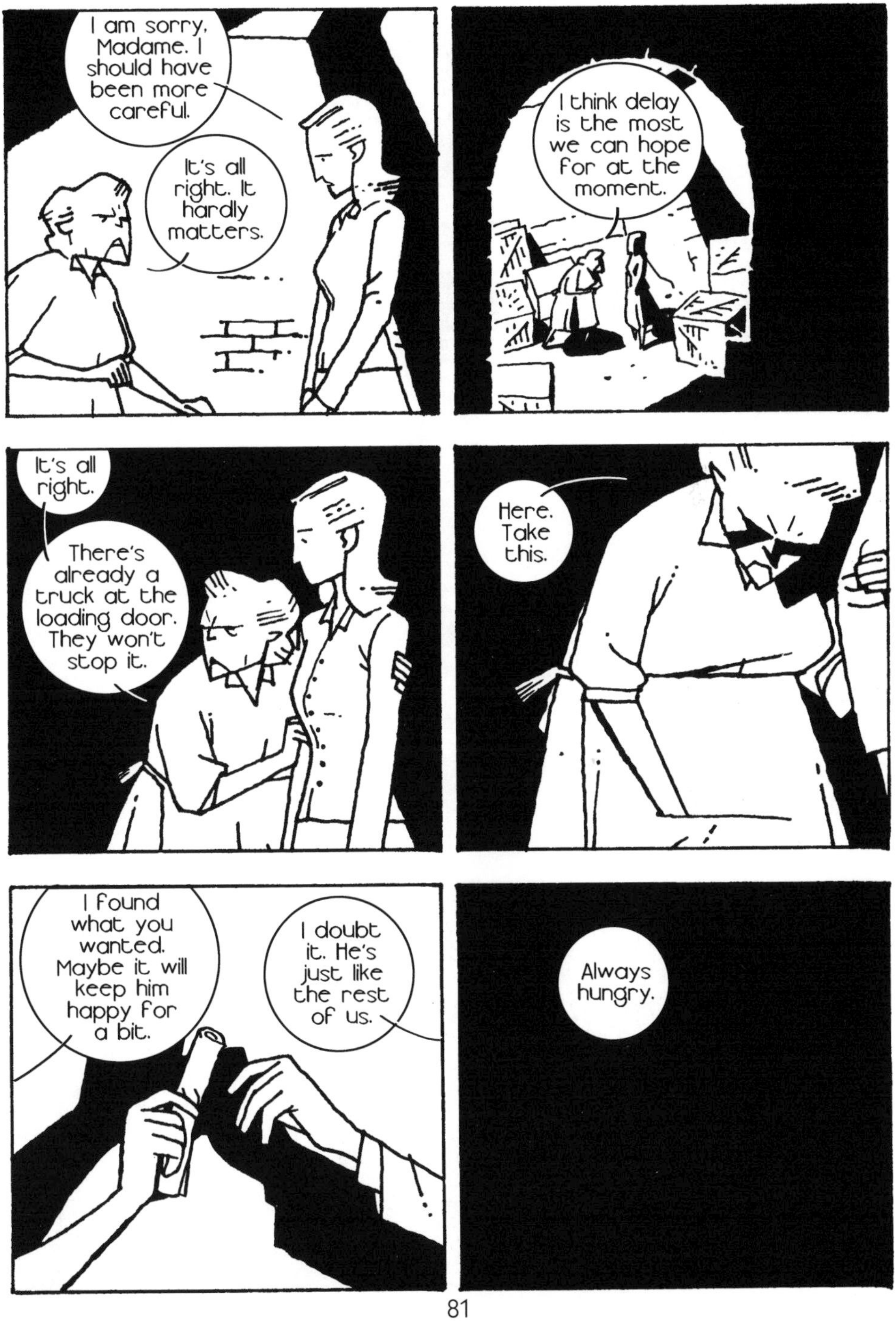
I am sorry, Madame. I should have been more careful.
It's all right. It hardly matters.
I think delay is the most we can hope for at the moment.
It's all right.
There's already a truck at the loading door. They won't stop it.
Here. Take this.
I found what you wanted. Maybe it will keep him happy for a bit.
I doubt it. He's just like the rest of us.
Always hungry.

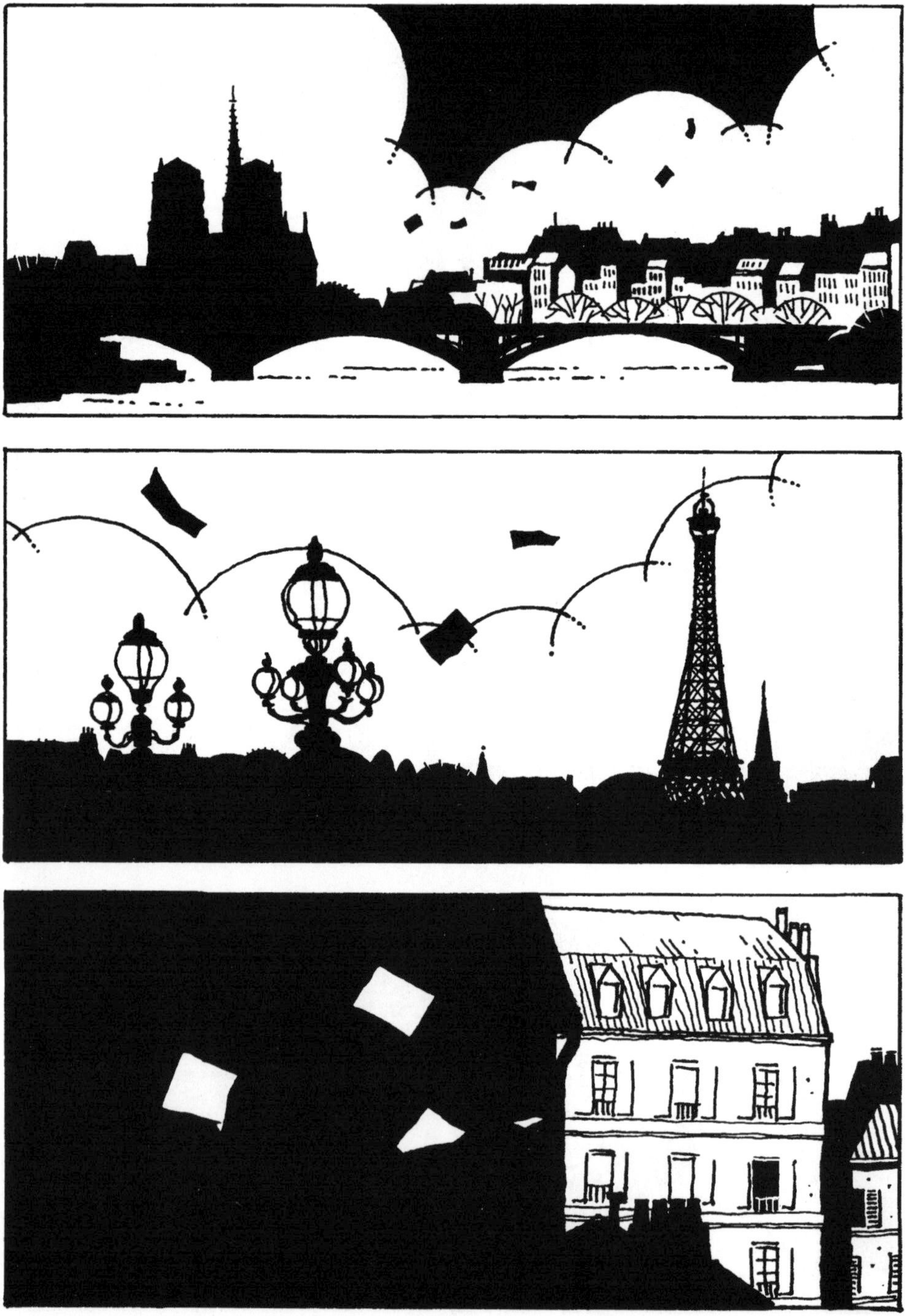

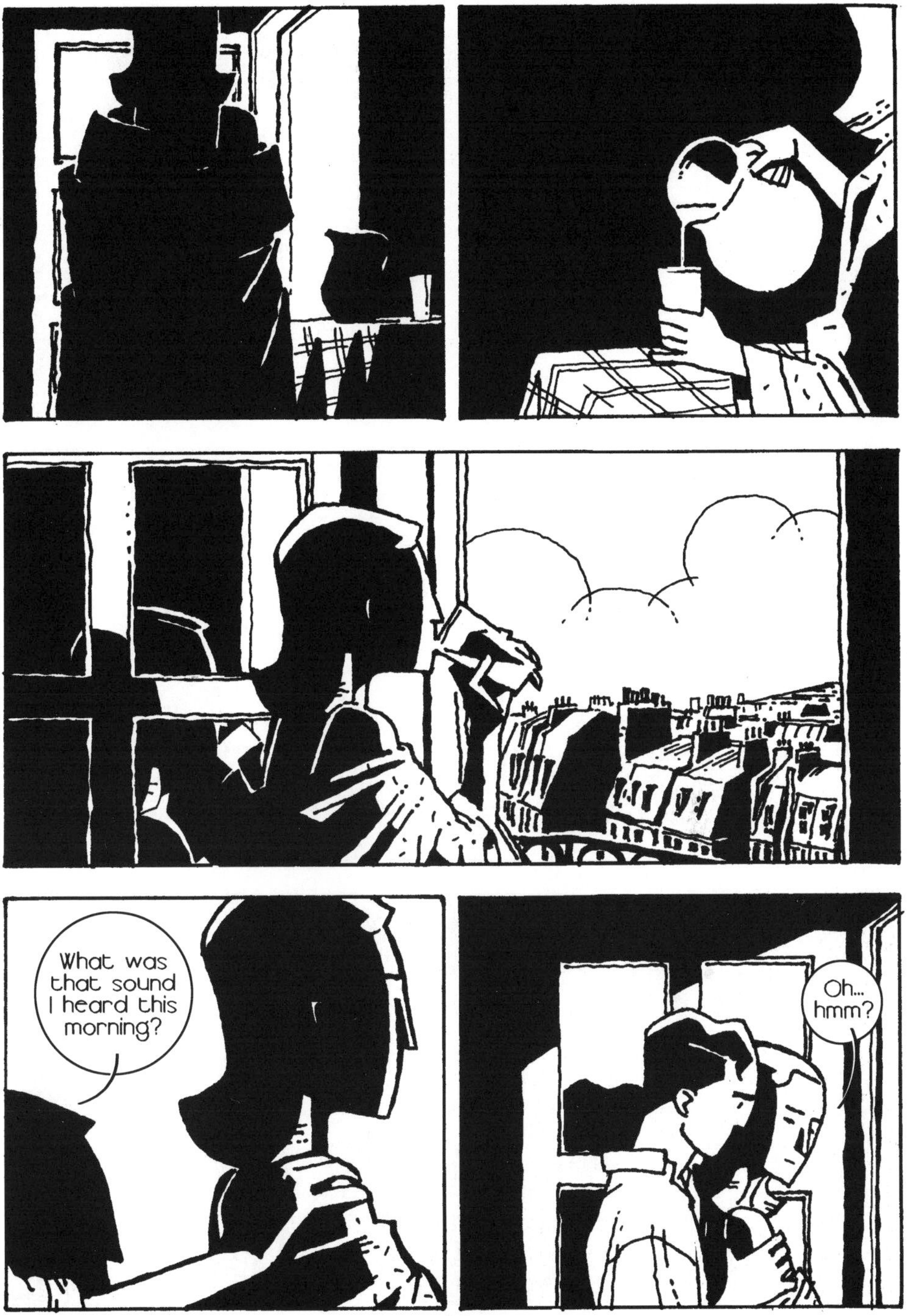
What was that sound I heard this morning?
Oh... hmm?

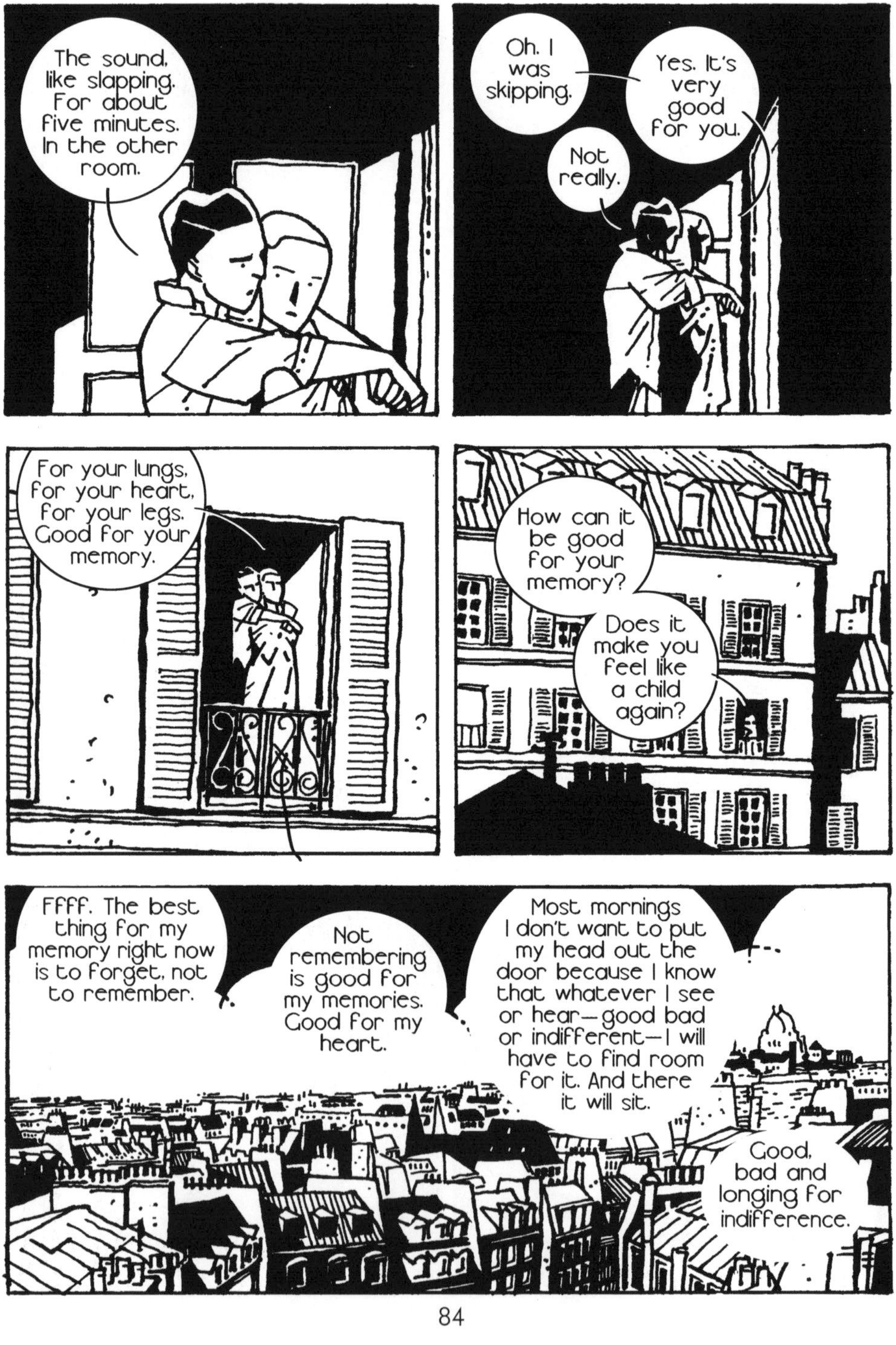
The sound, like slapping. For about five minutes. In the other room.
Oh. I was skipping.
Yes. It's very good for you.
Not really.
For your lungs, for your heart, for your legs. Good for your memory.
How can it be good for your memory?
Does it make you feel like a child again?
Ffff. The best thing for my memory right now is to forget, not to remember.
Not remembering is good for my memories. Good for my heart.
Most mornings I don't want to put my head out the door because I know that whatever I see or hear—good bad or indifferent—I will have to find room for it. And there it will sit.
Good, bad and longing for indifference.

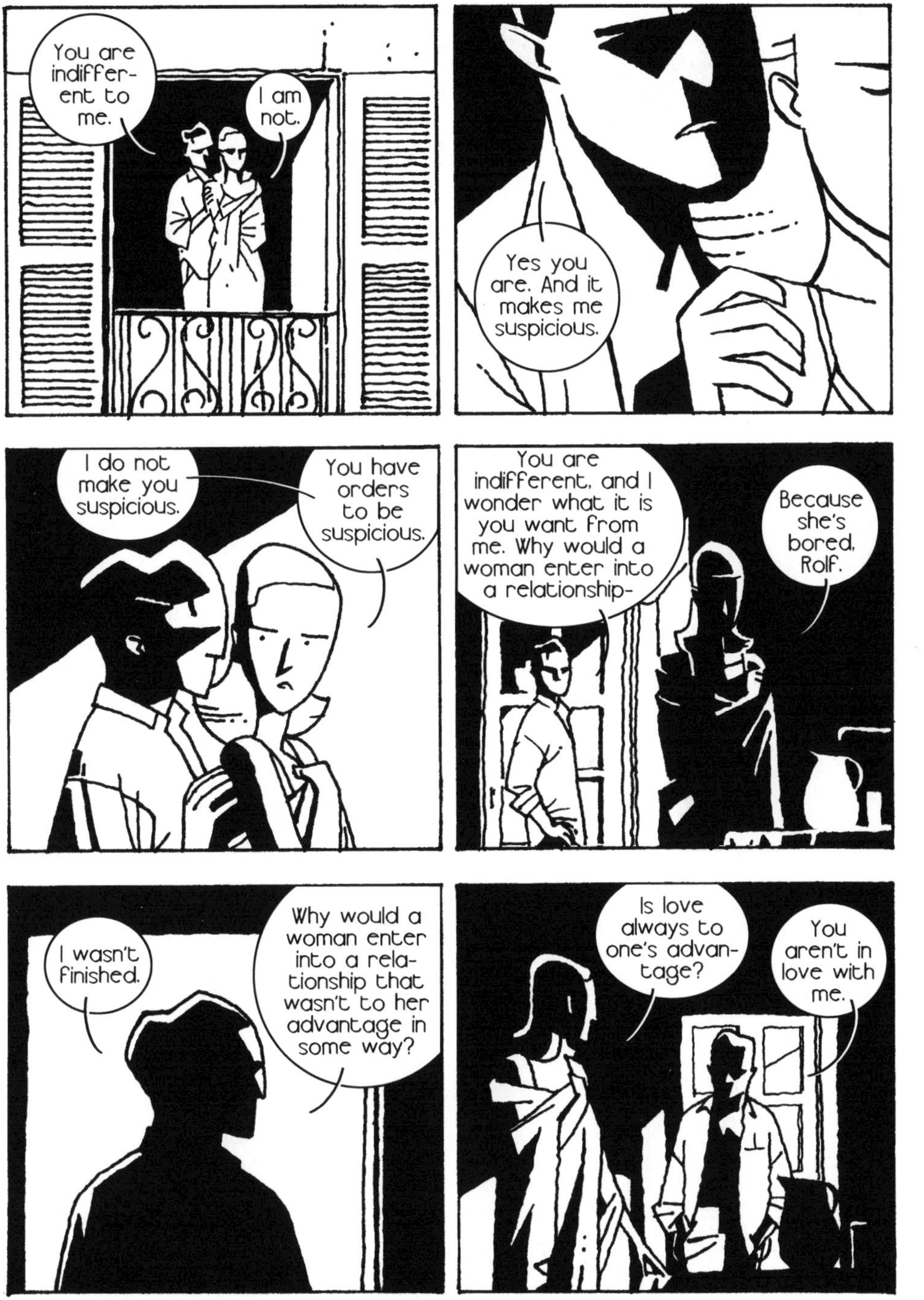
You are indiffer-ent to me.
I am not.
Yes you are. And it makes me suspicious.
I do not make you suspicious.
You have orders to be suspicious.
You are indifferent, and I wonder what it is you want from me. Why would a woman enter into a relationship-
Because she's bored, Rolf.
I wasn't finished.
Why would a woman enter into a rela-tionship that wasn't to her advantage in some way?
Is love always to one's advan-tage?
You aren't in love with me.

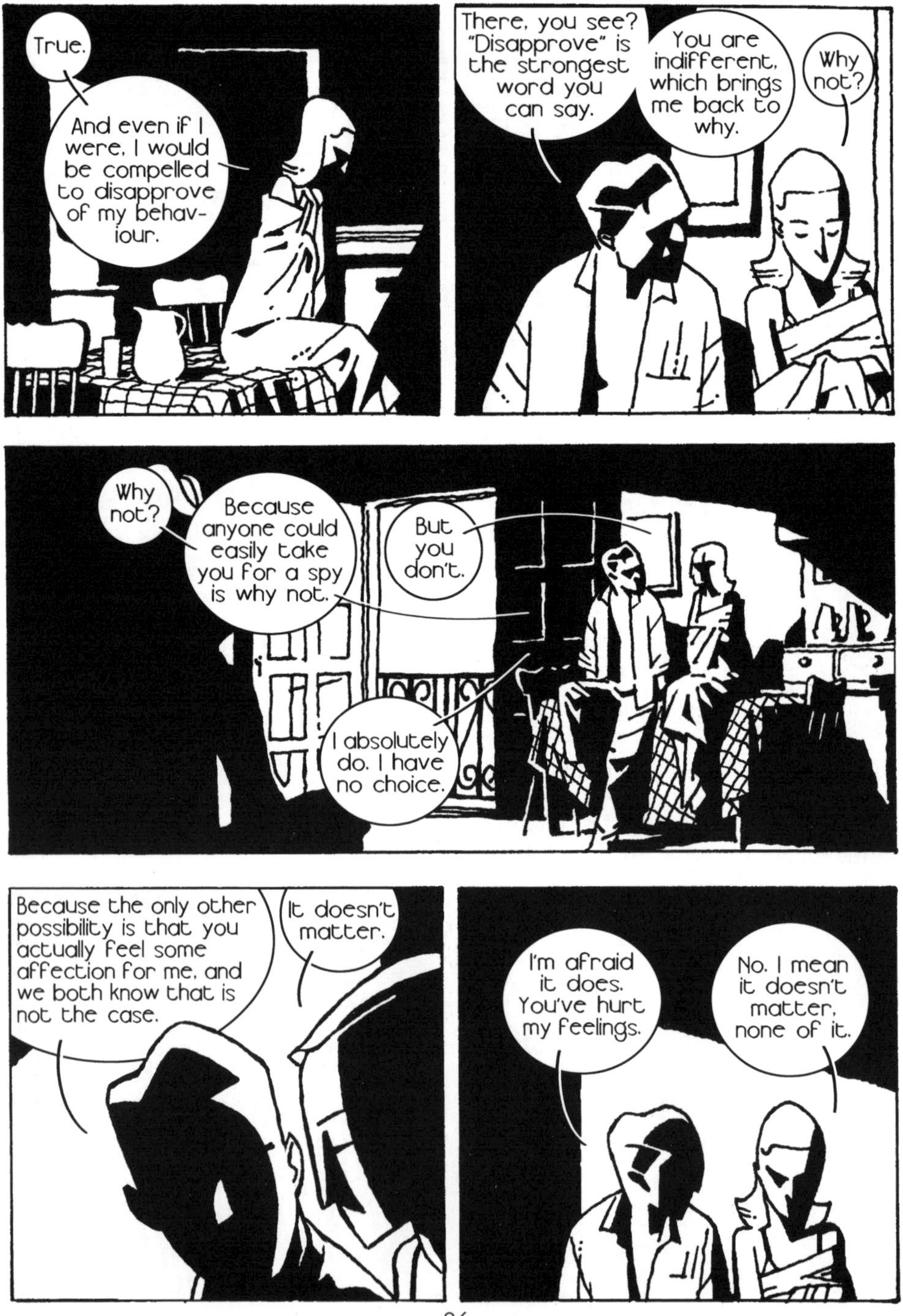
True.
And even if I were, I would be compelled to disapprove of my behaviour.
There, you see? "Disapprove" is the strongest word you can say.
You are indifferent, which brings me back to why.
Why not?
Why not?
Because anyone could easily take you for a spy is why not.
But you don't.
I absolutely do. I have no choice.
Because the only other possibility is that you actually feel some affection for me, and we both know that is not the case.
It doesn't matter.
I'm afraid it does. You've hurt my feelings.
No. I mean it doesn't matter, none of it.

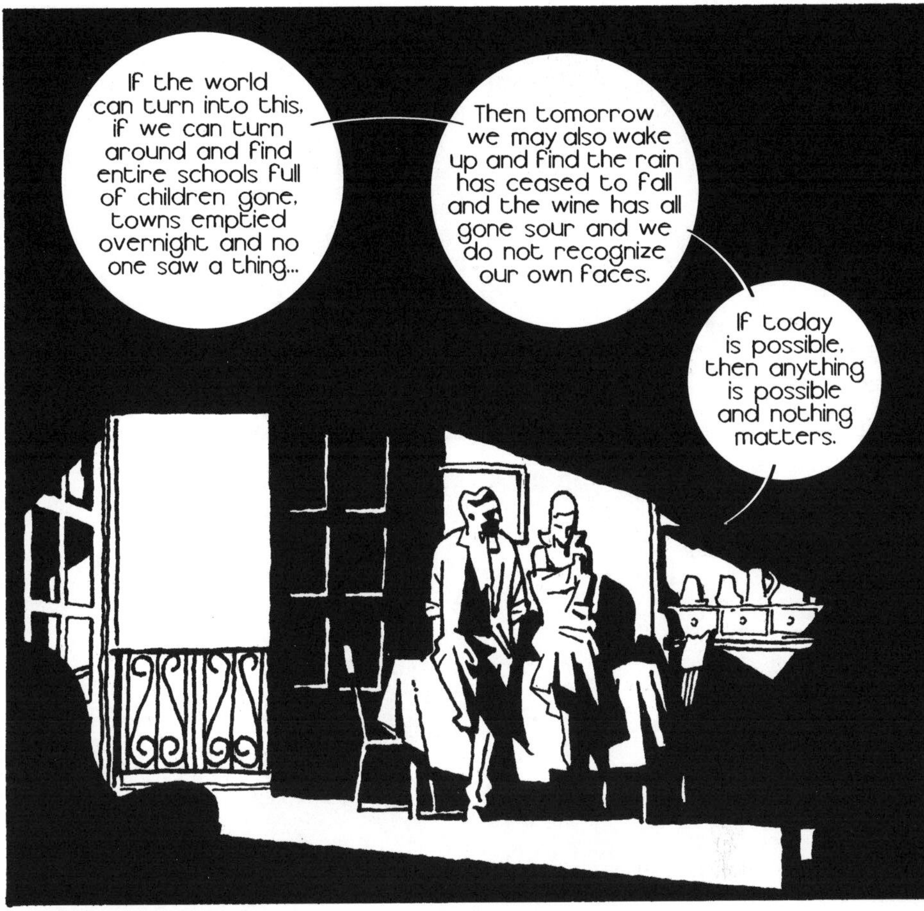
If the world can turn into this, if we can turn around and find entire schools full of children gone, towns emptied overnight and no one saw a thing...
Then tomorrow we may also wake up and find the rain has ceased to fall and the wine has all gone sour and we do not recognize our own faces.
If today is possible, then anything is possible and nothing matters.

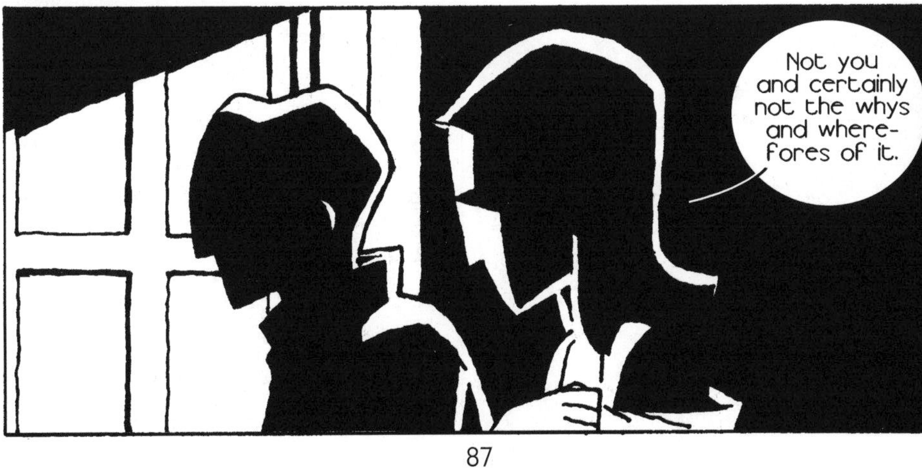
Not you and certainly not the whys and where-fores of it.

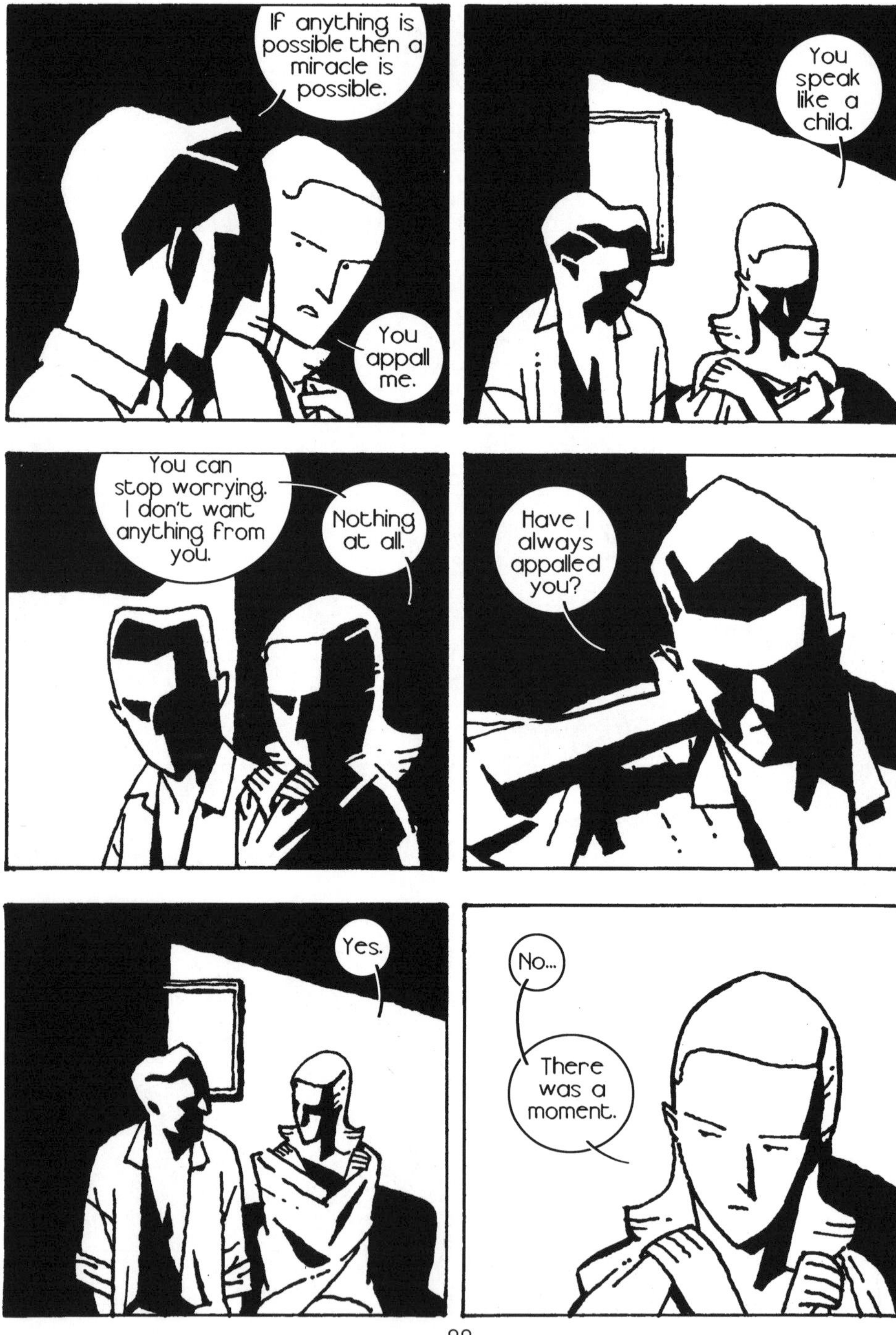
If anything is possible then a miracle is possible.
You appall me.
You speak like a child.
You can stop worrying. I don't want anything from you.
Nothing at all.
Have I always appalled you?
Yes.
No...
There was a moment.

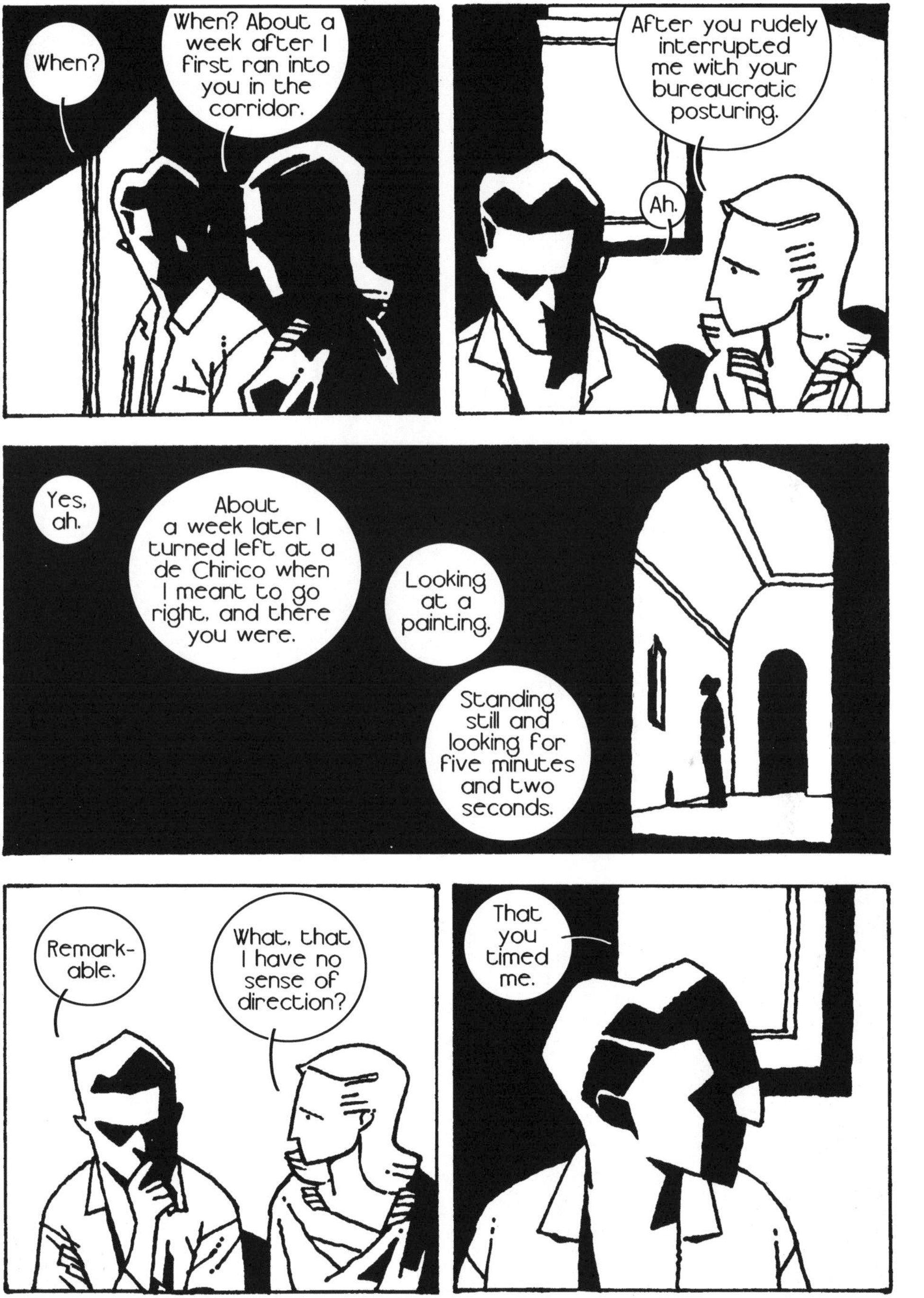
When?
When? About a week after I first ran into you in the corridor.
After you rudely interrupted me with your bureaucratic posturing.
Ah.
Yes, ah.
About a week later I turned left at a de Chirico when I meant to go right, and there you were.
Looking at a painting.
Standing still and looking for five minutes and two seconds.
Remark-able.
What, that I have no sense of direction?
That you timed me.

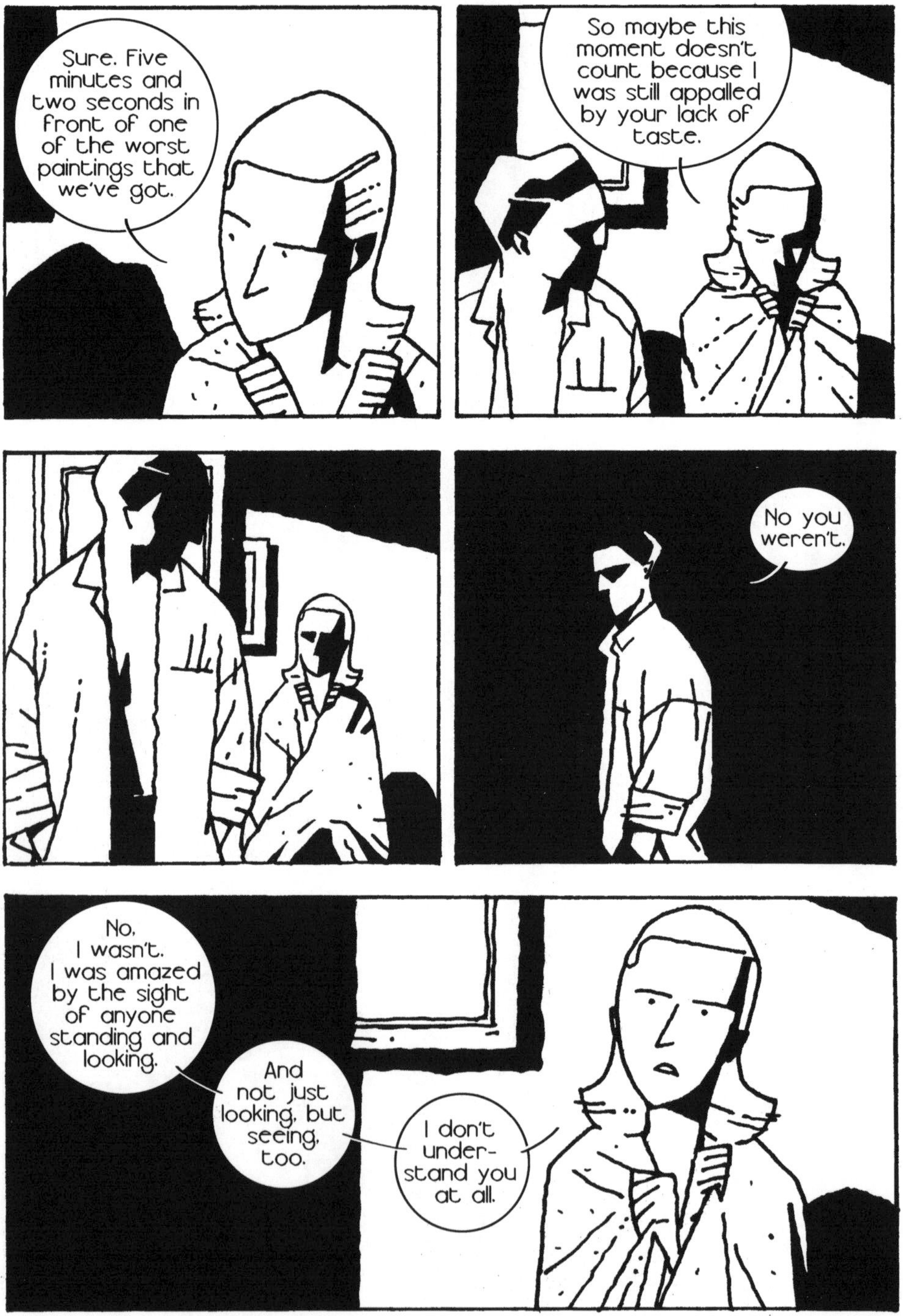
Sure. Five minutes and two seconds in front of one of the worst paintings that we've got.
So maybe this moment doesn't count because I was still appalled by your lack of taste.
No you weren't.
No, I wasn't. I was amazed by the sight of anyone standing and looking.
And not just looking, but seeing, too.
I don't under-stand you at all.

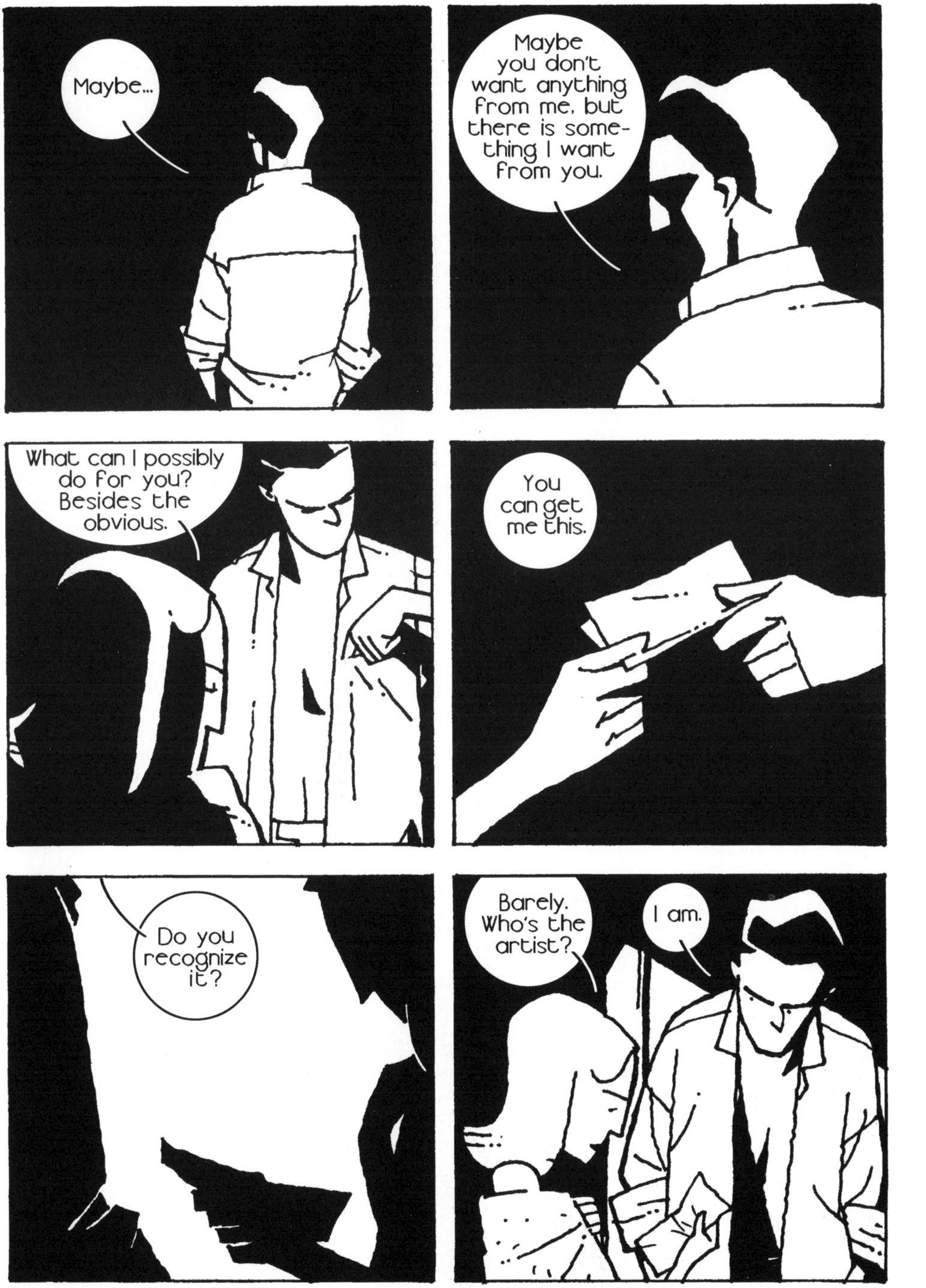

Maybe...
Maybe you don't want anything from me, but there is something I want from you.
What can I possibly do for you? Besides the obvious.
You can get me this.
Do you recognize it?
Barely. Who's the artist?
I am.

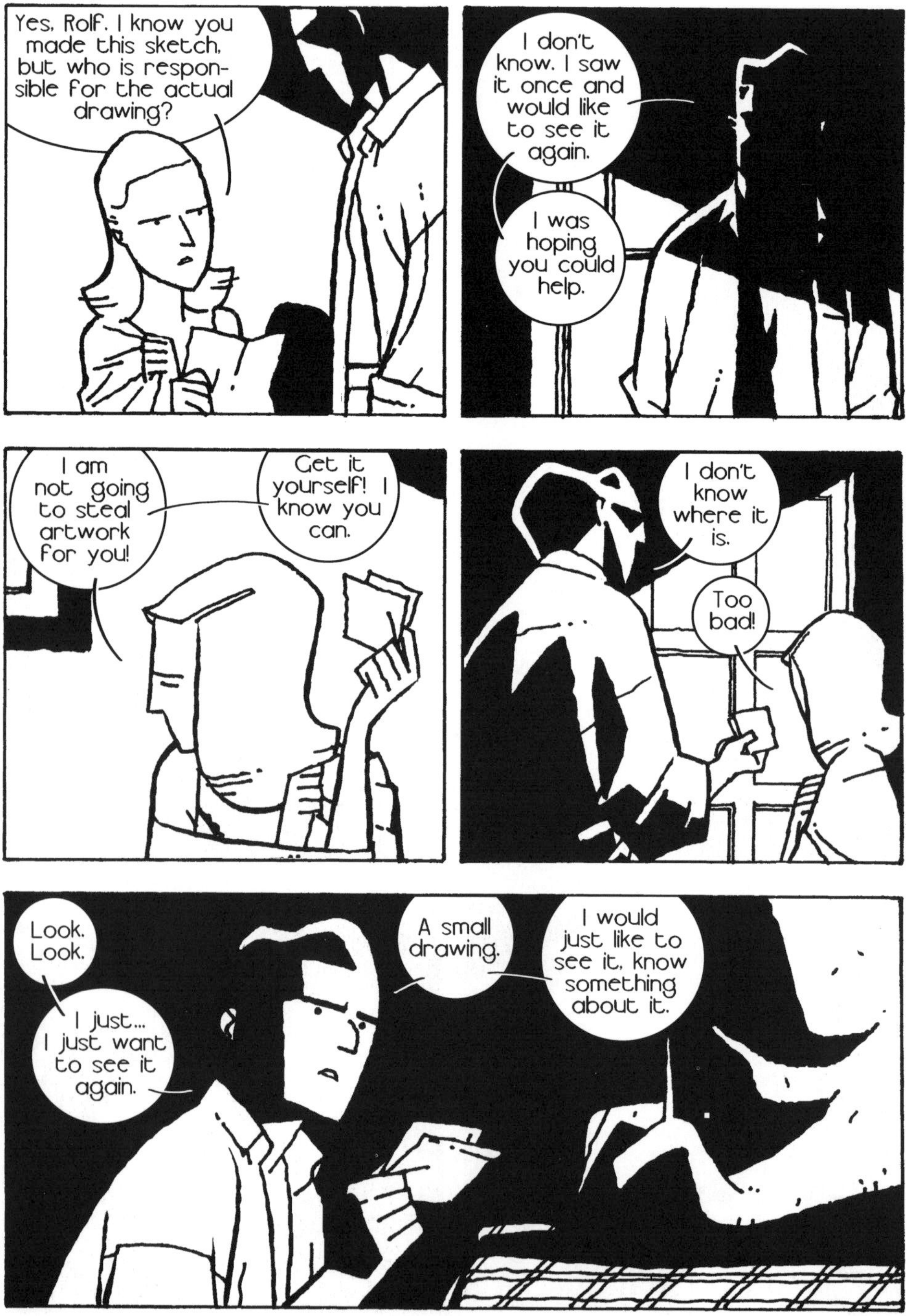
Yes, Rolf. I know you made this sketch, but who is responsible for the actual drawing?
I don't know. I saw it once and would like to see it again.
I was hoping you could help.
I am not going to steal artwork for you!
Get it yourself! I know you can.
I don't know where it is.
Too bad!
Look. Look.
I just... I just want to see it again.
A small drawing.
I would just like to see it, know something about it.

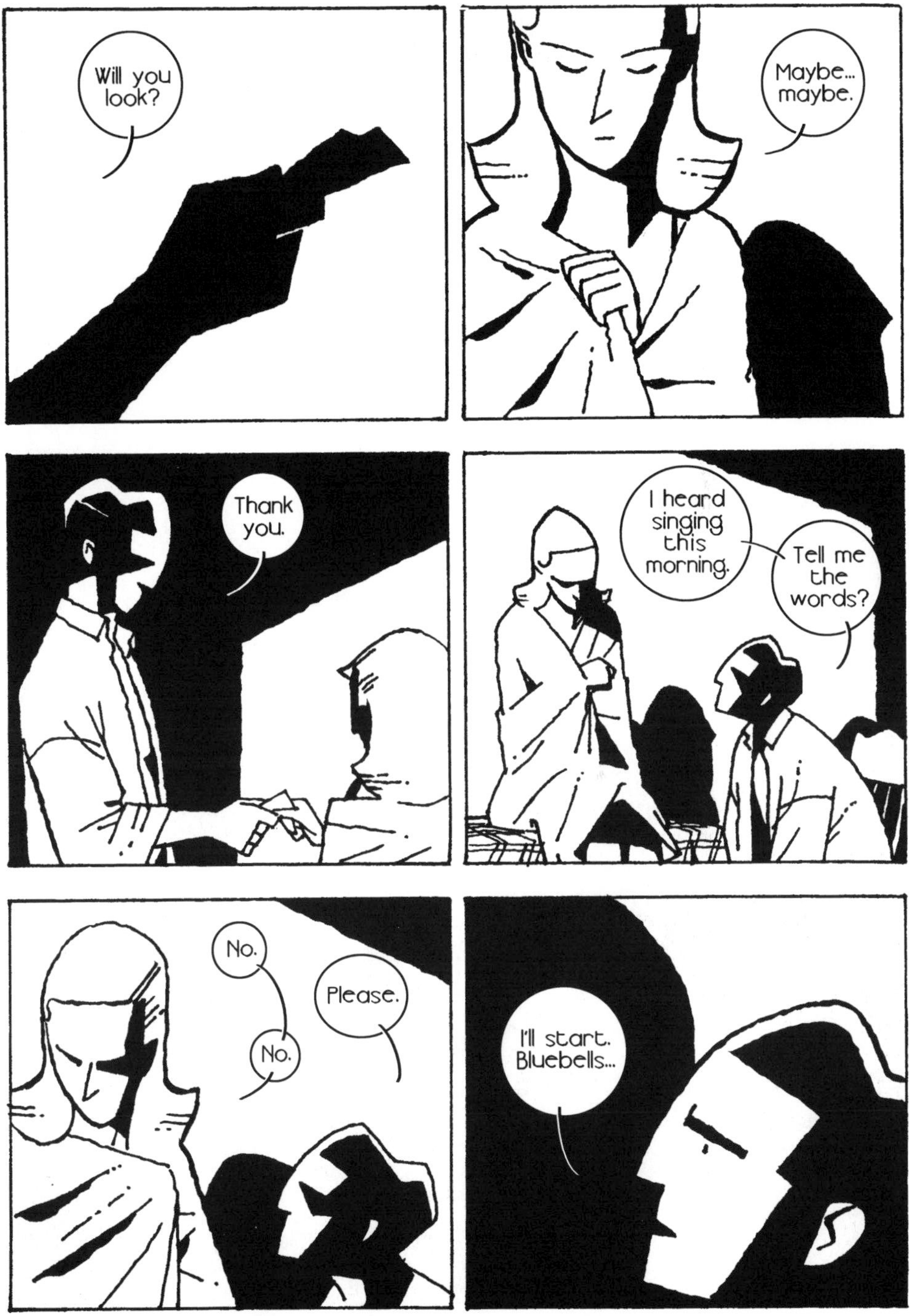
Will you look?
Maybe... maybe.
Thank you.
I heard singing this morning.
Tell me the words?
No.
No.
Please.
I'll start. Bluebells...

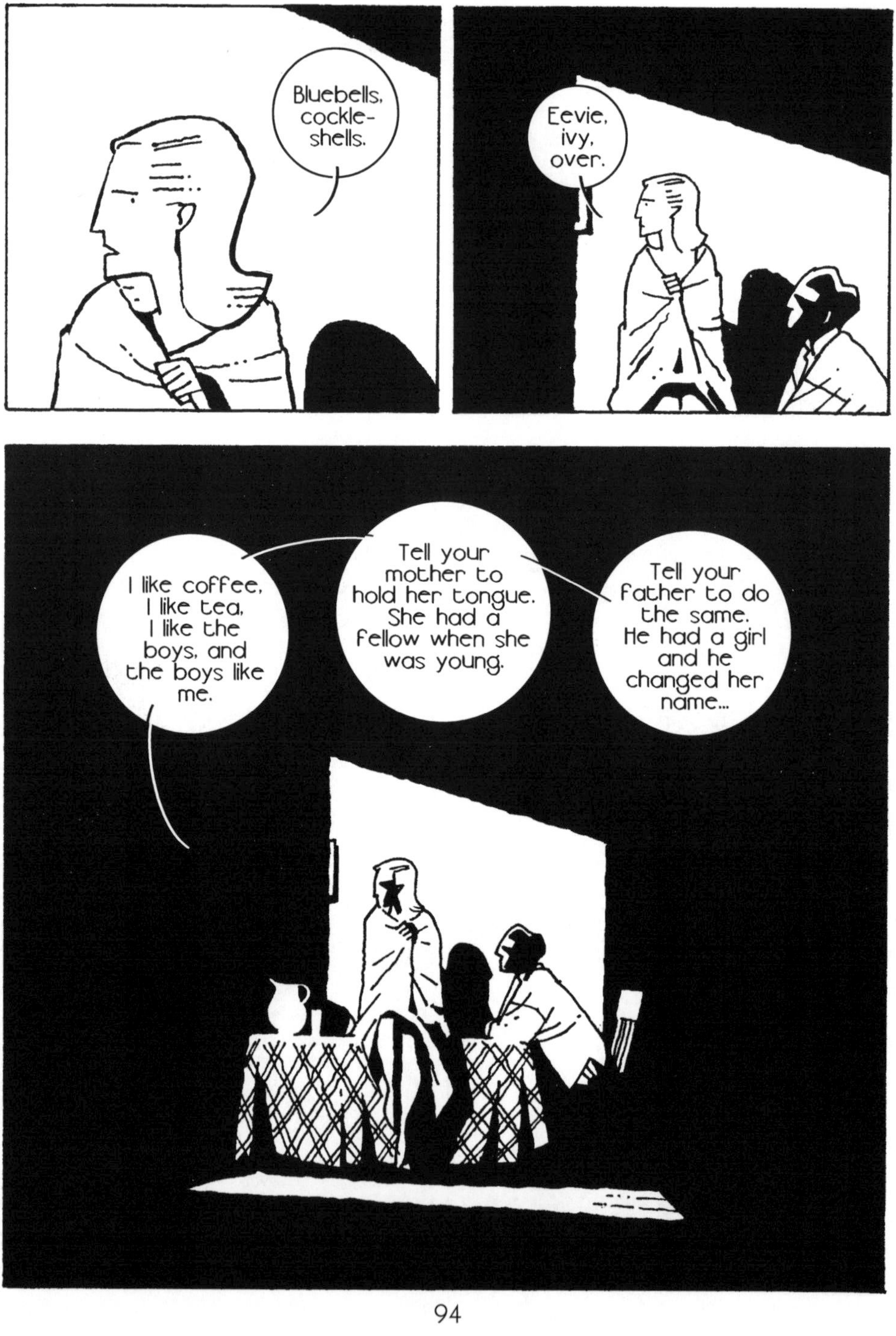
Bluebells, cockle-shells.
Eevie, ivy, over.
I like coffee, I like tea, I like the boys, and the boys like me.
Tell your mother to hold her tongue. She had a fellow when she was young.
Tell your father to do the same. He had a girl and he changed her name...

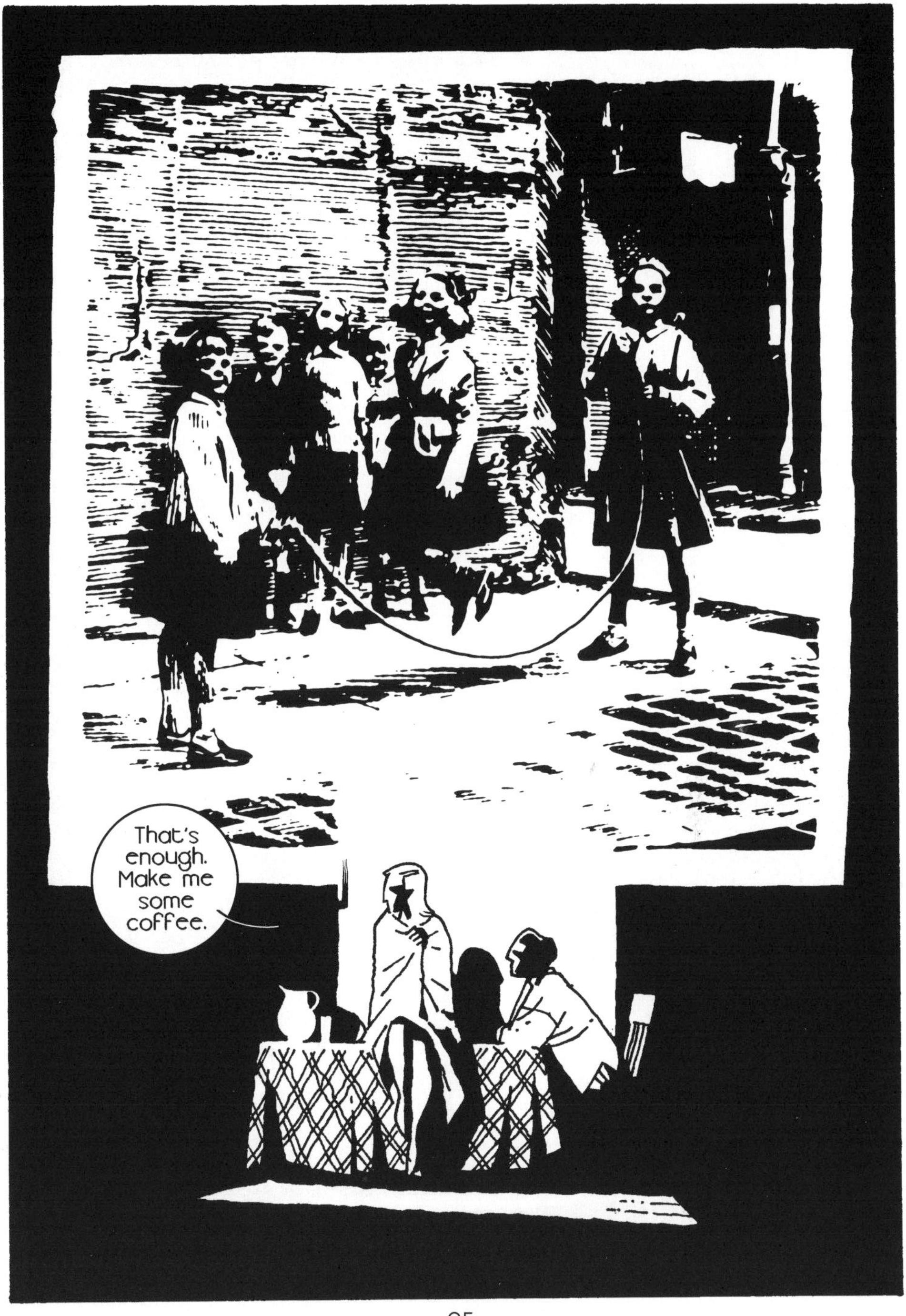
That's enough. Make me some coffee.

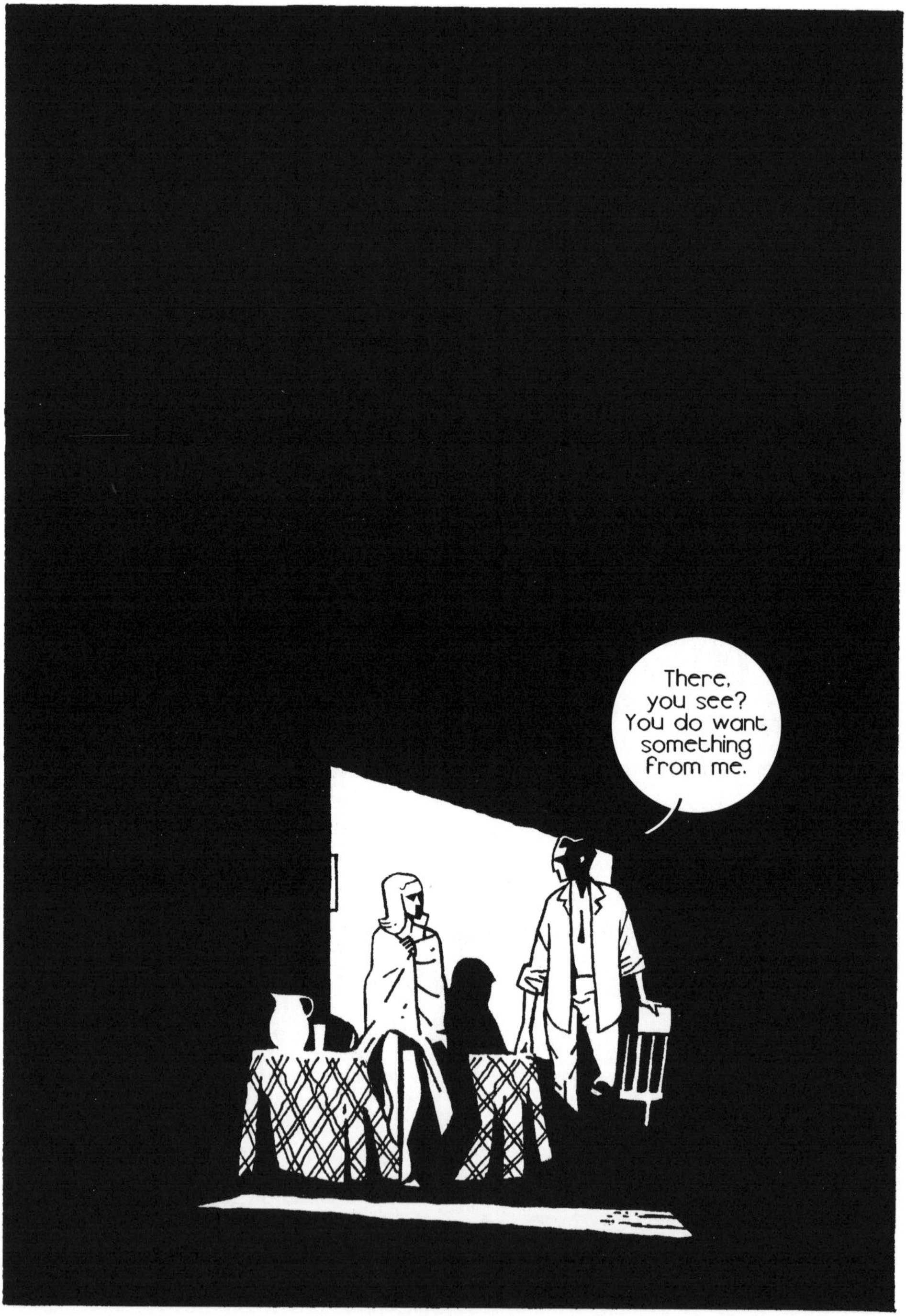
There, you see? You do want something from me.

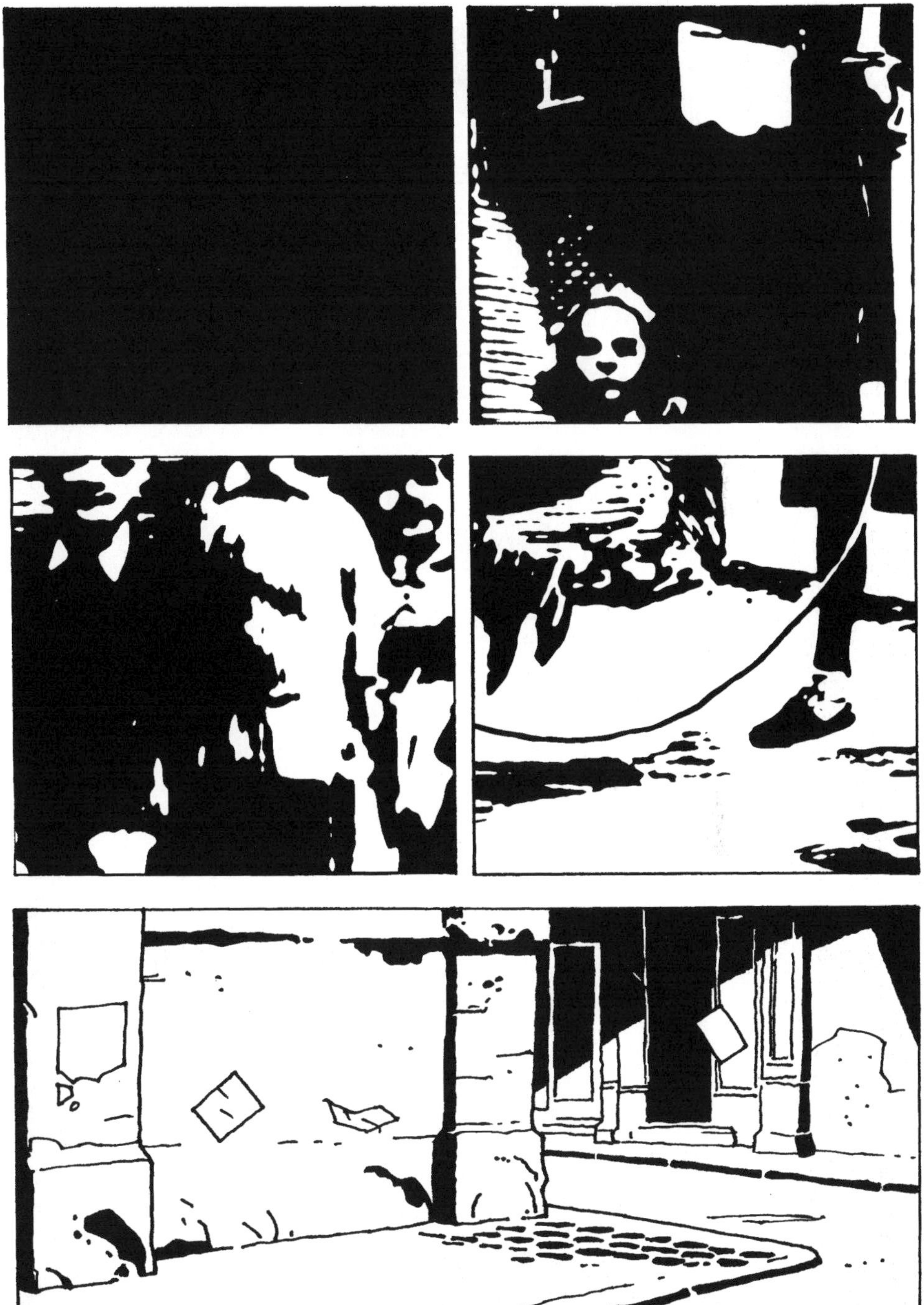

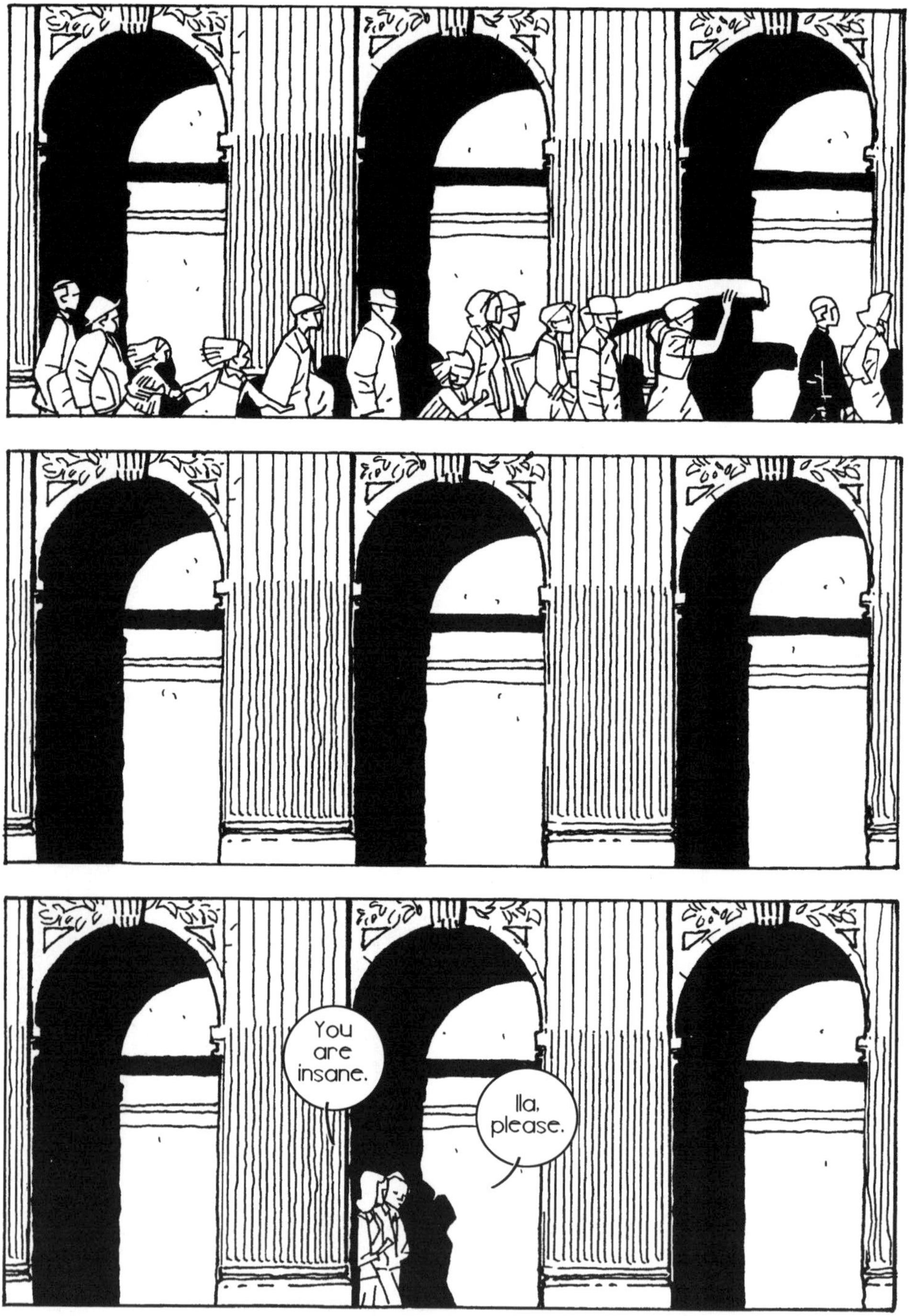
You are insane.
Ila, please.

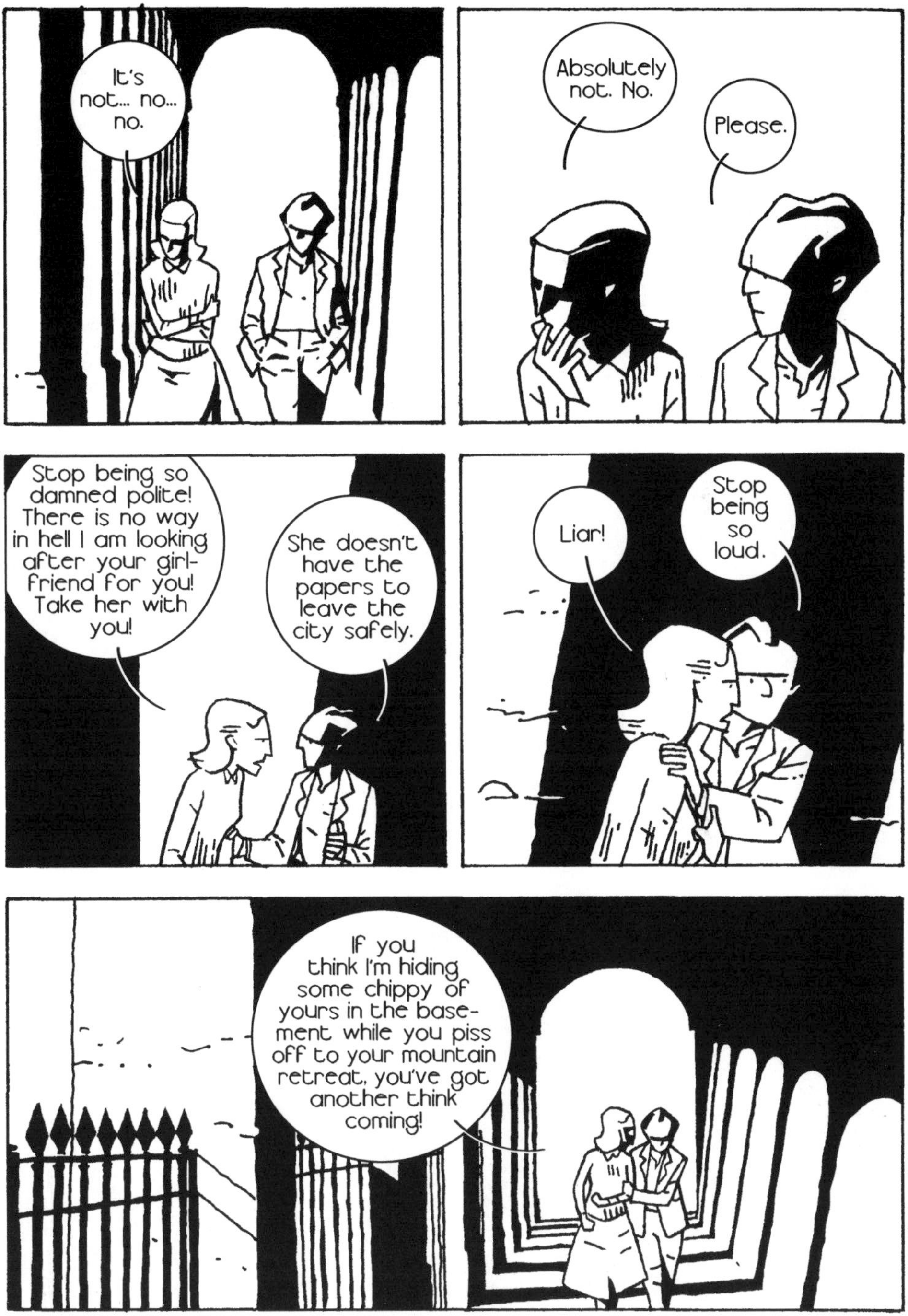
It's not... no... no.
Absolutely not. No.
Please.
Stop being so damned polite! There is no way in hell I am looking after your girl-friend for you! Take her with you!
She doesn't have the papers to leave the city safely.
Liar!
Stop being so loud.
If you think I'm hiding some chippy of yours in the base-ment while you piss off to your mountain retreat, you've got another think coming!

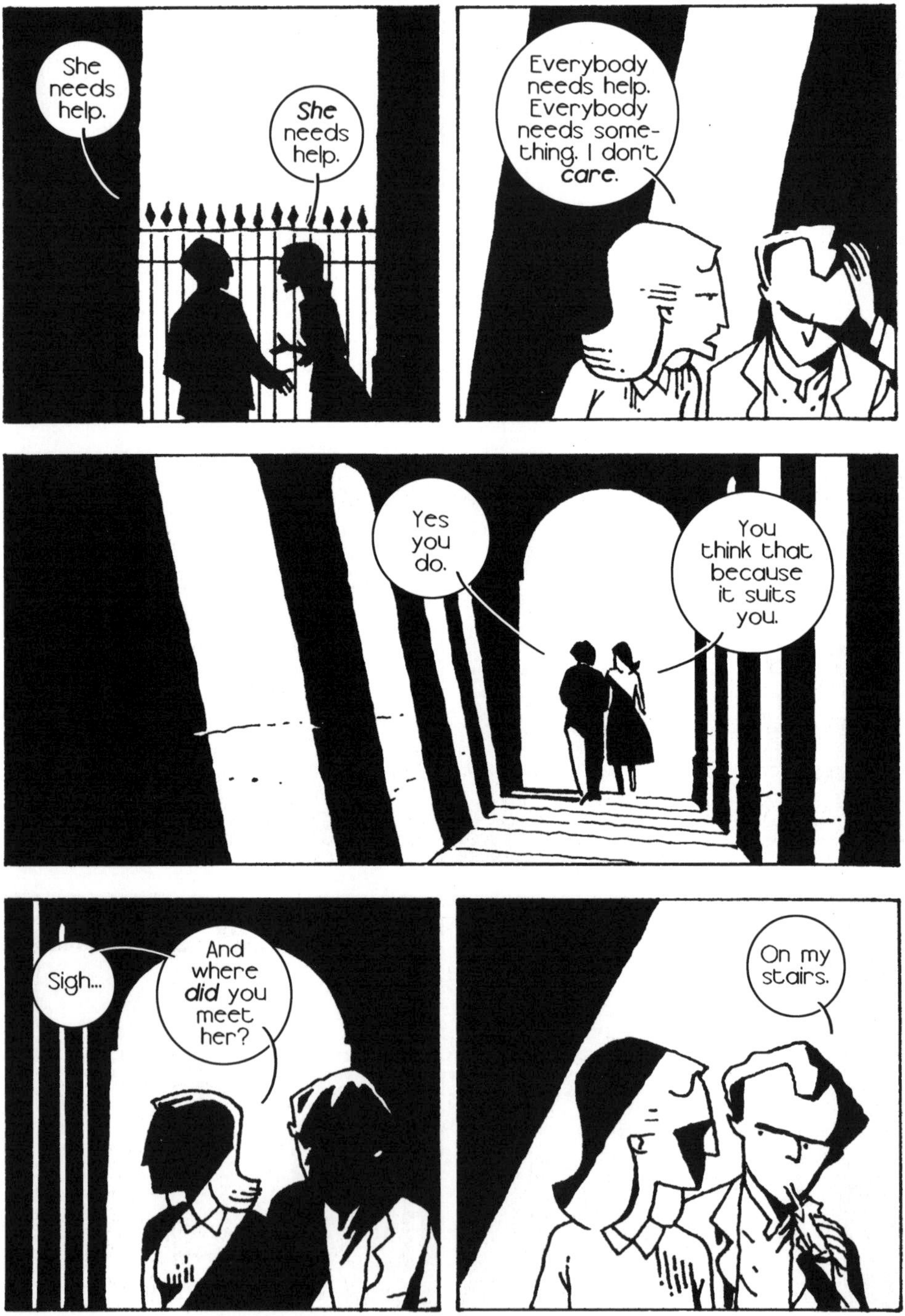
She needs help.
She needs help.
Everybody needs help. Everybody needs something. I don't **care**.
Yes you do.
You think that because it suits you.
Sigh...
And where *did* you meet her?
On my stairs.

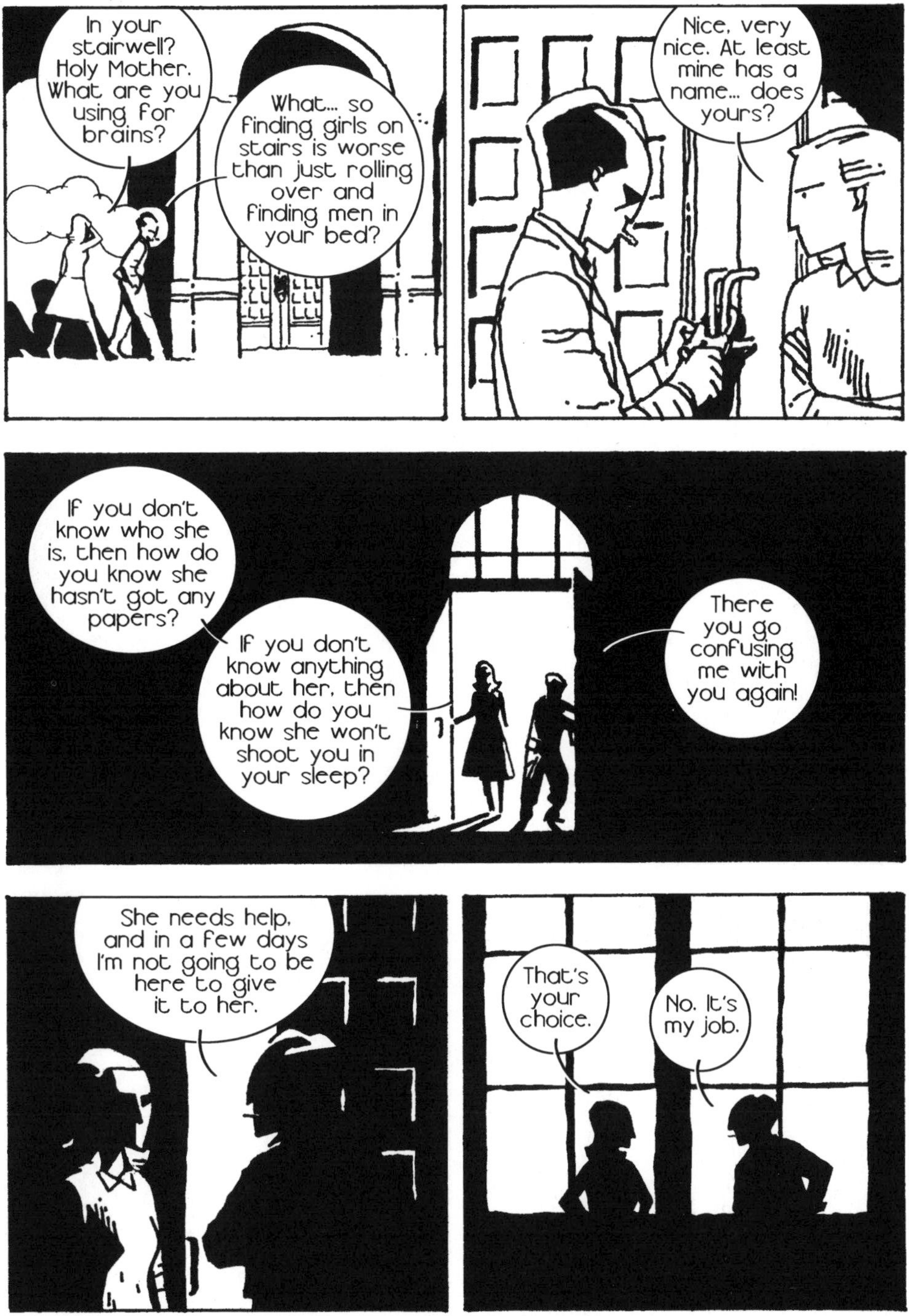
In your stairwell? Holy Mother. What are you using for brains?
What... so finding girls on stairs is worse than just rolling over and finding men in your bed?
Nice, very nice. At least mine has a name... does yours?
If you don't know who she is, then how do you know she hasn't got any papers?
If you don't know anything about her, then how do you know she won't shoot you in your sleep?
There you go confusing me with you again!
She needs help, and in a few days I'm not going to be here to give it to her.
That's your choice.
No. It's my job.

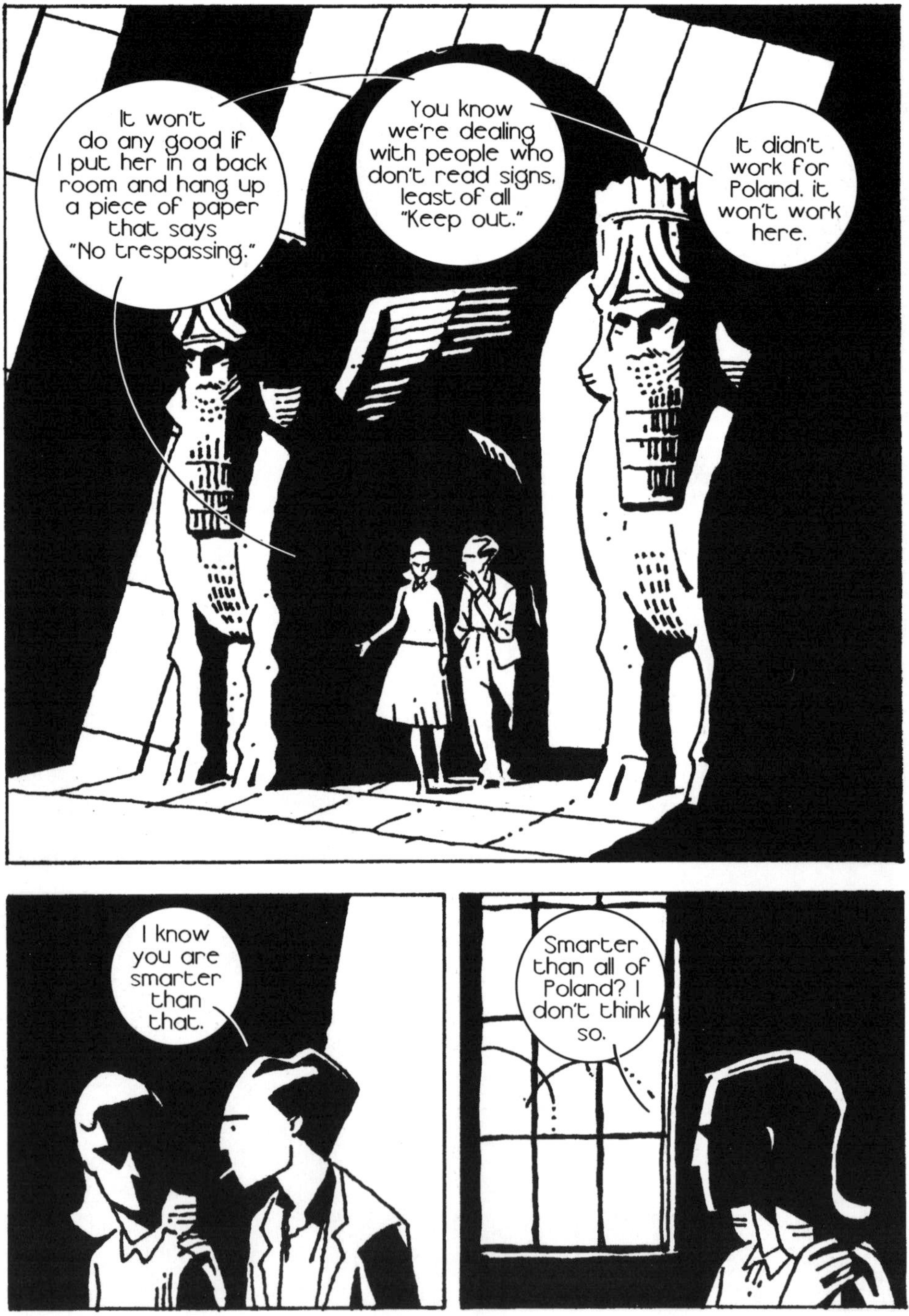
It won't do any good if I put her in a back room and hang up a piece of paper that says "No trespassing."
You know we're dealing with people who don't read signs, least of all "Keep out."
It didn't work for Poland. it won't work here.
I know you are smarter than that.
Smarter than all of Poland? I don't think so.

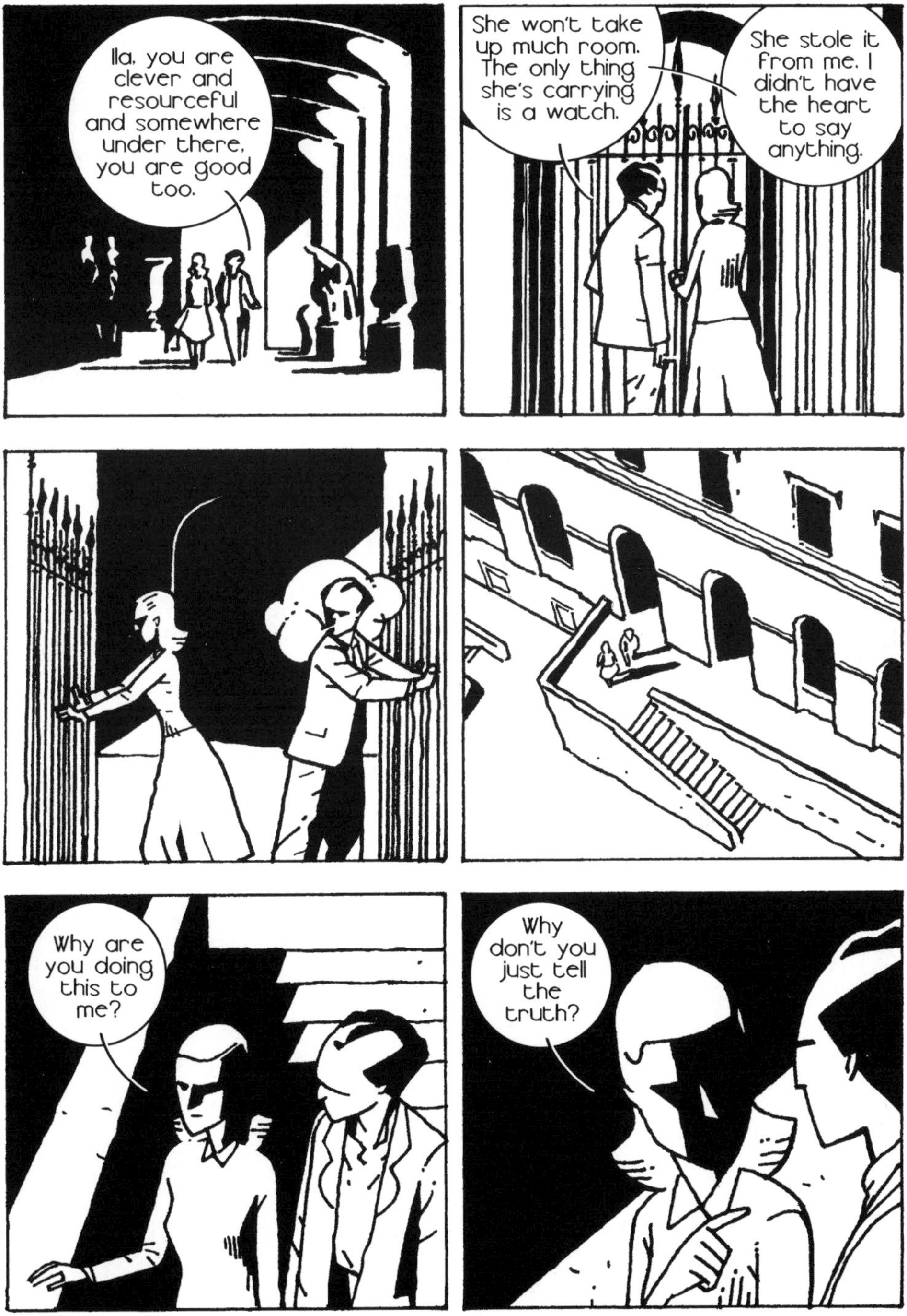
Ila, you are clever and resourceful and somewhere under there, you are good too.
She won't take up much room. The only thing she's carrying is a watch.
She stole it from me. I didn't have the heart to say anything.
Why are you doing this to me?
Why don't you just tell the truth?

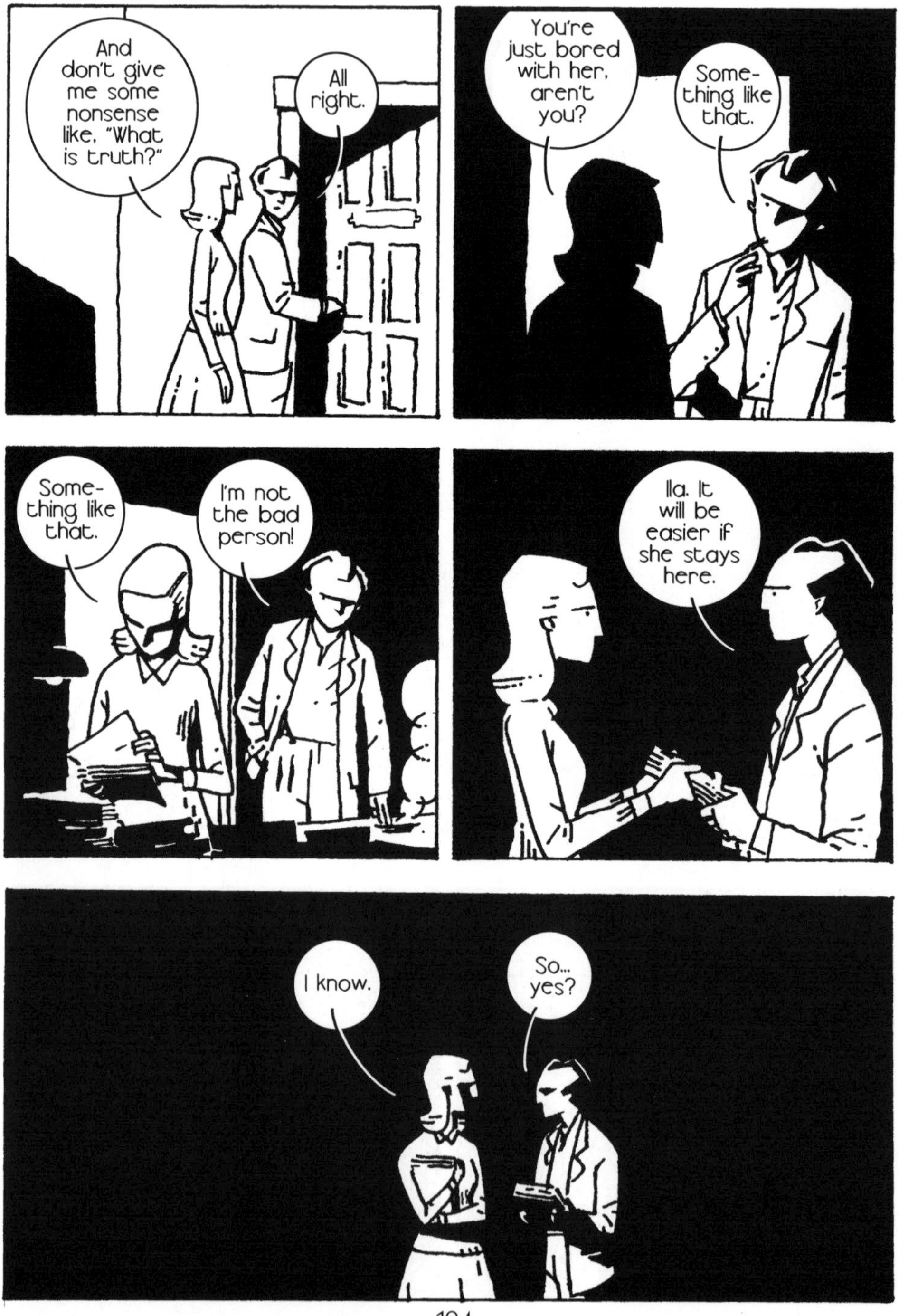

And don't give me some nonsense like, "What is truth?"
All right.
You're just bored with her, aren't you?
Some-thing like that.
Some-thing like that.
I'm not the bad person!
Ila. It will be easier if she stays here.
I know.
So... yes?

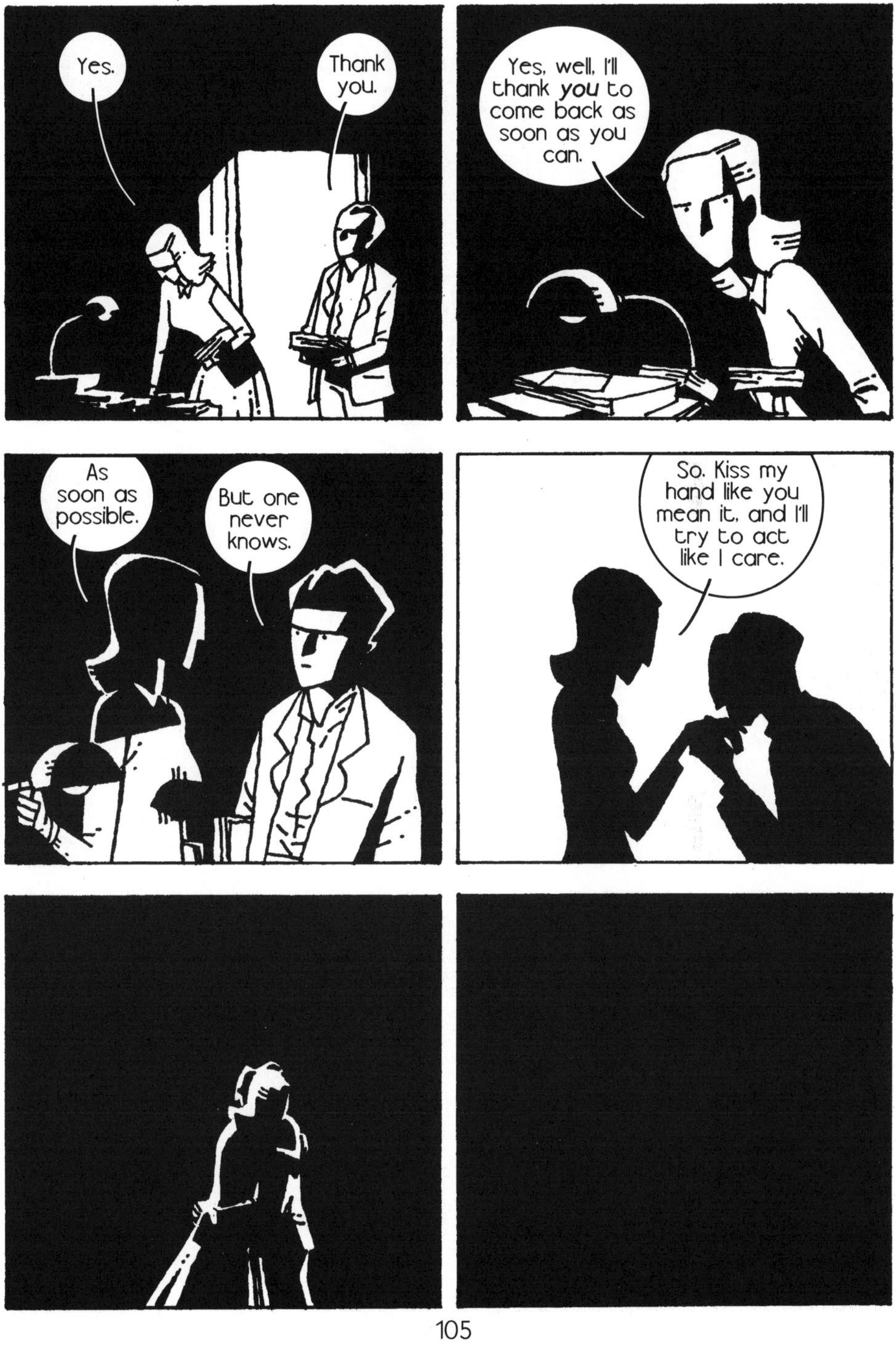
Yes.
Thank you.
Yes, well, I'll thank *you* to come back as soon as you can.
As soon as possible.
But one never knows.
So. Kiss my hand like you mean it, and I'll try to act like I care.

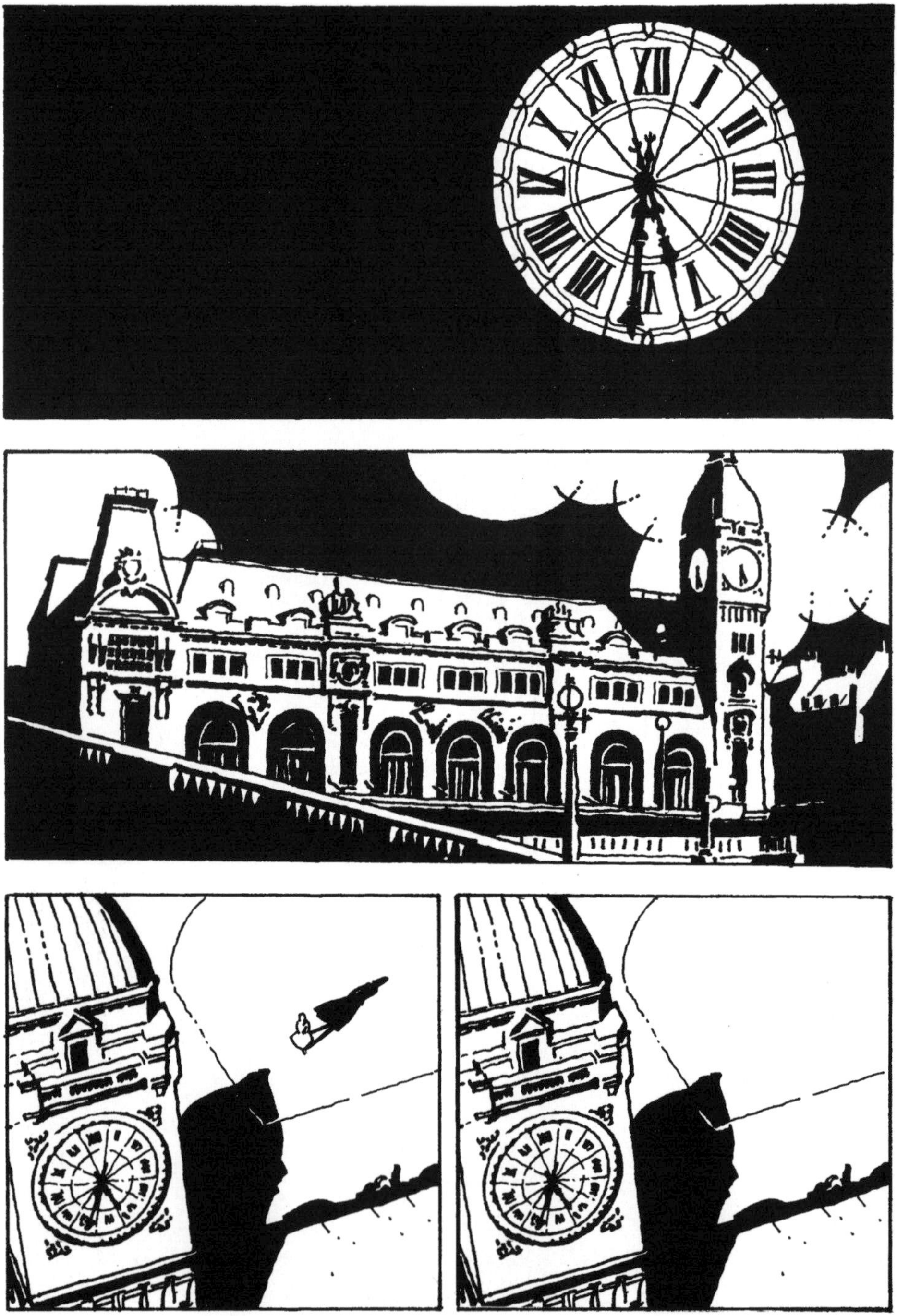

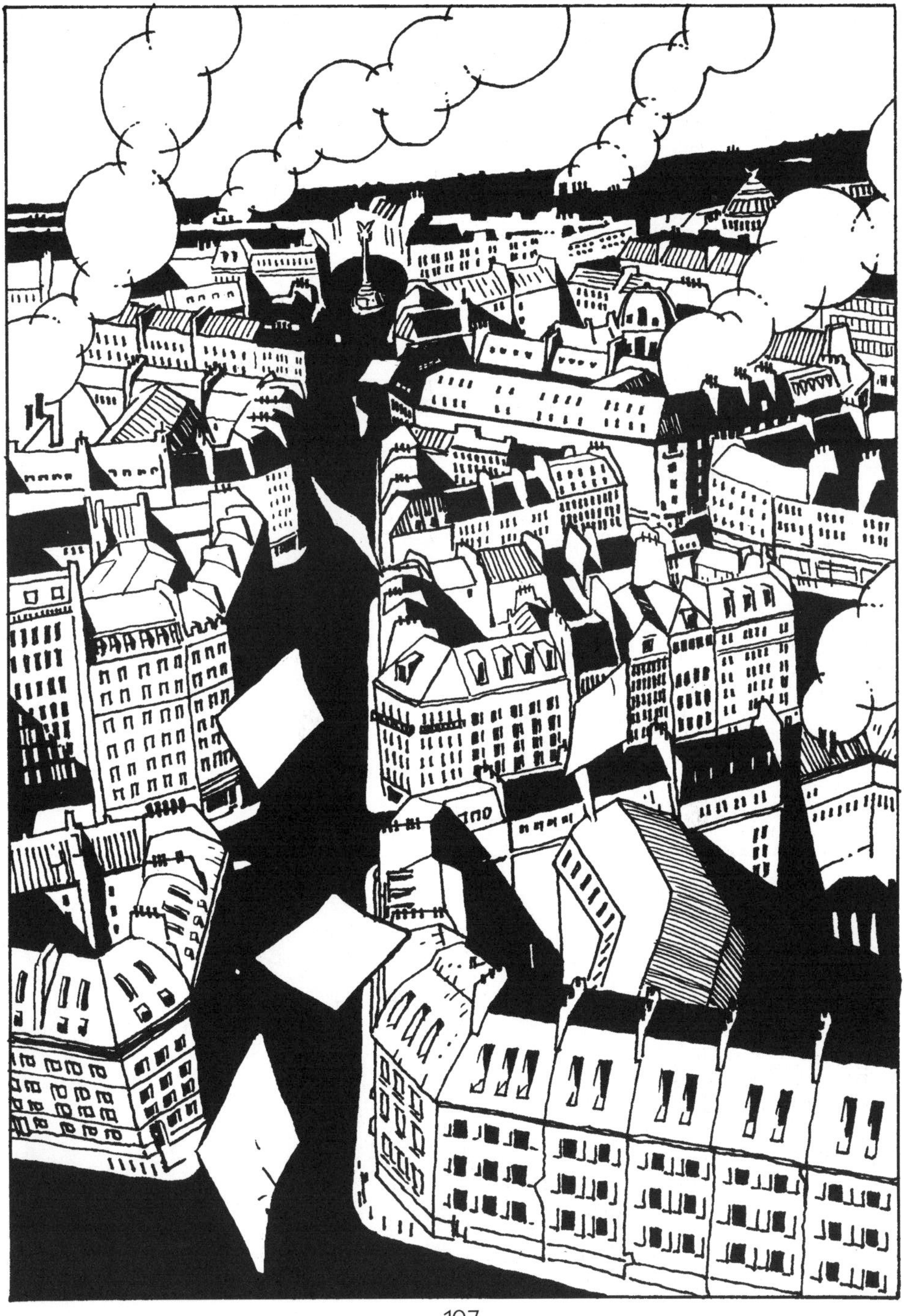

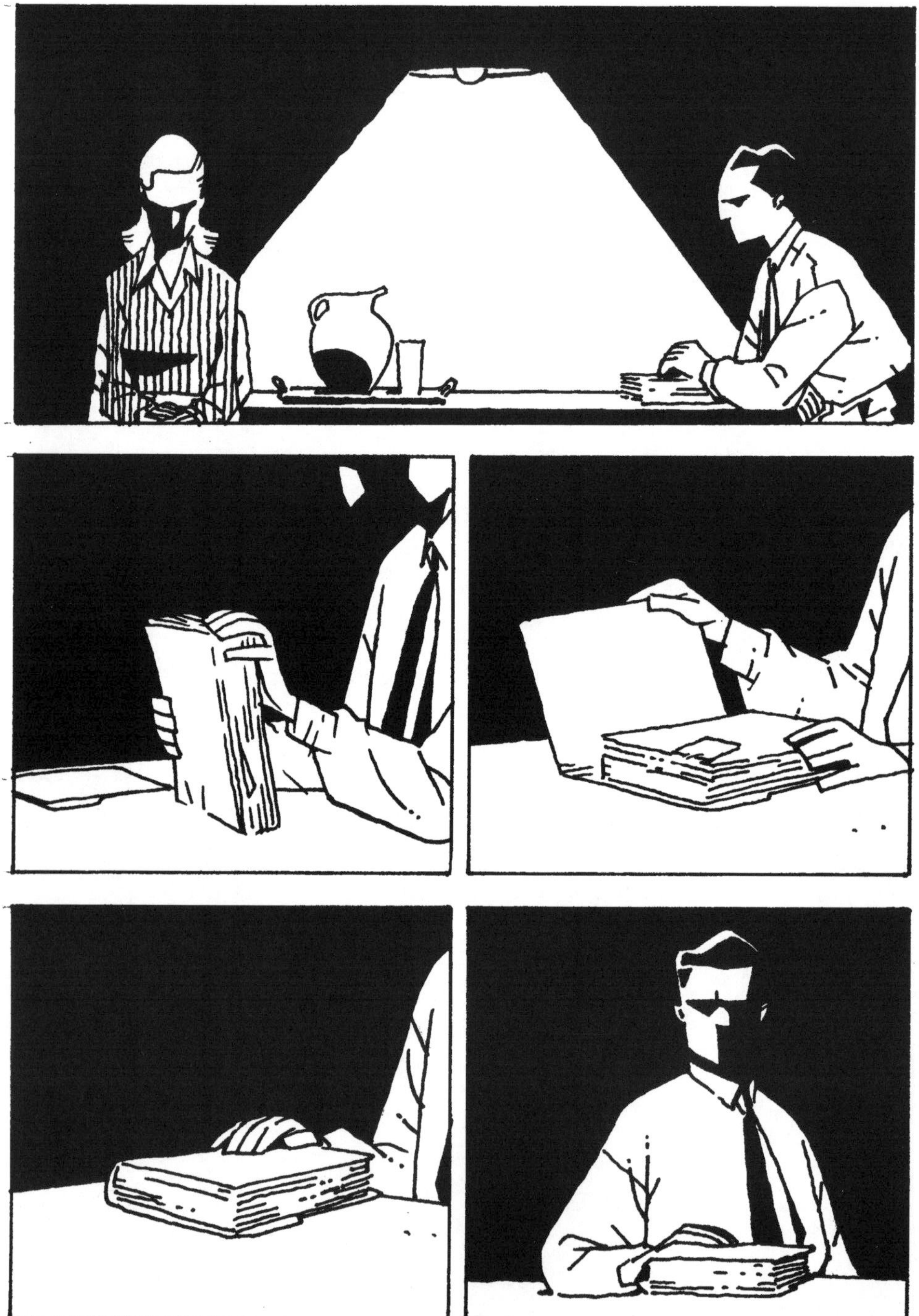

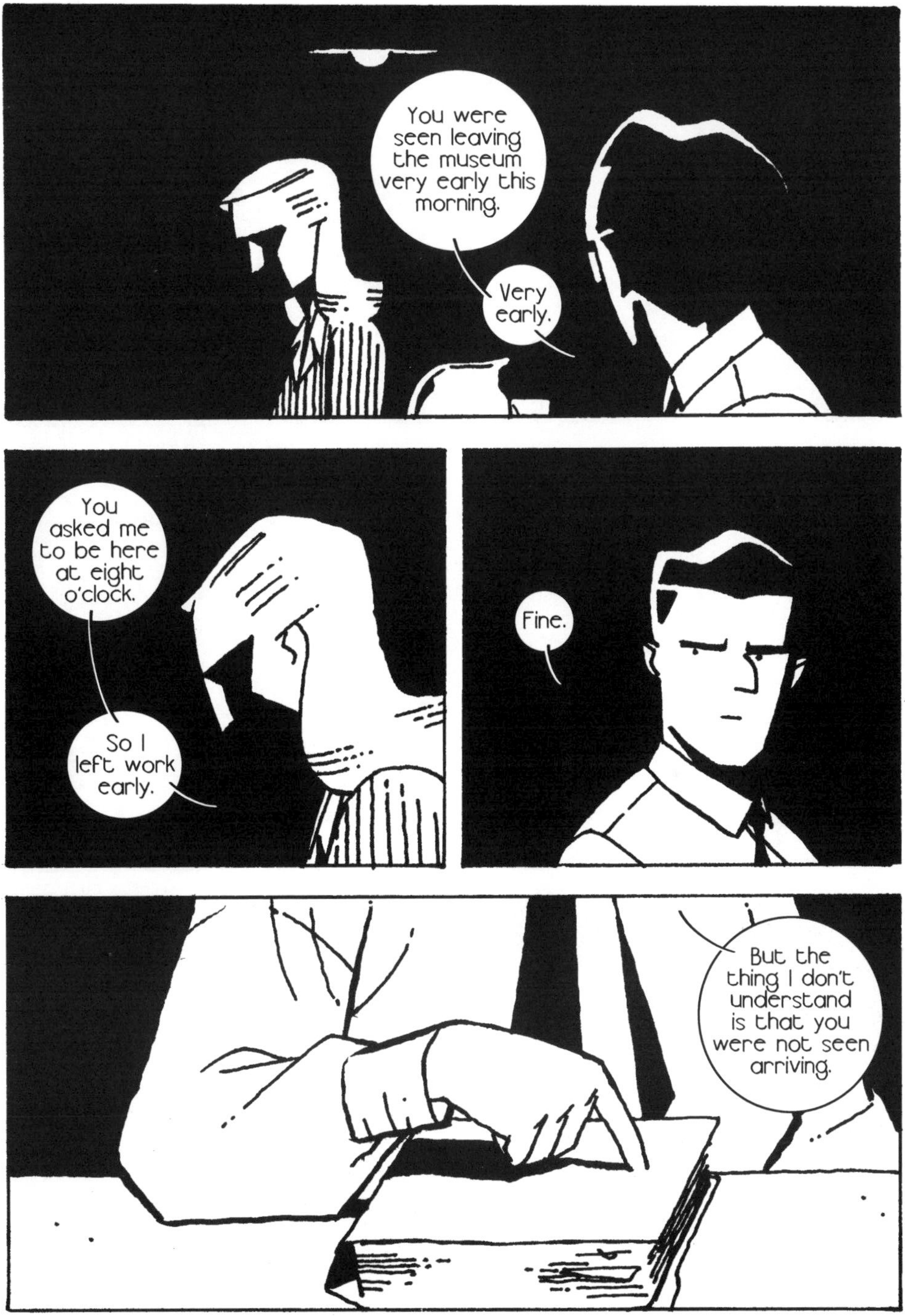
You were seen leaving the museum very early this morning.
Very early.
You asked me to be here at eight o'clock.
So I left work early.
Fine.
But the thing I don't understand is that you were not seen arriving.

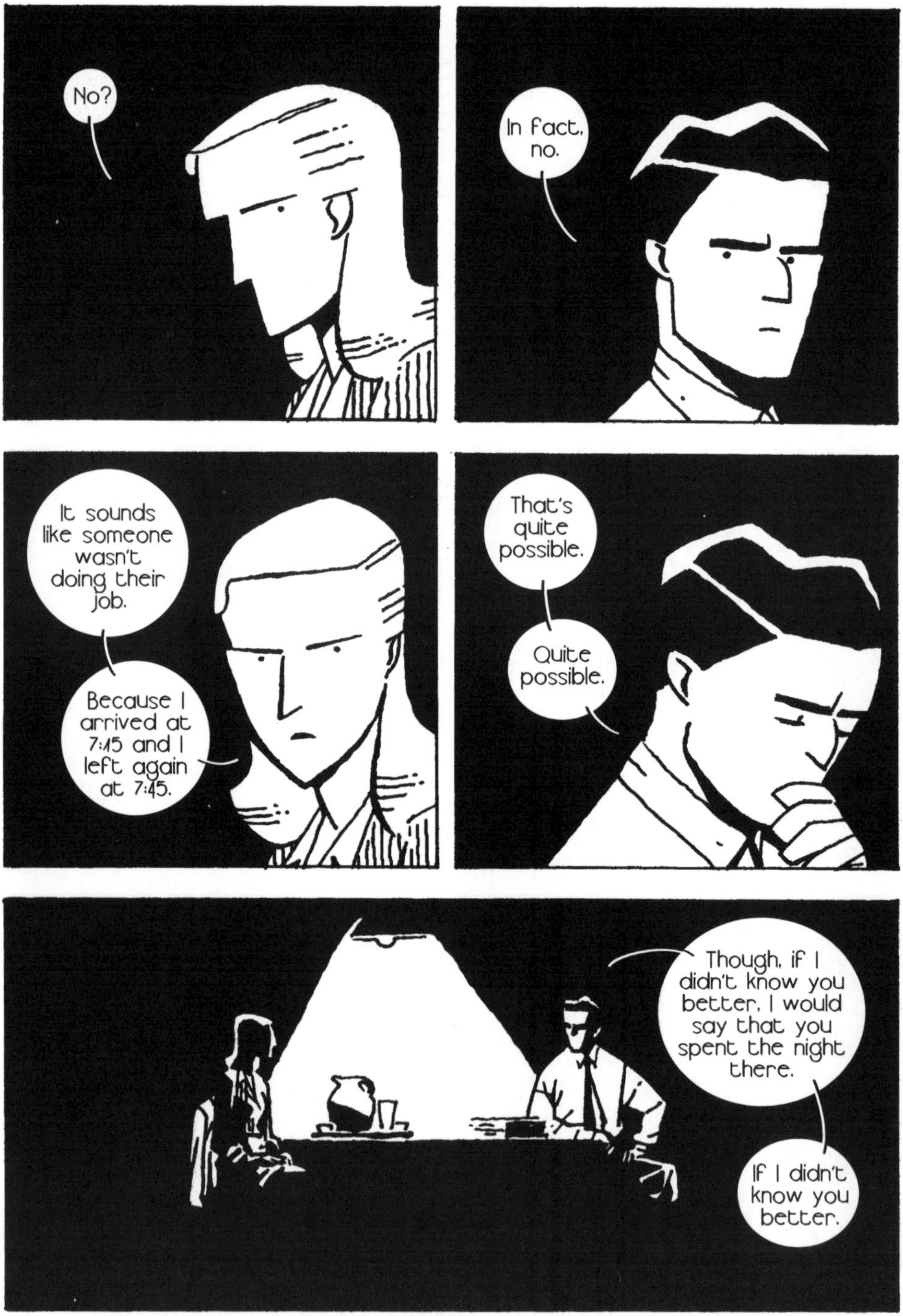
No?
In fact, no.
It sounds like someone wasn't doing their job.
Because I arrived at 7:45 and I left again at 7:45.
That's quite possible.
Quite possible.
Though, if I didn't know you better, I would say that you spent the night there.
If I didn't know you better.

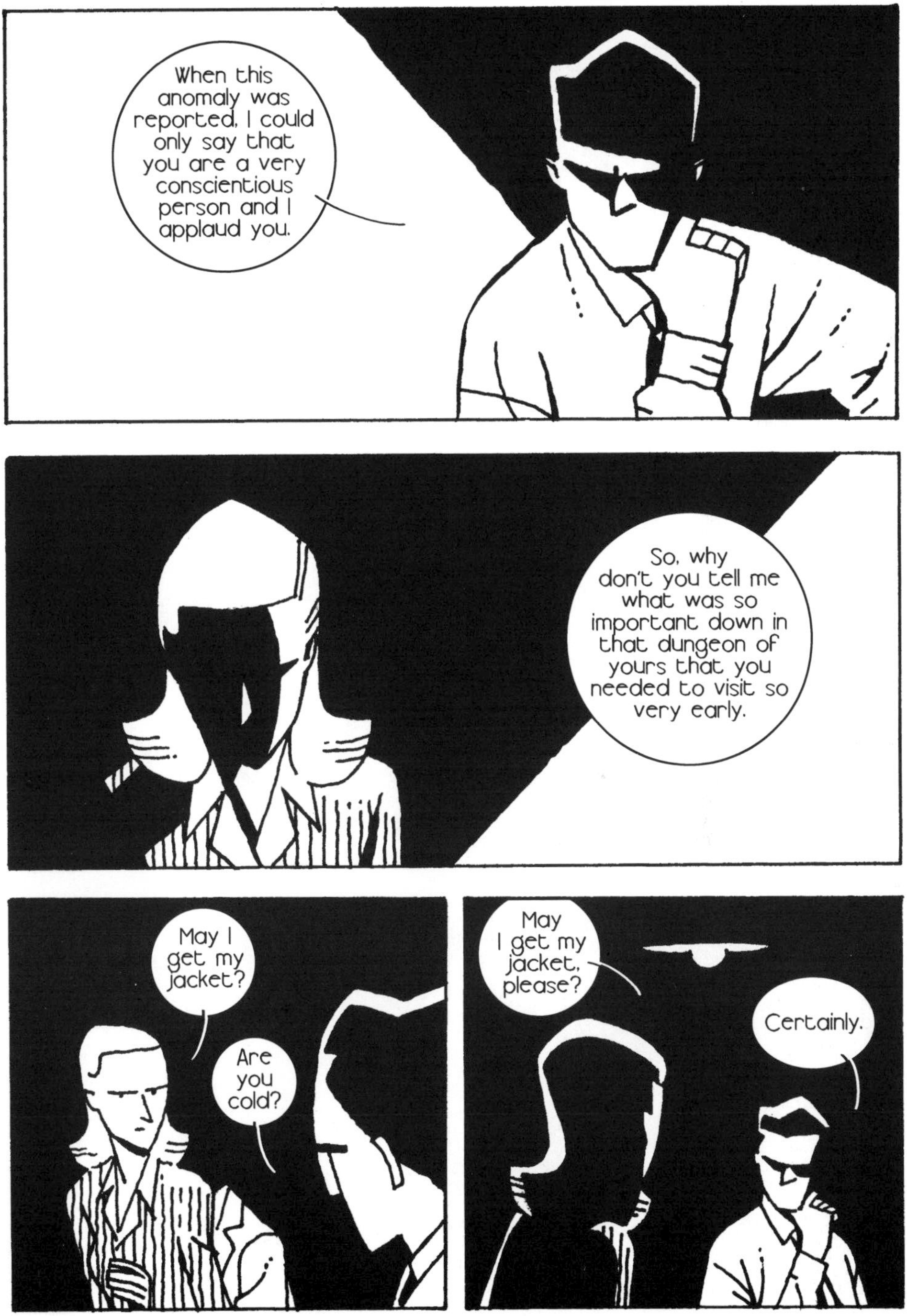
When this anomaly was reported, I could only say that you are a very conscientious person and I applaud you.
So, why don't you tell me what was so important down in that dungeon of yours that you needed to visit so very early.
May I get my jacket?
Are you cold?
May I get my jacket, please?
Certainly.

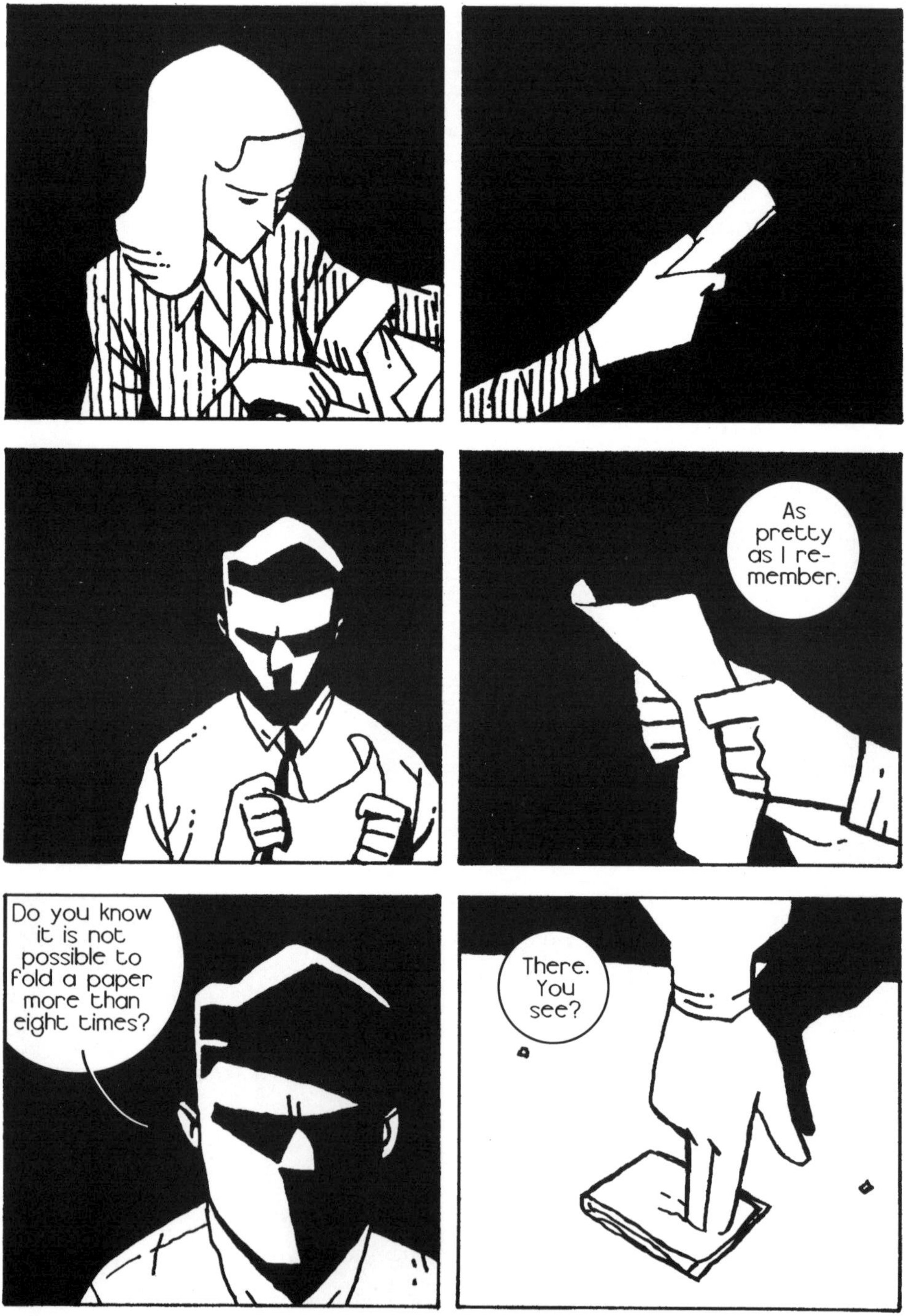
As pretty as I re-member.
Do you know it is not possible to fold a paper more than eight times?
There. You see?

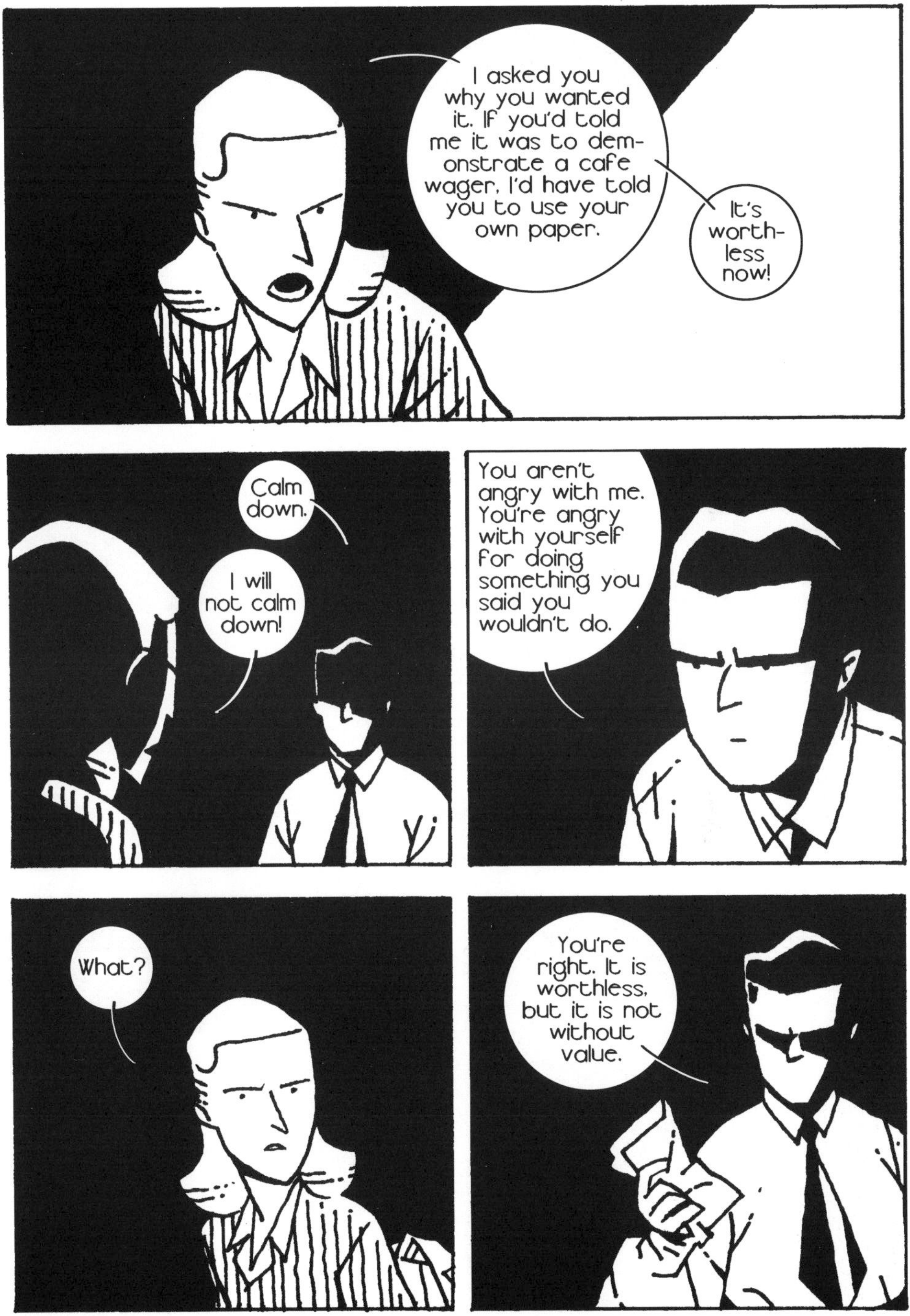
I asked you why you wanted it. If you'd told me it was to demonstrate a cafe wager, I'd have told you to use your own paper.
It's worthless now!
Calm down.
I will not calm down!
You aren't angry with me. You're angry with yourself for doing something you said you wouldn't do.
What?
You're right. It is worthless, but it is not without value.

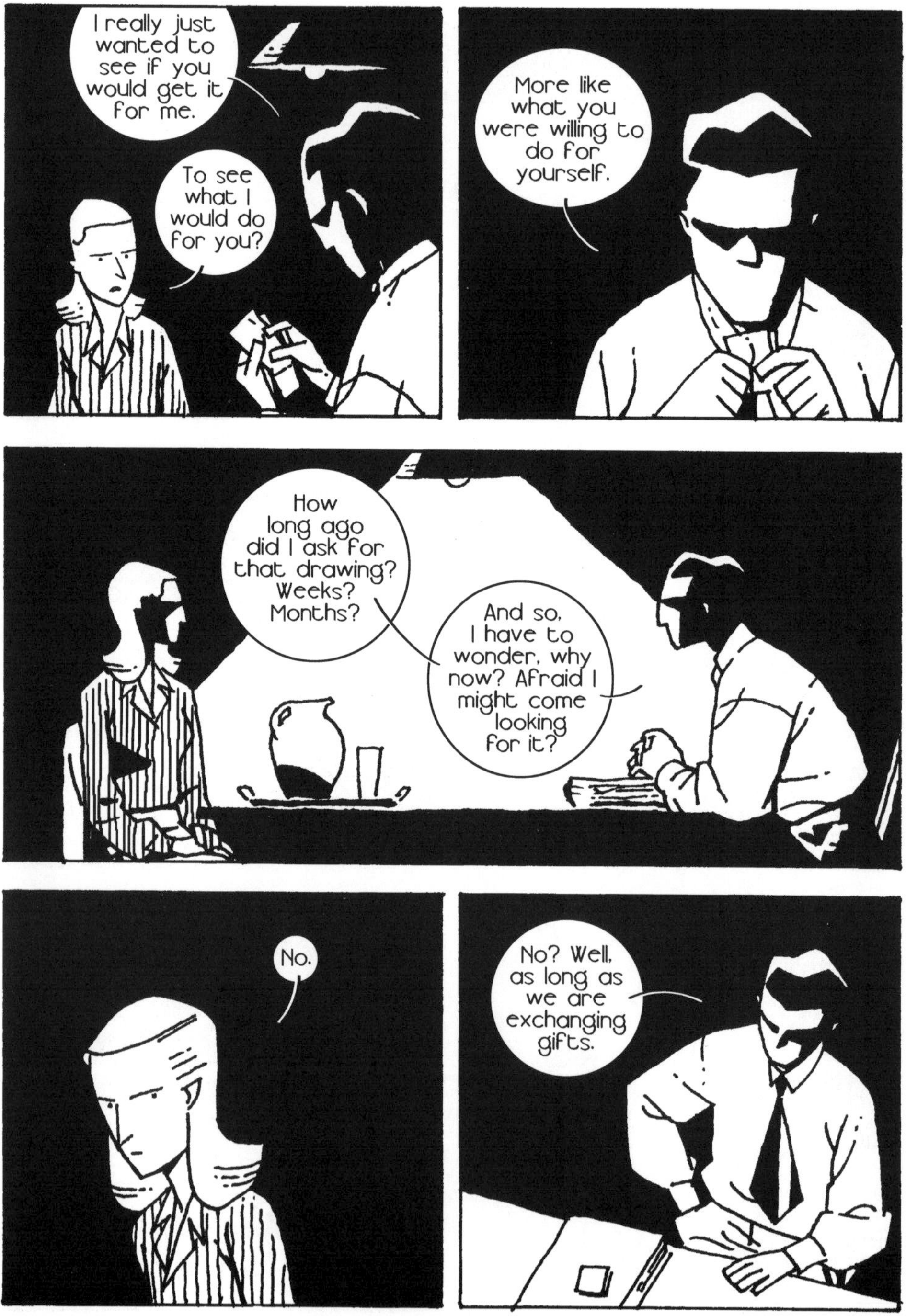
I really just wanted to see if you would get it for me.
To see what I would do for you?
More like what you were willing to do for yourself.
How long ago did I ask for that drawing? Weeks? Months?
And so, I have to wonder, why now? Afraid I might come looking for it?
No.
No? Well, as long as we are exchanging gifts.

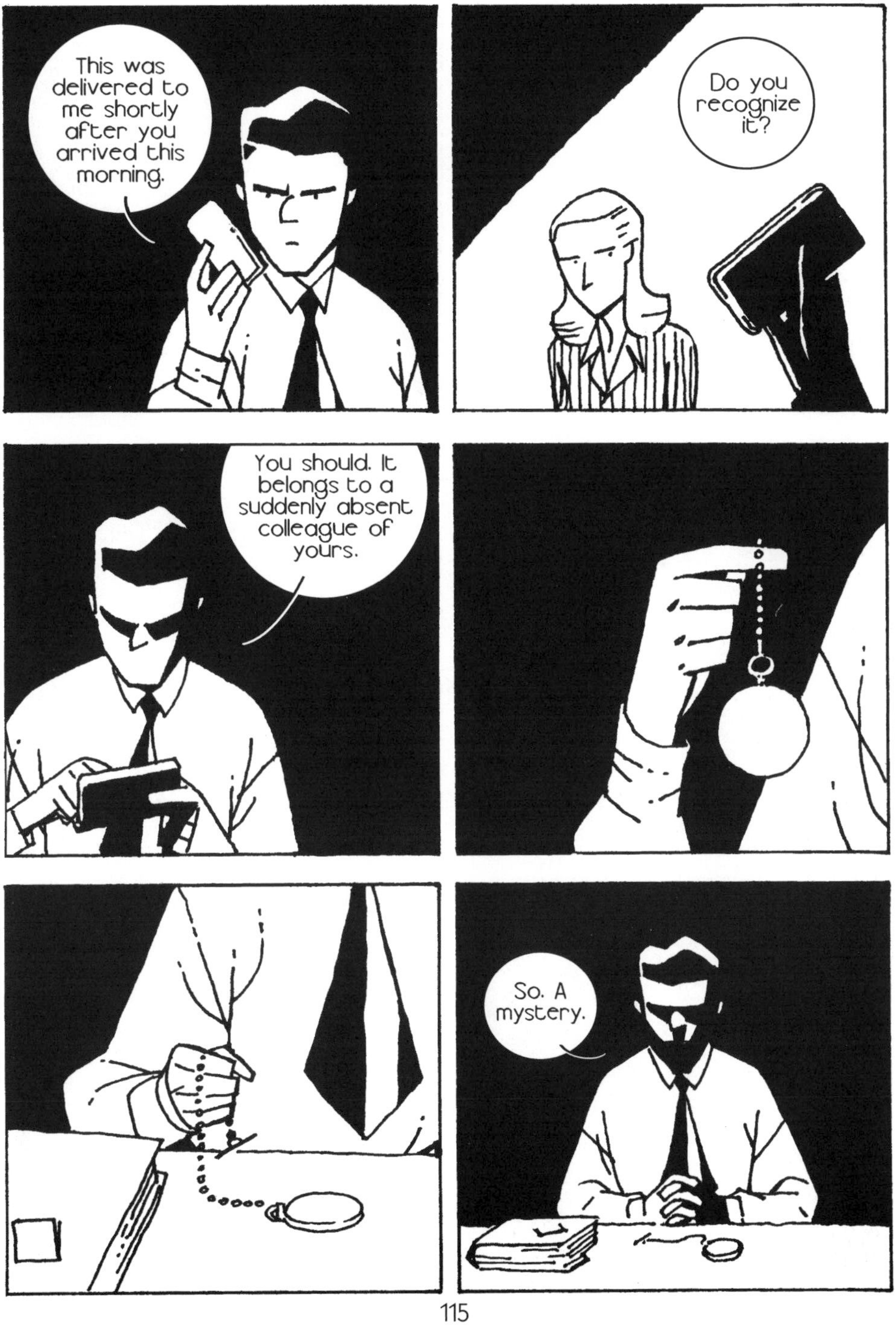
This was delivered to me shortly after you arrived this morning.
Do you recognize it?
You should. It belongs to a suddenly absent colleague of yours.
So. A mystery.

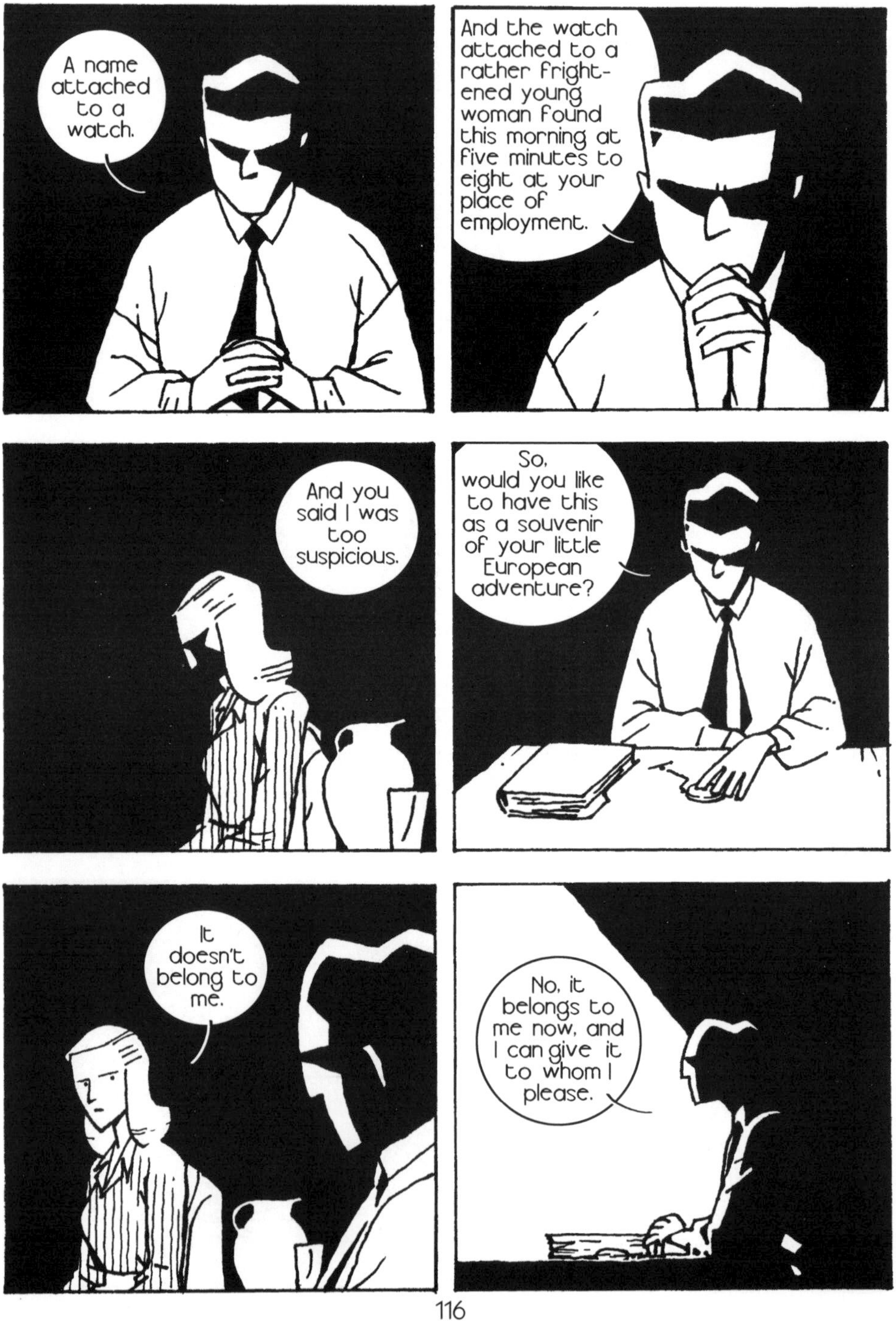
A name attached to a watch.
And the watch attached to a rather fright-ened young woman found this morning at five minutes to eight at your place of employment.
And you said I was too suspicious.
So, would you like to have this as a souvenir of your little European adventure?
It doesn't belong to me.
No, it belongs to me now, and I can give it to whom I please.

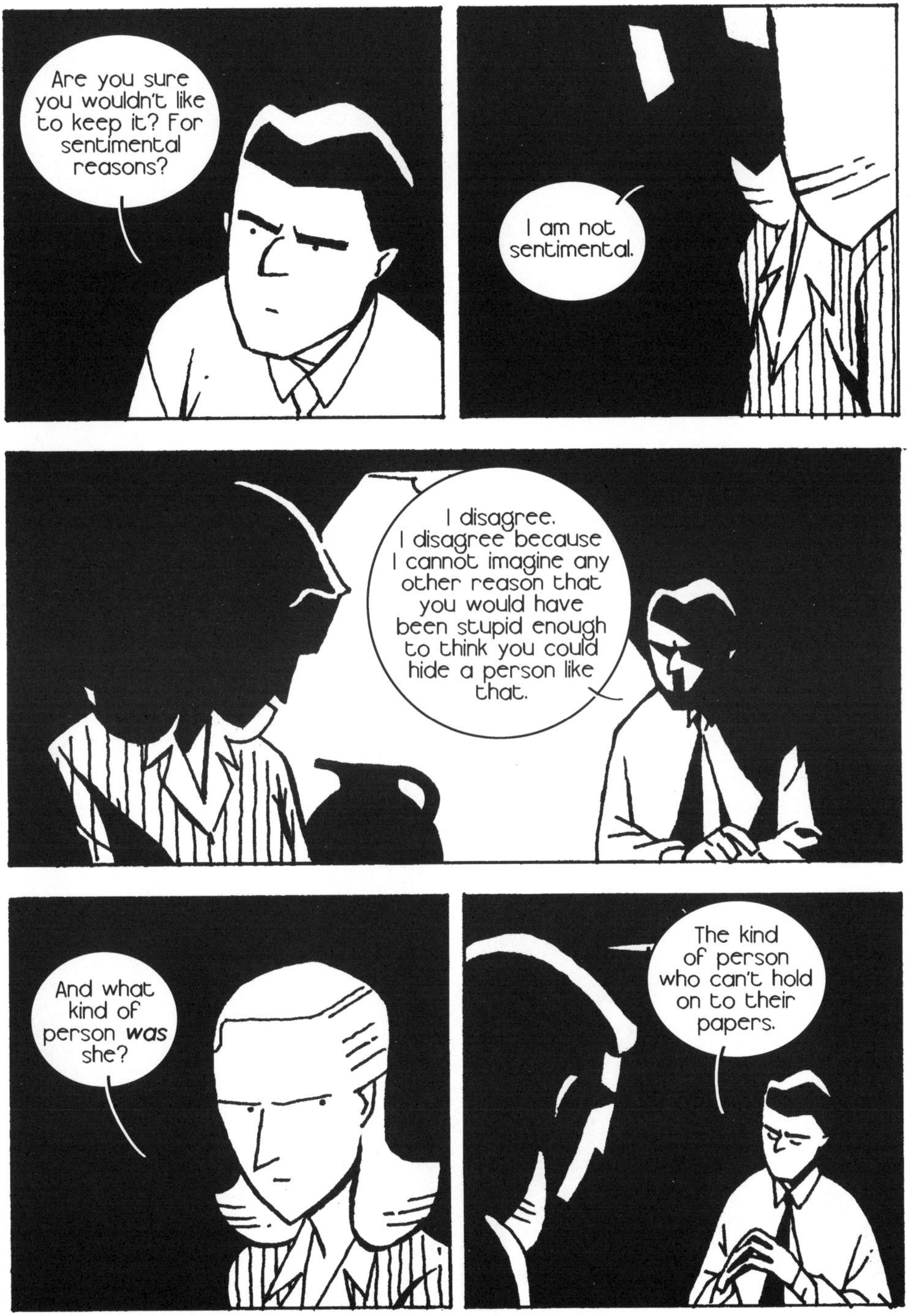
Are you sure you wouldn't like to keep it? For sentimental reasons?
I am not sentimental.
I disagree. I disagree because I cannot imagine any other reason that you would have been stupid enough to think you could hide a person like that.
And what kind of person *was* she?
The kind of person who can't hold on to their papers.

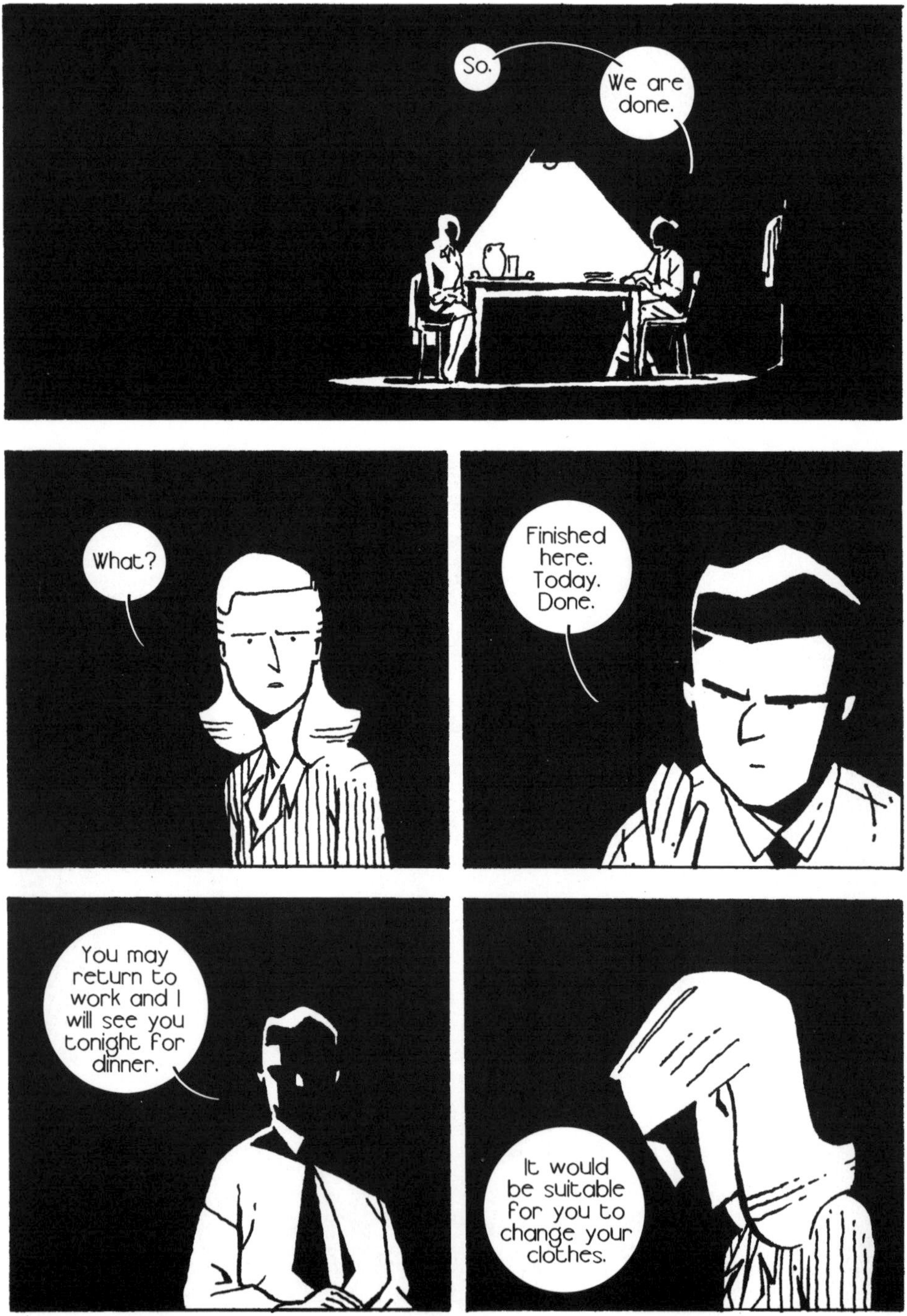
So.
We are done.
What?
Finished here. Today. Done.
You may return to work and I will see you tonight for dinner.
It would be suitable for you to change your clothes.

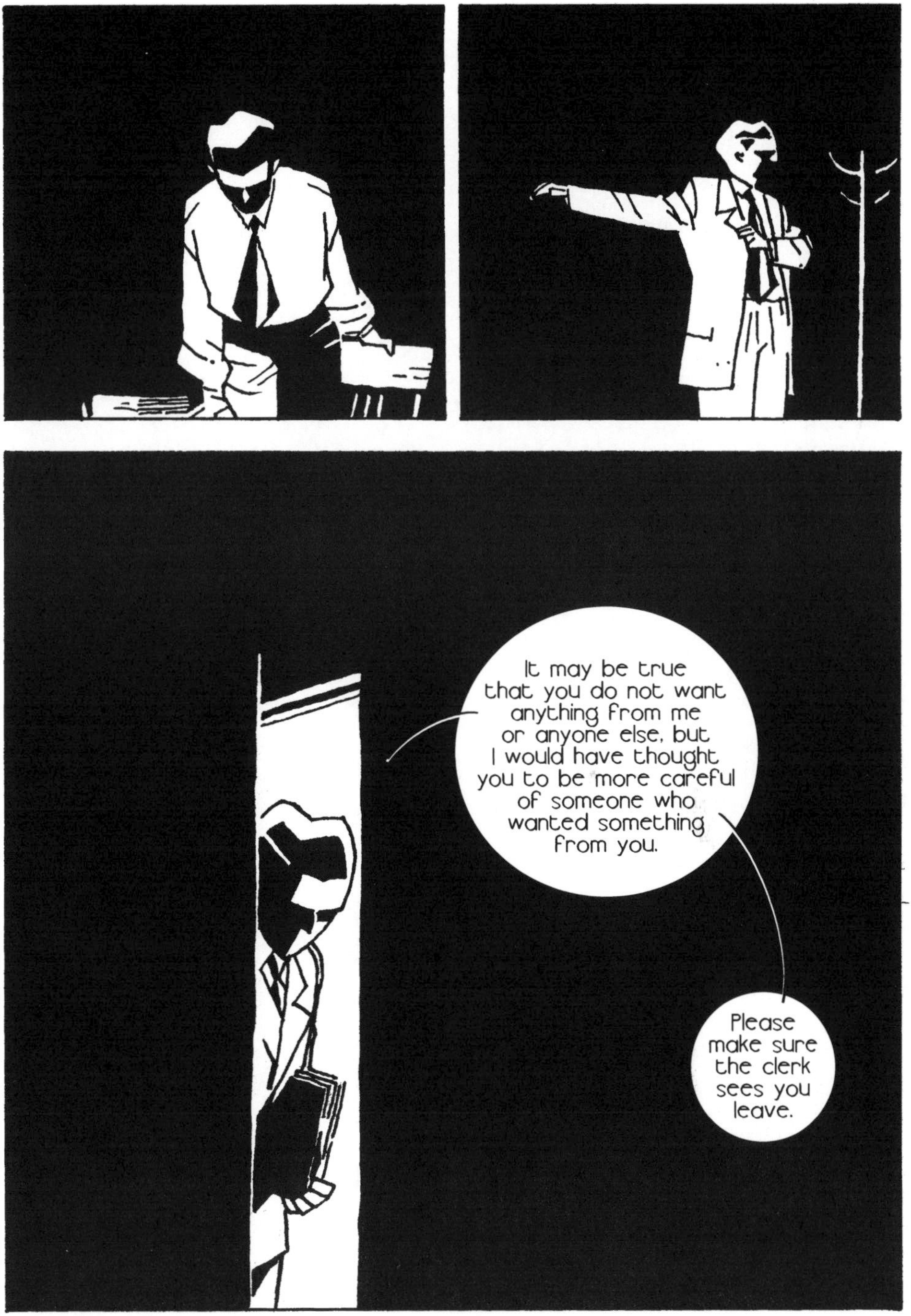
It may be true that you do not want anything from me or anyone else, but I would have thought you to be more careful of someone who wanted something from you.
Please make sure the clerk sees you leave.

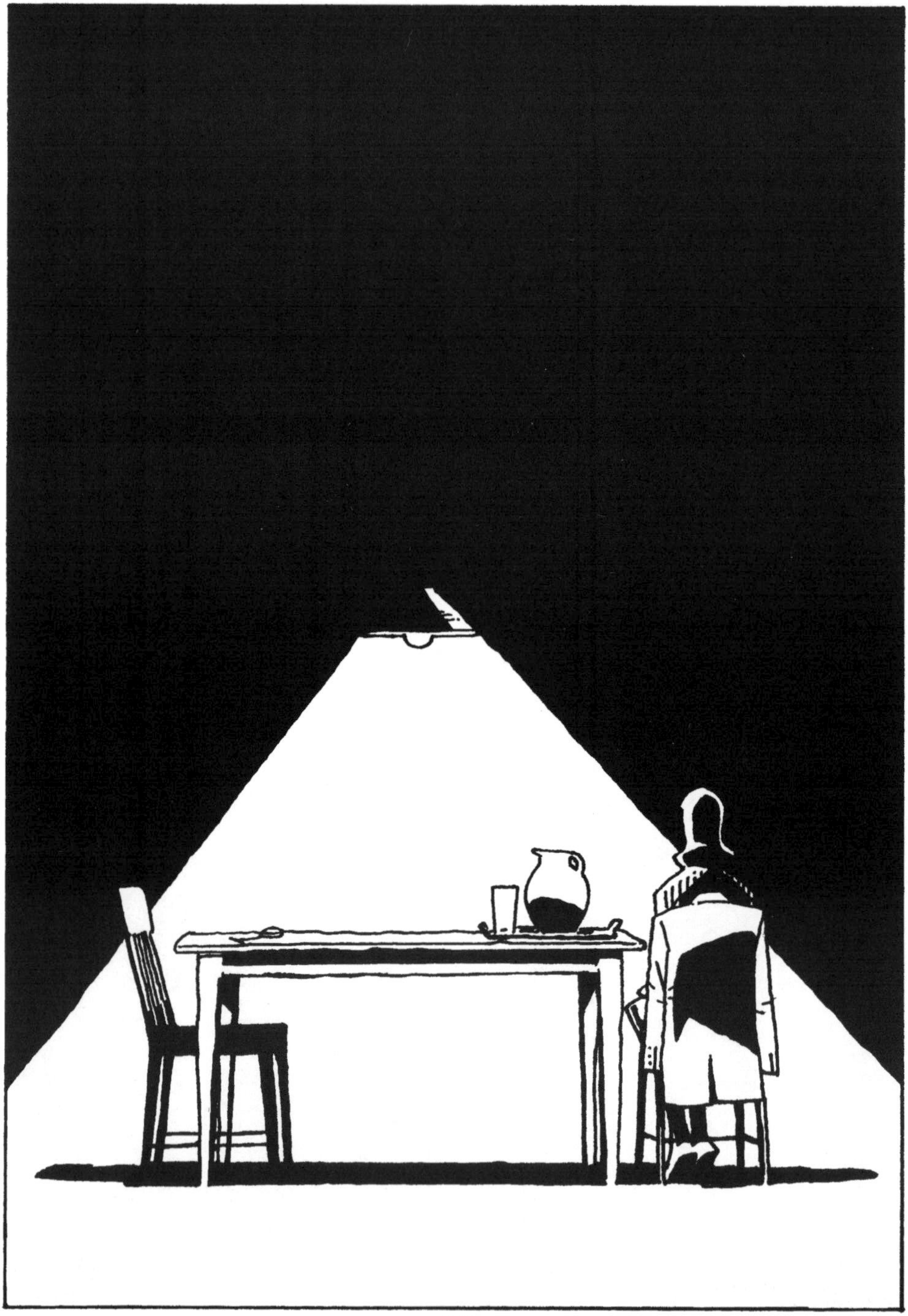

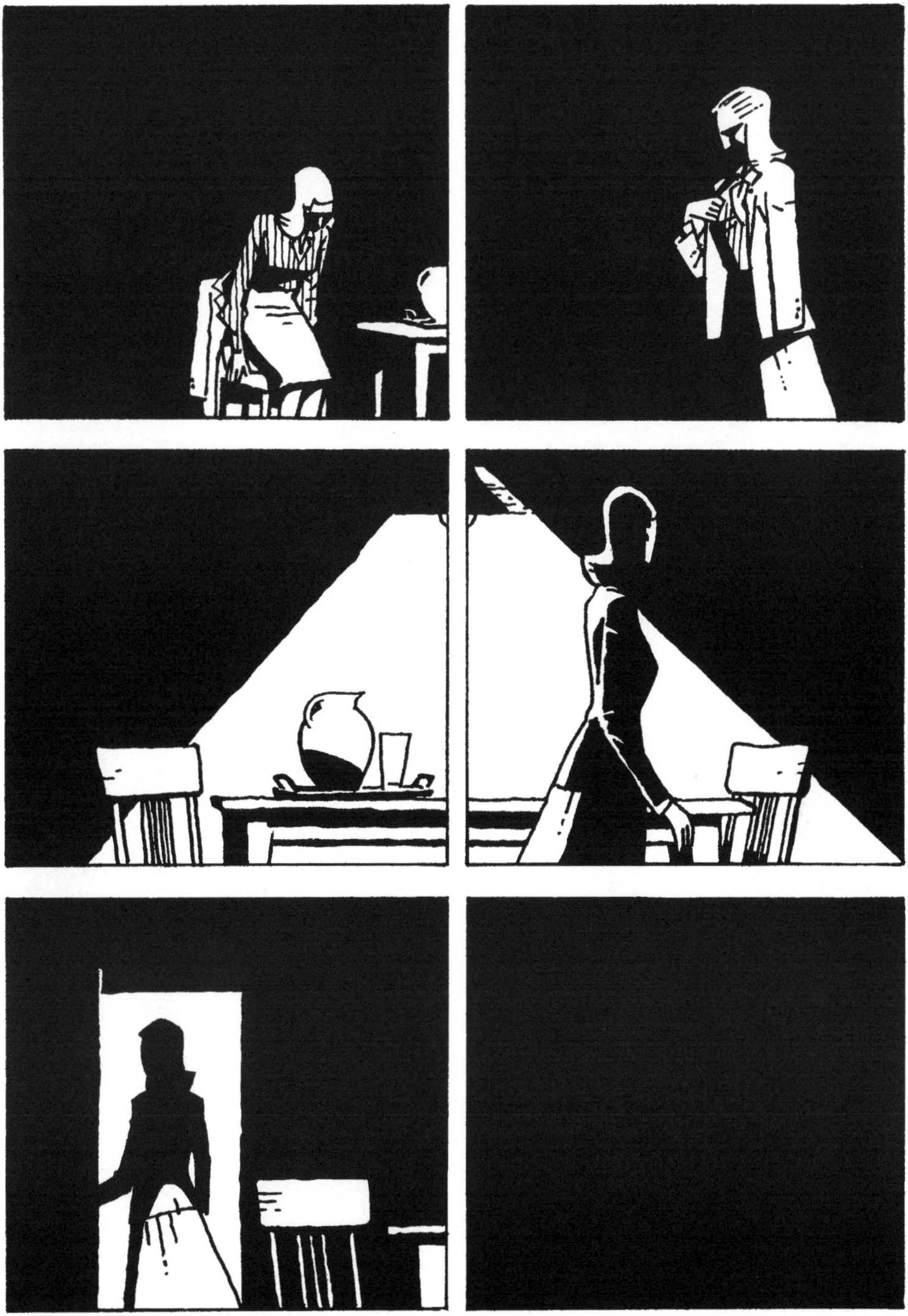

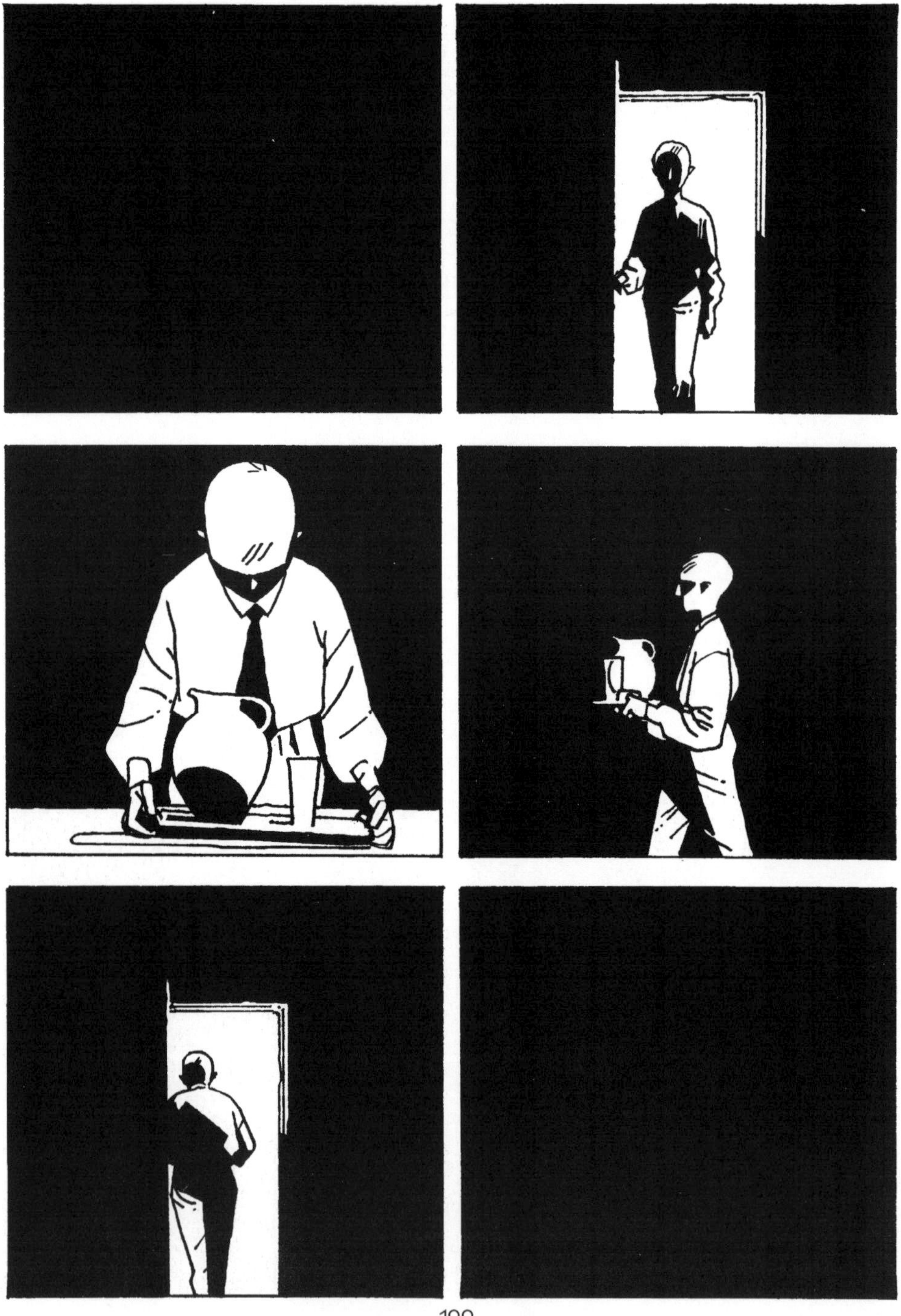

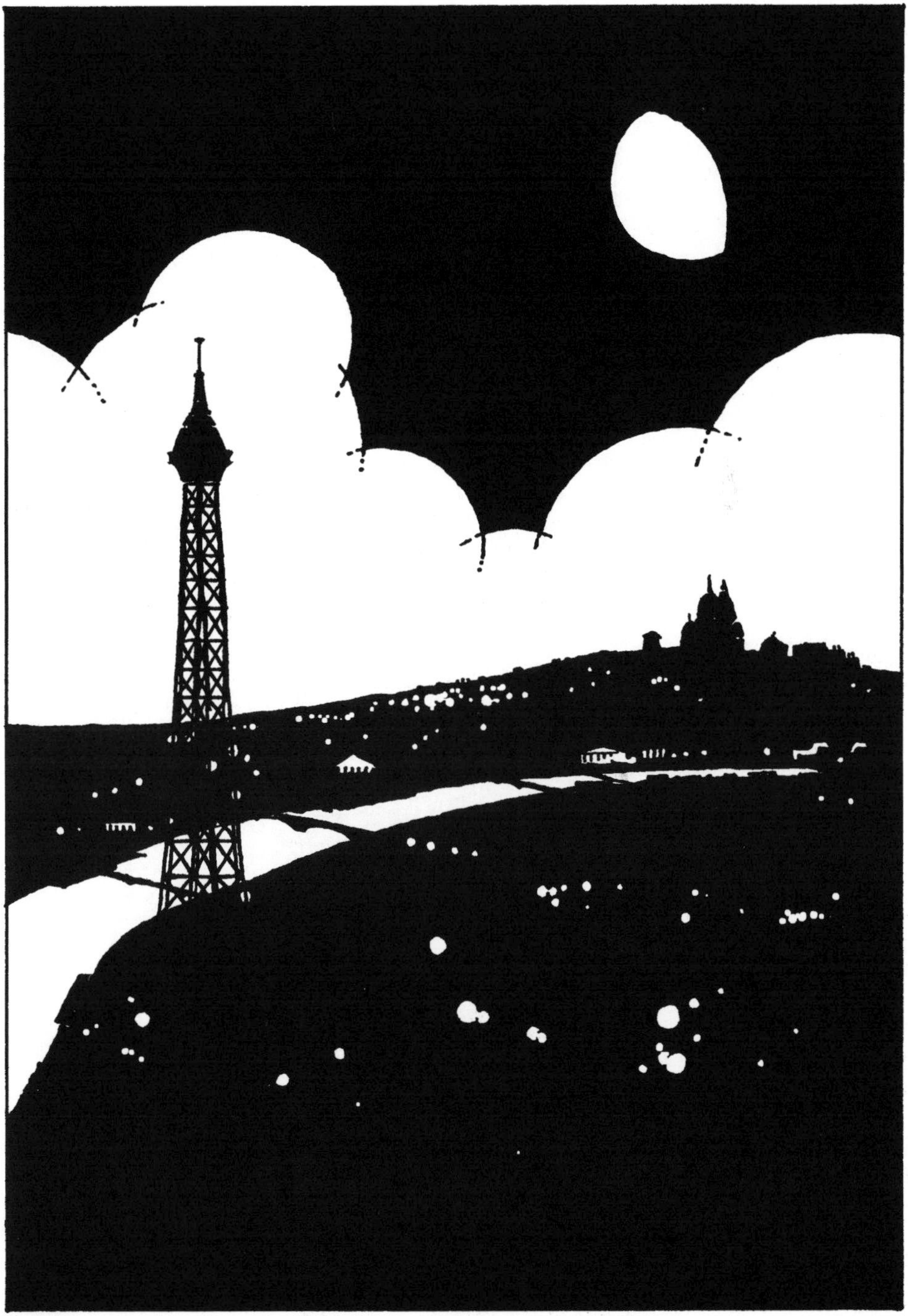

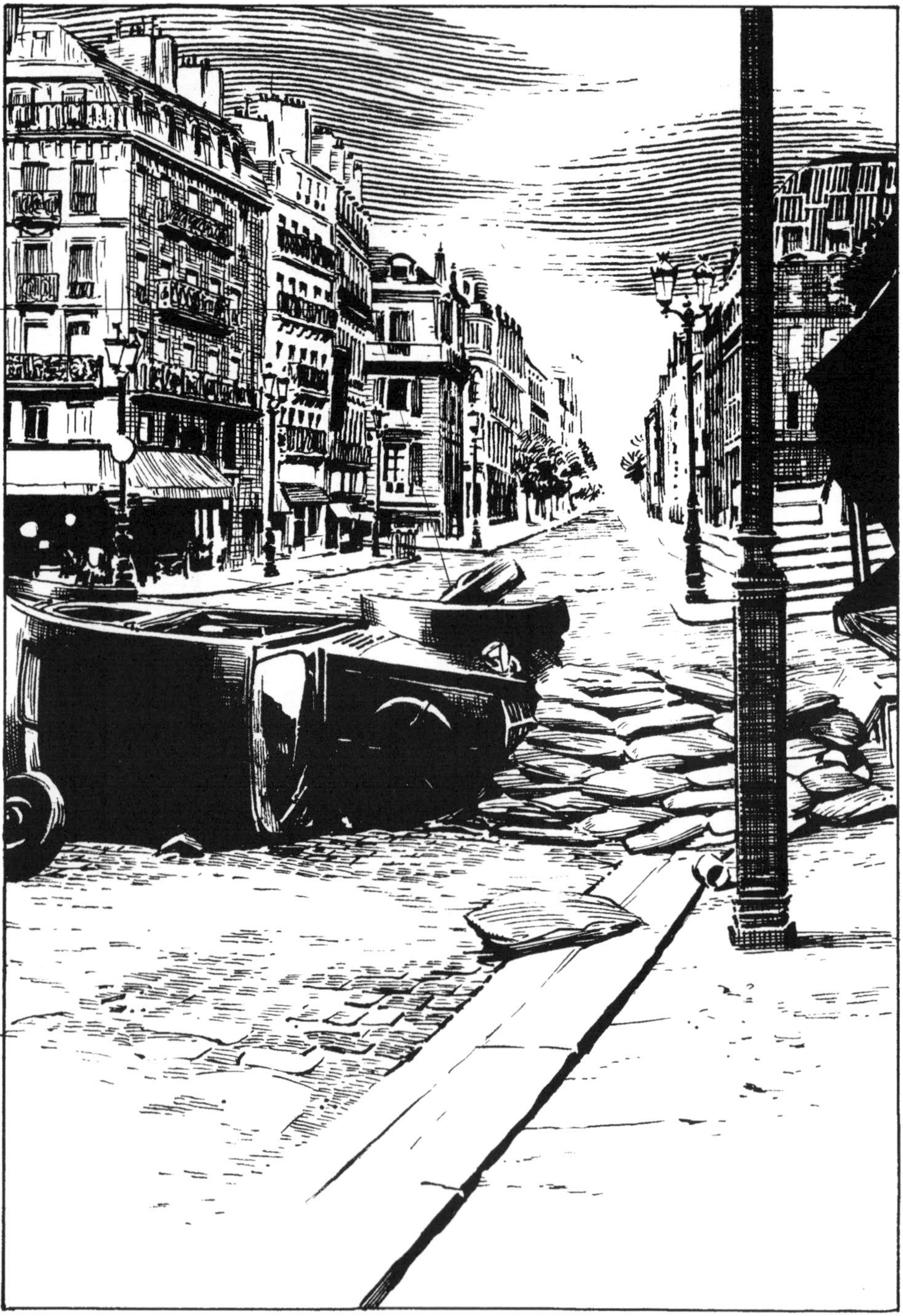

Hello, beautiful stranger.
Soon I will be sitting at a
long table staring out over
hills which have the look of
hiding something, and vine-
yards which would be
grateful for a rest. I think
even ten years from now,
people will drive themselves
along these roads and know
that the land was not
always so full of small hills and
matching small holes. When
you dig a trench, the earth
must go somewhere. Earth is
moved. Heaven, I fear, is not.
I can hear trucks starting up
in the courtyard. The walls
here are three metres thick,
and I would have to lean out
a long, long way to see who
it is coming or going. But I
am disinclined to stick my
neck out. As you know.

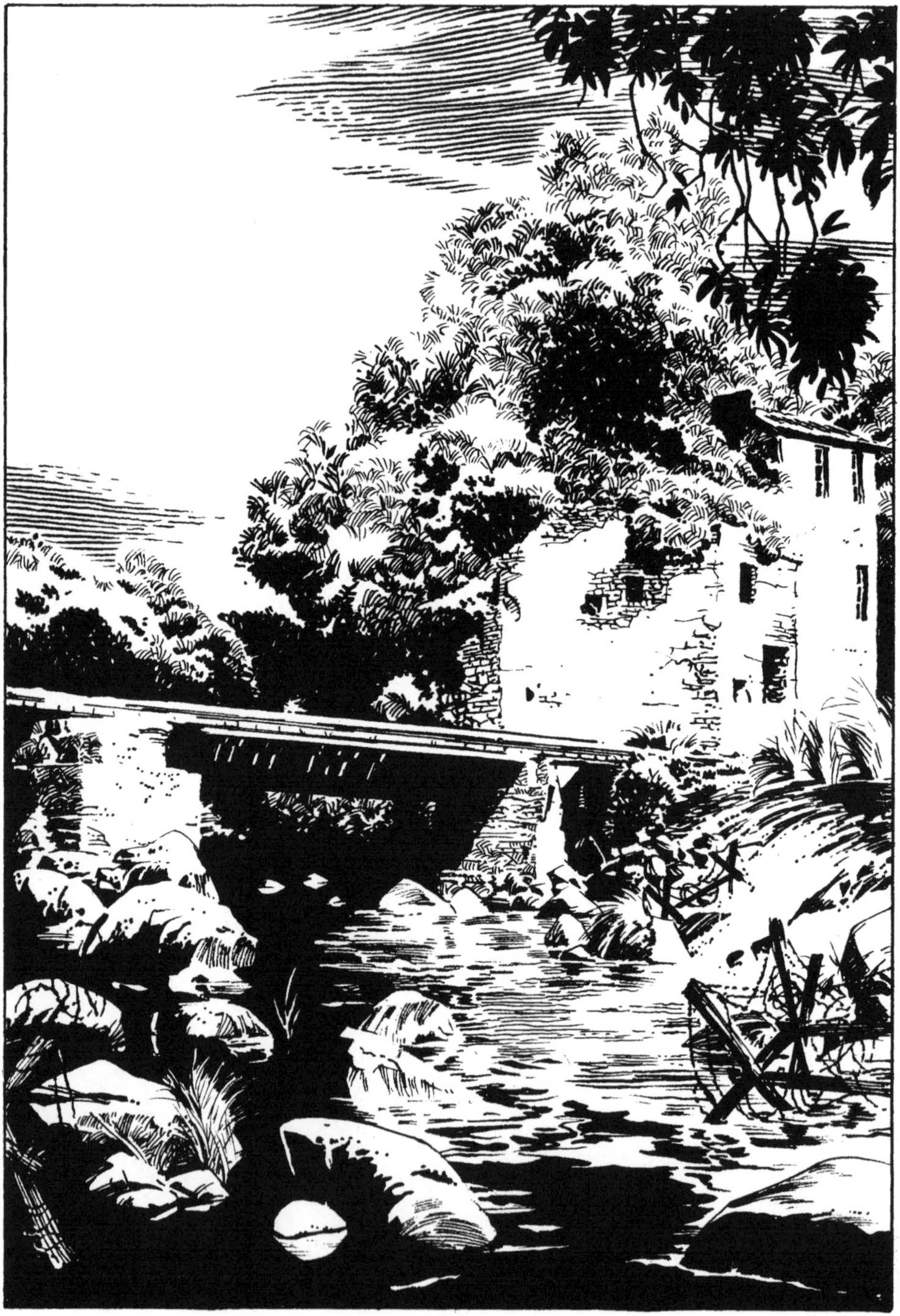

I am hoping for a château
big enough to wander in, so
that I may go for days
without seeing another soul.
All the work we've done. All
the works we've trans-
ported. Where will we find
the room for it all? Perhaps
in a wine cellar that this time
I will have the pleasure of
emptying first. You have
always said that headaches
were the price of organiza-
tion. I will gladly pay.

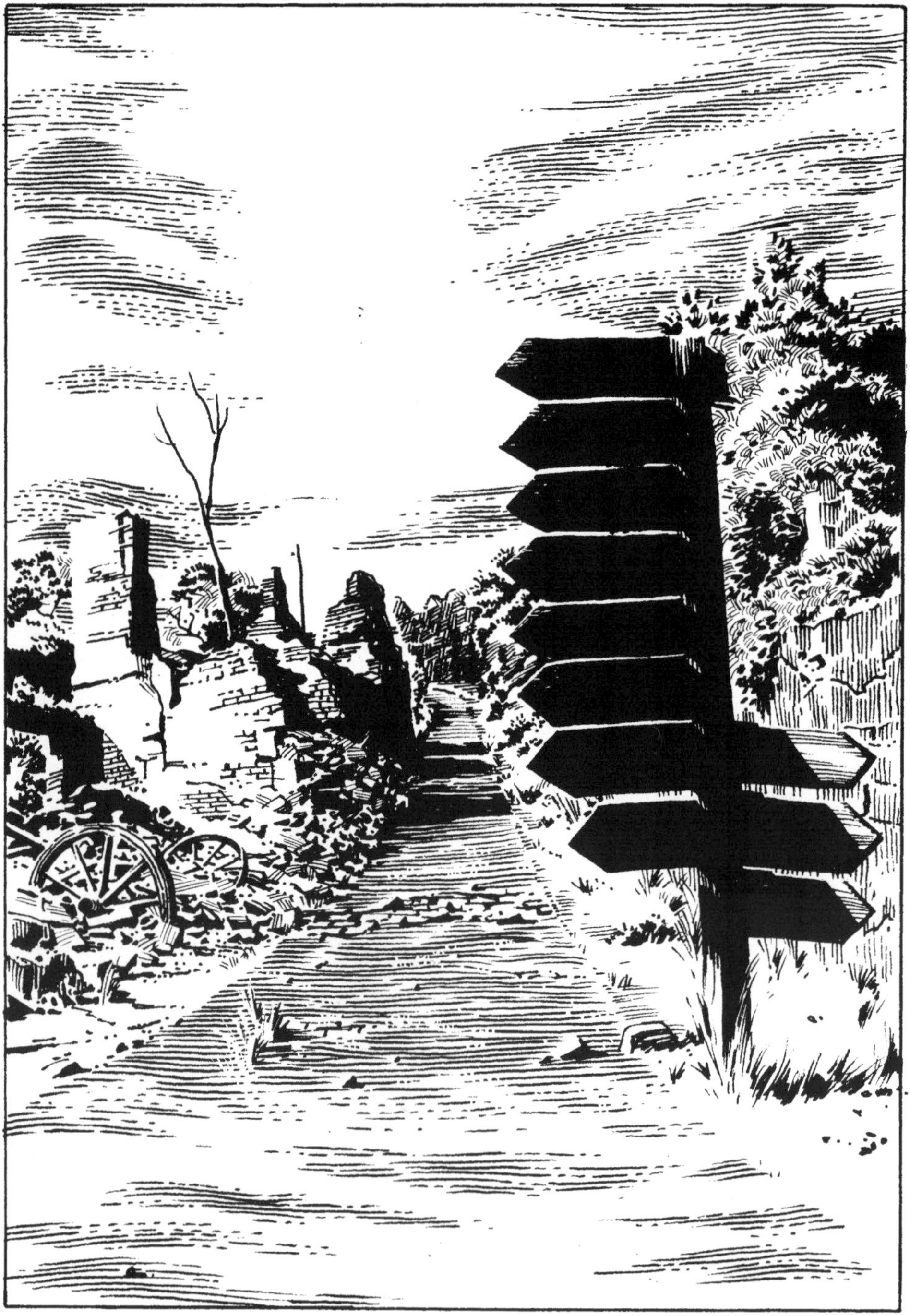

We are beginning to hear stories, rumours of paintings lodging even further underground. Rubens in a salt mine. De Chirico down a well. It's absurd. Of course, things will be lost. Much has been lost. I can only imagine what legends will be created. We see it starting already. But I think it is because what we see around us is so unimaginable that it cannot be real, but then I go down the stairs and there is a Tintoretto in between the bottles of Bordeaux, and I am reminded.

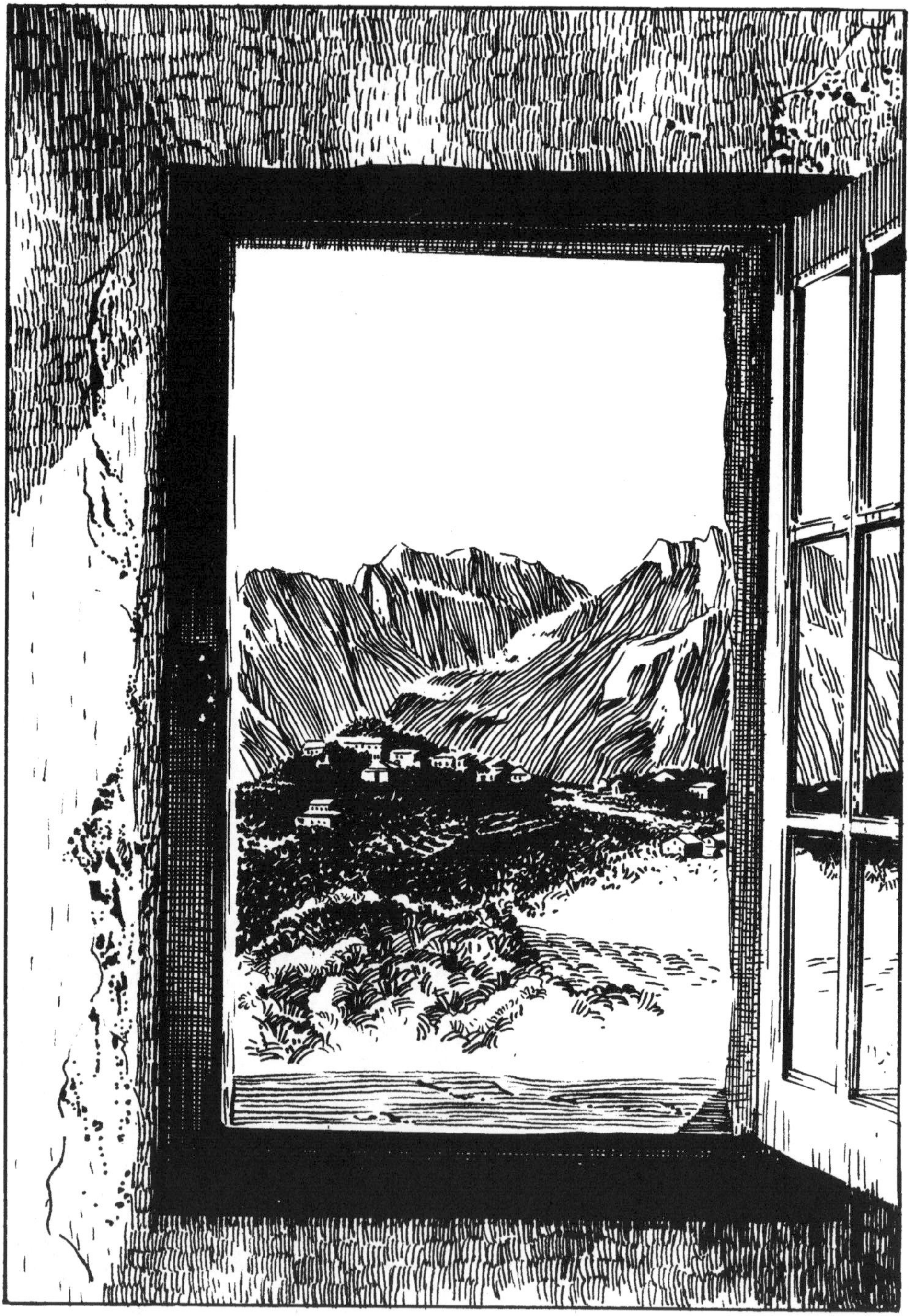

I have not slept so well these last few days. I awake in the middle of the night to the sound of trucks moving in the hills beyond the town. Maybe I hear them. Maybe. But then last night the sound was a terrible ticking, like an enormous clock. You know, I had an uncle who built clocks. Extraordinary things, like in a church. I can imagine this was the sound he heard always. But the ticking and the ticking, and I woke with a cold wind beginning to braid my spine. It was a terrible ache.

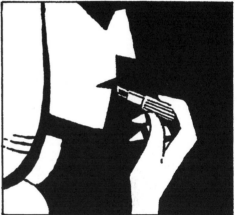

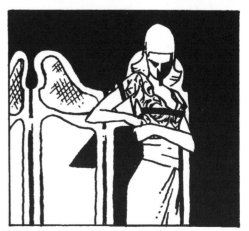

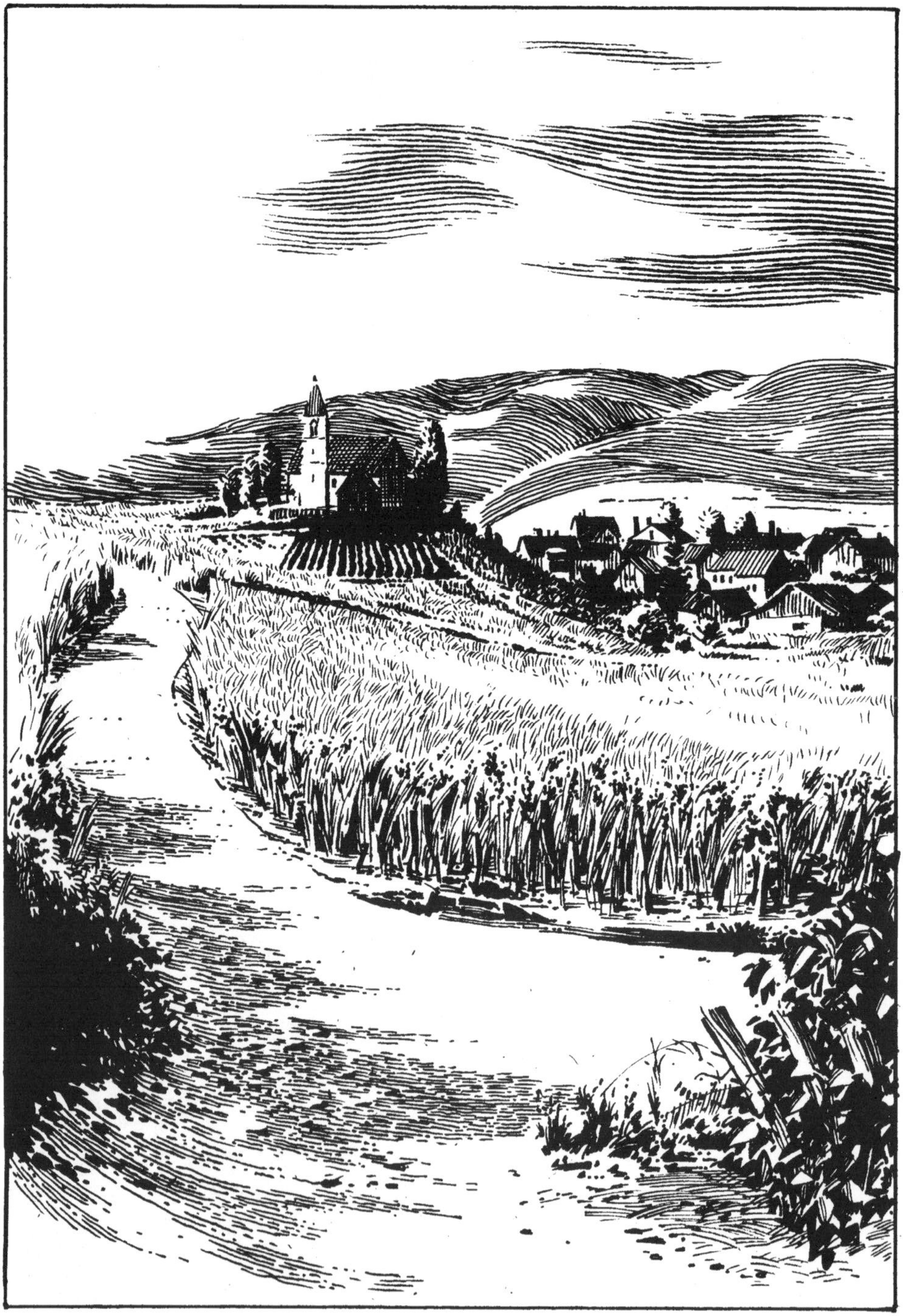

My shoulder blades pushing through my skin. And then the sound was coming from something in my hand. Something so small. Ila. I dreamt I held a watch in my hand and it was small and smooth and cold like a stone. Like a coin from a fountain. And now, in the daylight, I feel I know our project has failed.

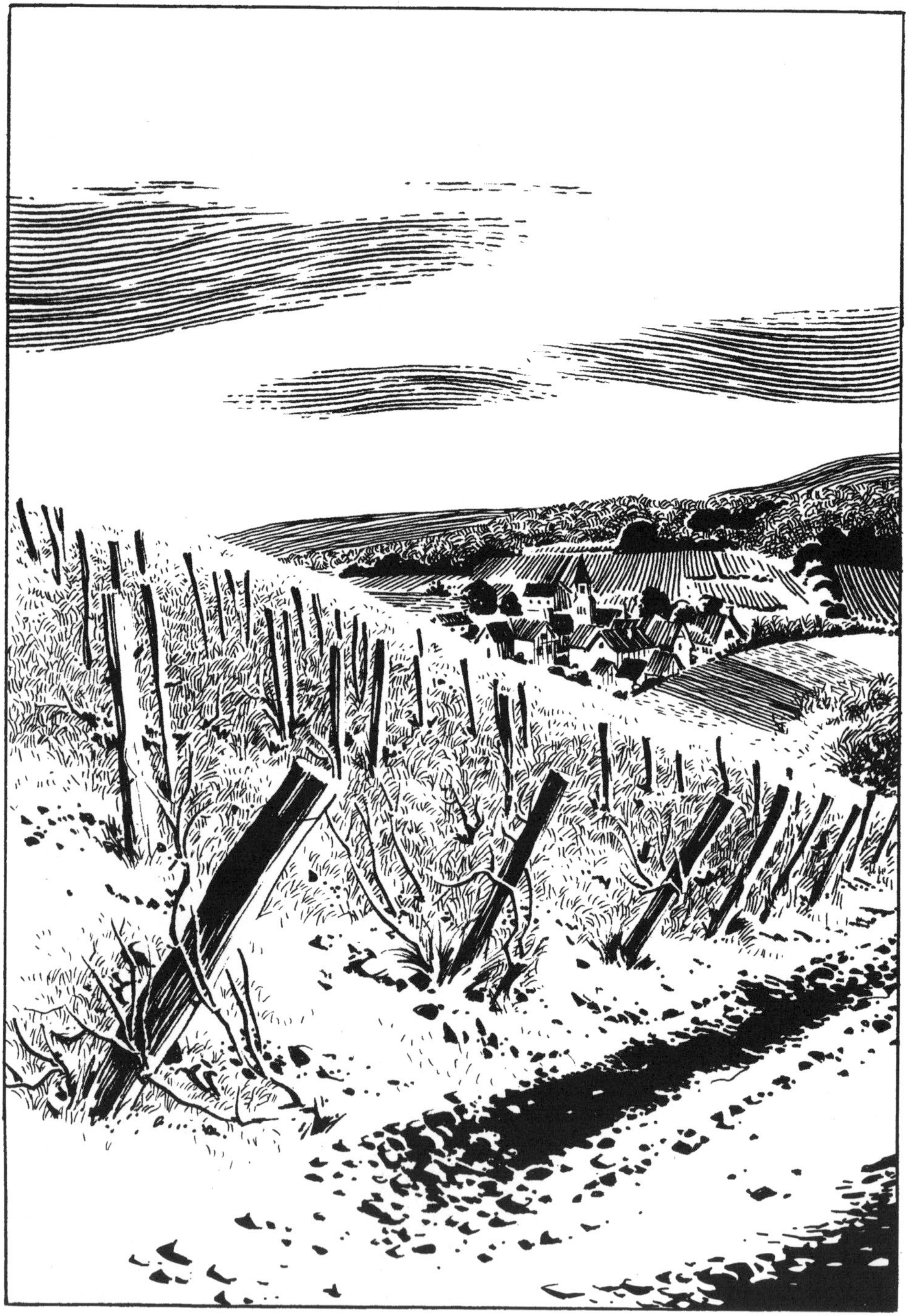

I look around me, and if I slide my hand forward on the table, my fingers edge into the sunlight, but the feel of the wood dragging on my wrist makes me feel so ill. Ila, be careful. I find myself making lists upon lists. On and on until my pockets are stuffed and paper is scarce. But we both know, no one cares. Not really. Not for always. What remains, remains. What goes is gone and it should be. If these works, these tempered images were mine, I would sell them. I would sell them all and never be heard from again. If I had anything of value, I would vanish. But then I look again, and I see that I already have. And you have. How else could it end? Because we surely can't simply go on, after this. My page is finished. My glass is empty. I advise you to take what you can and never be heard from again. To do otherwise is a mistake.
Je t'embrasse.

Marc

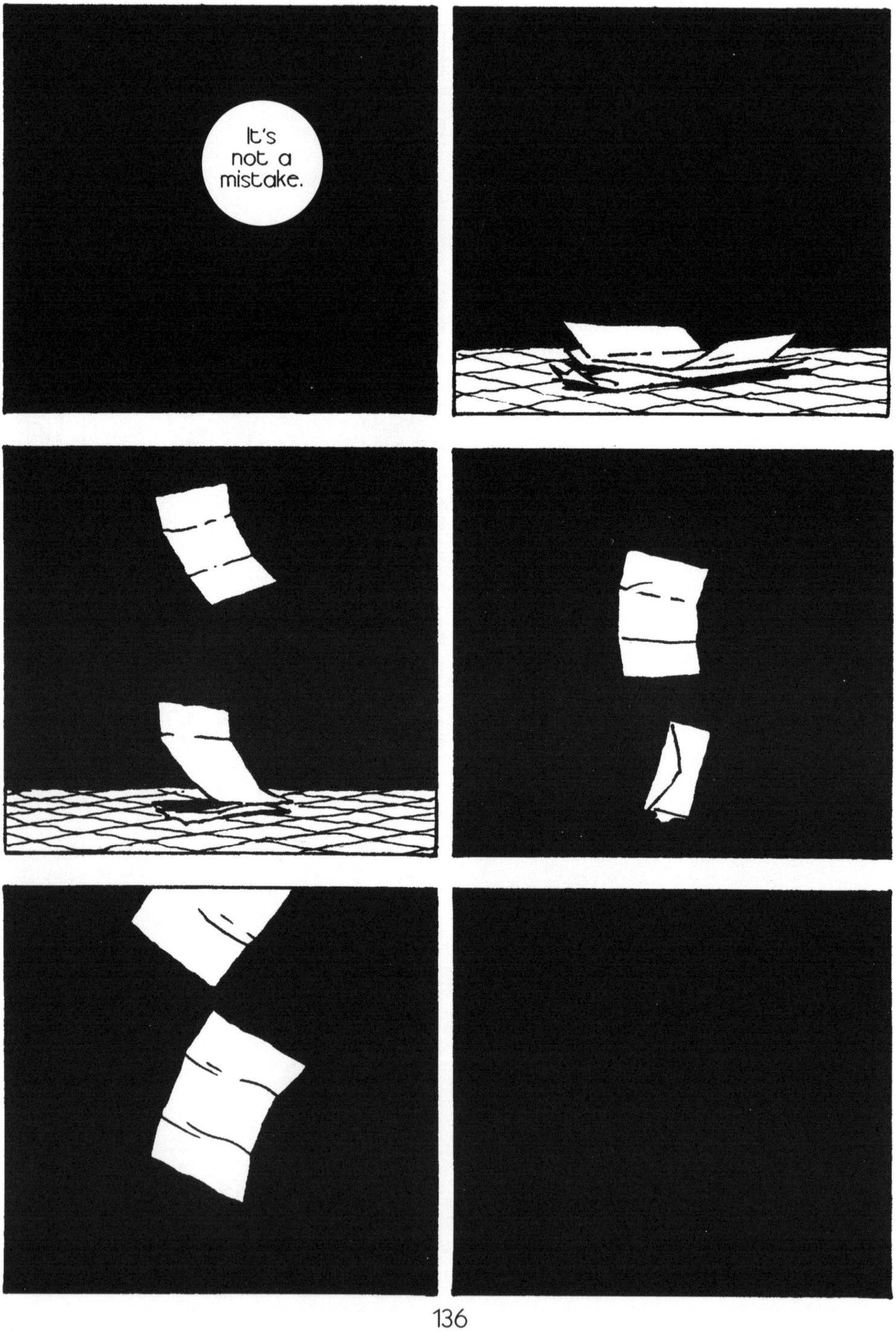
It's not a mistake.